Drugs and Youth:

The Challenge of Today

Drugs and Youth:
The Challenge of Today

Editor

ERNEST HARMS, Ph.D.

Addiction Service Agency
New York City

PERGAMON PRESS INC.

New York · Toronto · Oxford · Sydney · Braunschweig

PERGAMON PRESS INC.
Maxwell House, Fairview Park, Elmsford, N.Y. 10523

PERGAMON OF CANADA, LTD.
207 Queen's Quay West, Toronto 117, Ontario

PERGAMON PRESS, LTD.
Headington Hill Hall, Oxford

PERGAMON PRESS (AUST.) PTY. LTD.
Rushcutters Bay, Sydney, N.S.W.

VIEWEG & SOHN Gmbh
Burgplatz 1, Braunschweig

Printed in the United States of America

0-08 017063 3

Contents

The Contributors

D. Vincent Biase, Ph.D. is Director of Research Development and Evaluation, Resource Planning Corporation, Washington, D.C.

Roderic V. O. Boggs, is Executive Director, Washington Lawyers' Committee for Civil Rights, Washington, D.C.

Edward M. Brown is Executive Director, Lower East Side Service Center, New York City.

James V. DeLong is Director of Program Development, Drug Abuse Council, Washington, D.C.

George R. Gay, M.D. is Director, Haight-Ashbury Free Medical Clinic, San Francisco.

Erich Goode, Ph.D. is Associate Professor, Department of Sociology, State University of New York at Stony Brook, Stony Brook, N.Y.

Arthur Gruber, B.A. is Instructor in Social Work and Freelance Writer, New York City.

Ella J. Hughley, M.S.W. is Lecturer, York College, City University of New York, and Consultant, Department of Health, New York City.

Bernard Lander, Ph.D. is President, Touro College, New York City.

Nathan Lander, Ph.D. is Associate Professor, St. John's University, Jamaica, N.Y.

John Langrod, Ph.D. is Director of Research, Bronx State Hospital, New York City.

Gabriel V. Laury, M.D. is Director of Education and Training, Kings Park State Hospital and Associate Professor of Psychiatry, New York School of Psychiatry, New York City.

Lois L. Neumann, M.D. is Associate Professor of Clinical Pediatrics, New York University School of Medicine, New York City.

Stuart L. Nightingale, M.D. is Chief, Treatment and Rehabilitation, Office of Programs, Special Action Office for Drug Abuse Prevention, Washington, D.C.

Edward Preble, M.A. is Associate Research Scientist, Rockland Children's Psychiatric Hospital, and Professor of Anthropology, New York School of Psychiatry.

Charles W. Sheppard, M.D. is Co-Director of Medical Services, Haight-Ashbury Free Medical Clinic, San Francisco.

Jacob Sokol, M.D. is Assistant Clinical Professor of Medicine, University of Southern California Medical School, and Chief Physician, Juvenile Hall, Los Angeles County Probation Department.

Harold L. Trigg, M.D. is Associate Professor of Clinical Psychiatry, Mt. Sinai School of Medicine, City University of New York, and Associate Director of Psychiatry, Bernstein Institute, Beth Israel Medical Center, New York City.

Introduction

In 1964 we edited and published *Drug Addiction in Youth*. What follows here is a collection of studies, with a similar focus, that highlights more recent professional speculations.

The impulse of this editor to cut through the unknowns that surrounded the issue of drug addiction in youth began in the 1950s when he was Director of a major Child Guidance Clinic in New York which served several high schools. During that decade the increase in the use of drugs by teen-agers was so alarming that it seemed proper to term it an epidemic.

An effort to bring this to the attention of New York's mental health and educational authorities met with frustration. They denied that drug addiction was a widespread problem. However, our deep concern persisted and we were not dissuaded from pursuing our study of adolescent drug use in New York City and its suburbs. This study was published in the New York State *Journal of Medicine*.* It also roused certain professional circles to begin to face the reality of the menace of teen-age drug dependency. A number of workers wrote reports of their observations, and these were considered important enough to publish. The result was *Drug Addiction in Youth*.

Although our contributors were seriously engaged in attempts to scrutinize and curb addiction, for the most part their experience was still limited, blocked by the bureaucratic and human failure to face facts in

*December 15, 1962.

ix

time to prevent tragedy. The contributors had received their scientific credentials from various schools of psychology and sociology, and they researched and described the phenomena from behavioristic, psycho-analytical, and other views. Nothing had yet been developed that could be called a real psychology of addiction, presenting its dynamic functional processes, its pathology and therapy. Everyone talked about addiction, but no one really understood it. Our book had great value in opening the door for professional and lay minds to approach the problem.

Another decade has passed, during which fumbling attempts have been made to advance progress. We had to unlearn our dogmatic, behavioristic, psychoanalytic, or genetic concepts. We had to learn a more sophisti-cated, subtle psychology of complicated processes. We had to confess mistakes in treatment. All approaches to prevention in the social context had to be given as much and even more attention than treatment itself. We had to reach out for educational and sociological insights to get to the root of the impulses to dependence on drugs.

During the last ten years, the aspect of drug addiction has changed. It has widened to a degree never anticipated; yet we must confess that we are still ignorant of definite basic factors that might lead to an unraveling of the mystery of addiction. There are years of research ahead which may alter our presently held views.

However, in this volume we are able to show that progress has been made since publication of *Drug Addiction in Youth*. We have learned to "listen" to the addict and have begun to comprehend his psychology. We have begun to view teen-agers, not by our subjective older standards of behavior, but with some insight into the dynamics of their needs. We have begun to learn not to be against them, not to try to "reform" them by appealing to what they consider an outmoded morality, but to be "with them," by trying to help them through the labyrinth in which they are suffering and of which they are as aware as we are of their being there.

This volume expands the range of vision on drug addiction, especially from two perspectives: the social cultural and the psychological. Our improved understanding will help us overcome society's punitive attitude, which must be considered an error in dealing with teen-agers. The psycho-logical perspective will give us our first glimpse of what may be potential cure. We know we will not relieve the addict by merely attempting to thwart delinquent or criminal activities that contribute to his being a social danger. We know we may cure him if we help him to find individual, healthy identity, and support him in his struggles toward self-autonomy. This is our goal in psychotherapy.

At present, areas that demand very special attention from us are the sniffing of chemical solvents and other similar materials, and the methadone treatment. Since sniffing mind-changing fumes is the earliest form of drug abuse in our youth, it appears that this should have received considerable attention from past investigators. Strangely enough, it did not. There are very few fact-finding observations at our command and also very few concrete studies of a psychological and educational nature. It is important that more interest be concentrated on this addiction. Dr. Sokol, who contributed a chapter to our first book, has since done a considerable amount of work in the area which he summarizes for us in a chapter here. I also offer a paper with somewhat deepened insight into the problem.

Methadone treatment, introduced with the hope that it would eliminate heroin addiction, has not as yet fulfilled its early promise. In recent years, more and more skepticism has been voiced about its possible success; it has been found to have limited value as a real cure. However, in order to give a balanced survey of opinion, the Director of the Bernstein Institute in New York City, which is making outstanding attempts to alleviate drug dependence by methadone maintenance, outlines their treatment, and another chapter addresses itself to criticism from various views — giving the reader an objective insight into methadone use.

In preparing this collection of studies and opinion, the editor has sought help from as many sources as possible to enable him to offer the results of valid research. All the contributors have had first-hand experience with addicts and are devoting themselves to the cause of relieving suffering victims. Thanks are due to those who gave us the benefit of their knowledge. Special personal appreciation must be extended to Dr. John Langrod whose insight and advice have been most constructive.

ERNEST HARMS

Drug Abuse in Pregnancy: Its Effects on the Fetus and Newborn Infant

LOIS L. NEUMANN

INTRODUCTION

There has been increasing concern in recent years over the problems of drug abuse among adolescents and young adults. Approximately 15–20 percent of narcotic addicts(91) and an unknown, but probably larger percentage of habitual users of sedatives, stimulants, and hallucinogens are female. An unfortunate and often unappreciated consequence of the abuse of drugs among females in the childbearing age group is the passive exposure of infants *in utero* to drugs taken by their mothers.

There is ample clinical and chemical evidence that many drugs cross the placenta. While the rate of diffusion of a drug across placental membranes depends upon several factors, including molecular size, degree of ionization, protein-binding, and, most importantly, lipid solubility, virtually any drug present in the circulation of a pregnant woman can be transmitted to her fetus(4, 79, 112). Among the drugs known to cross the placenta are morphine and its derivatives and a number of the other drugs subject to abuse. Respiratory depression of newborn infants following administration of morphine to their mothers has been recognized for many years(9, 135), and withdrawal symptoms in infants of morphine- or heroin-addicted mothers have been described in numerous reports since the late nineteenth century(25, 49, 69, 75). Analysis of blood, tissues, or urine of newborn infants has confirmed the presence of morphine, meperidine, methadone, barbiturates, and other drugs taken before delivery or the metabolites of these drugs(111).

1

Drugs which cross the placenta may exert two types of effects on the fetus—those which can be predicted on the basis of effects observed in adults, and those which are unique to the particular developmental stage of the fetus at the time of exposure. The former is exemplified by the neonatal narcotic withdrawal syndrome which in many respects resembles narcotic withdrawal as it is seen in adults. Less is known about the effects of drugs of abuse on fetal development or the influence of different fetal developmental stages on the action of some of these drugs. Thus, it is important to document drug exposure during pregnancy as accurately as possible and to be alert to the possibility of abnormalities or alterations of physiology in infants of mothers with a history of such exposure.

The medical problems related to drug abuse in pregnancy are compounded by the adverse social circumstances of the majority of habitual drug abusers in our culture. The areas of our cities in which most narcotic addicts live are also the areas with the highest rates of the whole spectrum of social pathology(91). Poverty, malnutrition, inadequate housing, unstable or non-existent family life, criminal activity, and prostitution are common in the lives of addicted women and greatly add to the difficulty of caring for them and their babies.

GYNECOLOGIC AND OBSTETRIC CONSIDERATIONS

Effects of Narcotic Addiction on Menstruation and Fertility

Narcotic addicts commonly experience abnormalities of menstruation. Ninety percent of a group of 81 pre-menopausal female addicts admitted to the United States Public Health Service Research Center in Lexington, Kentucky, gave a history of menstrual abnormalities beginning after a few to several months of regular heroin use(149). A similarly high incidence is reported in other series(24, 62, 160). Amenorrhea is the most frequent disturbance. It has been postulated that heroin or morphine causes a neural block between the hypothalamus and the pituitary gland, resulting in a lack of stimulus for the secretion of gonadotropin, and the absence of a normal menstrual cycle(62). It is also possible that the poor nutritional state of many addicts is a contributing factor, as it is known that severe malnutrition commonly results in amenorrhea(118). Regular menses return in most addicted women soon after withdrawal from narcotics in an institutional setting(24, 149). It is of interest that 82 of 83 women who had abnormalities of menstruation while on heroin resumed regular menses within a short time after being admitted to a methadone maintenance program(160). This occurred in spite of their daily intake of 60–120 mg of methadone. Their return to a normal menstrual pattern may be due to differences in neuro-endocrine effects of methadone as compared to other narcotics, or, more likely, to the improved nutrition, environment, and medical care available under a supervised maintenance program.

The frequent occurrence of amenorrhea among addicts has led to the assumption that infertility is similarly frequent. Infertility, defined as failure to conceive within one year, despite adequate sexual exposure without contraception, was reported in 63 percent of a group of addicts during regular drug use. However, 39 of the 81 patients in this series had had a total of 77 pregnancies since beginning their drug habits(149). Conception often seems to take place at times when the addict is on relatively low doses or drug-free, as following recent discharge from jail or hospital. Conception has occurred sufficiently often following admission to a methadone maintenance program for one commentator to refer to pregnancy as a "side-effect of methadone"(19). Once again, however, it is difficult to separate the effects of the drug from those of the improved environmental circumstances of the addict in a maintenance program.

That the absence of menses does not necessarily imply lack of ovulation or fertility is illustrated well by a case cited by Pettey(122). A woman, addicted to morphine during her third pregnancy, subsequently delivered an additional 10 infants, while continuing a regular intake of 20 grains of morphine per day. Menses never reappeared following her third pregnancy.

In spite of a reduced libido often associated with addiction, frequent sexual exposure of female addicts is assured by the high rate of prostitution resorted to, to support costly drug habits.

Management of the Narcotic Addict During Pregnancy

While addicts could be expected to be a high risk group, some authors note a surprisingly low incidence of serious complications of pregnancy (18, 151). On the other hand, Stern(148) found an increased frequency of toxemia and placental abnormalities as compared to the non-addict population delivered at the same hospital. An increased proportion of premature labors and breech deliveries has been observed in all reported series(119,148,151). The frequency of breech presentation is probably secondary to the high proportion of low birth weight infants.

Most addicts who become pregnant do not seek prenatal care(24,92, 119,151). If an addict is seen during her pregnancy, a decision must be made as to the management of her addiction. Factors which should be considered in making this decision include the stage of the pregnancy, the general health of the addicted woman, the possibility of follow-up (either in an institution or as an outpatient), and the wishes of the addict herself.

It was suggested in earlier literature that attempts at withdrawal be limited to the first months of gestation because of violent fetal activity (50) sometimes observed when a pregnant addict is overdue for a dose of narcotic. Abrupt withdrawal has also been felt to increase irritability of the uterus and to be a possible cause of premature labor (24, 123). With modern methods of substitution and gradual withdrawal, however, there is probably no medical contraindication to withdrawal at any stage of pregnancy except when labor is imminent or in progress. A number of pregnant addicts do voluntarily present themselves for "detoxification." Some are motivated by genuine concern over possible harmful effects of drugs on the baby and others by the increasing difficulty with advancing pregnancy of obtaining money to buy drugs. Blinick *et al.* (18) in one large series, found a 10-day schedule of methadone in decreasing doses to be very successful in avoiding severe withdrawal symptoms in pregnant addicts. However, attempts at long-range rehabilitation, despite follow-up psychiatric and social services, met with consistent failure. Drug intake was usually resumed shortly after discharge from the hospital, and several patients returned repeatedly for "detoxification." Except for patients who remain in prison or in other institutions for the balance of their pregnancy, little seems to be accomplished by withdrawal except a temporary decrease in the cost of the addict's "habit."

The relative success of methadone maintenance treatment in rehabilitating narcotic addicts (44, 46) has led a few groups to establish methadone maintenance programs for pregnant addicts (33, 160). Potential benefits of these programs include: regular medical supervision and improved nutrition during pregnancy, avoidance of the stresses of drug-seeking behavior and periodic withdrawal by stabilization of the drug intake, lessened exposure to the contaminants and unknown adulterants of "street drugs," and possible reduced severity of neonatal withdrawal symptoms. Most importantly, engaging the mother in a treatment program during pregnancy increases the possibility of continued medical and social service supervision of mother and child after delivery (17).

The initial report from the methadone maintenance program at New York's Beth Israel Medical Center (160) indicated that "there was no significant evidence of 'withdrawal syndrome'" among 8 live born infants, although treatment was given to 2 of the infants for unspecified indications. A more recent report from this program indicates that of 19 babies born to women on methadone maintenance, usually at a dose of 100 mg daily, 8 were asymptomatic, 6 were mildly and 5 moderately affected, and none had severe symptoms(17). As of this writing, this series has been expanded to 30 infants, of whom approximately 50 percent have shown symptoms of withdrawal in the neonatal period(16). Most babies were free of symptoms by 10 days. Their average hospital stay was 15 days, compared to 40 days for infants of addicts not in the maintenance program, with the longer period for the most part due to social problems and need for placement. Most infants of mothers on methadone maintenance have been discharged to their own mothers and have been available for follow-up, in some instances for as long as 6 years(16, 17).

Finnegan(57) has observed moderate symptoms in infants of mothers on high maintenance doses of methadone (80–100 mg daily) but few if any symptoms in infants of mothers receiving only 20–60 mg daily.

Recently Rajegowda et al.(123b) have observed that a group of infants of mothers receiving 80–160 mg of methadone daily had a higher incidence and longer duration of withdrawal symptoms than did a group of infants of heroin addicts (6–16 days and 2–8 days respectively). This difference may be accounted for by a lower intake of narcotic by many heroin addicts, and by delayed excretion of methadone as compared to heroin. Of greater concern has been the occurrence of convulsions and sudden death at 1–2 months of age in several infants who had undergone methadone withdrawal(61a, 123a). Intensive investigation is required to determine whether these serious reactions are caused by methadone, other drugs taken by the mothers, or some unrelated factor.

Management of Labor and Delivery

Recommendations regarding the use of drugs for the relief of pain during labor and delivery have varied. Some physicians feel that narcotics should be withheld or used sparingly, apparently out of fear of fostering the patients' addiction(114, 152). Others recommend that no distinction should be made between addicts and other patients in the use of analgesia and anesthesia during labor(18, 119). Surgeons and anesthesiologists with experience in the management of addicts urge that narcotic dependent individuals who develop acute medical or surgical conditions should be given maintenance doses of narcotic drugs until the acute illness subsides (1, 52, 143). It would seem inhumane as well as medically unwise to superimpose the physiological and psychological disturbance of withdrawal on the stress of labor and delivery. Regional analgesia is advised (2) for delivery of addicts. If a specific situation demands the use of general anesthesia, hepatotoxic agents such as halothane should be avoided in those patients, who are known to have a high incidence of liver dysfunction. Sudden hypotension, which sometimes complicates the course of general anesthesia in addicts, may respond to an intravenous dose of narcotic if the usual measures are not effective(2, 104).

ASSOCIATED MEDICAL PROBLEMS OF POSSIBLE SIGNIFICANCE TO THE FETUS

Various medical problems occur with increased frequency among addicts(23, 97, 128). The majority of these, including viral hepatitis, syphilis, tetanus, abscesses, septicemia, and bacterial endocarditis, are due to infections, some of which may secondarily affect infants born to addicted women.

Hepatitis

Hepatitis is one of the most common illnesses complicating the course of drug addiction, with shared injection equipment serving as a mode of transmission of the virus(23, 97, 128). There seems to be little doubt that most cases of acute hepatitis in addicts are serum hepatitis (hepatitis B, long-incubation hepatitis). Hepatitis B antigen (Australia antigen, HAA), which is associated with the causative agent of serum hepatitis(98), has been found in the sera of over two-thirds of drug abusers with acute hepatitis(153).

Until recently the effect of hepatitis in pregnancy upon the fetus or new-born infant has been poorly understood. The possibility of transmission of maternal serum hepatitis to infants has been suggested by several scattered case reports(6, 10, 150). However, the majority of infants born to mothers with hepatitis in pregnancy do not develop overt disease (80, 108).

New information is now accumulating on the possible transmission of hepatitis virus from mother to infant, using the presence of hepatitis B antigen as a marker. Several studies of infants whose mothers were anti-genemic at the time of delivery(37, 95, 116, 131, 137, 140, 157) have thus far revealed only one instance of an infant whose cord blood was positive for antigen(116). Follow-up for 3–5 months by Skinhøj et al.(137) of 28 infants born to healthy hepatitis B antigen carriers has failed to reveal antigenemia or evidence of hepatitis in any of the children. In contrast, follow-up of infants whose mothers had antigen-positive hepatitis late in pregnancy has revealed antigenemia in several previously antigen-negative infants at intervals of 3–4 weeks(37), 49 days(131), 59 days (157), and 3 months(137) following delivery.

Clinically apparent hepatitis and cirrhosis have not been reported among the infants who were followed from birth and who developed hepatitis B antigen in the serum. However, in several instances elevated serum enzyme levels (glutamic oxalacetic transaminase, glutamic pyruvate transaminase, or alanine transferase) gave evidence of subclinical hepatitis soon after the appearance of antigen in the serum (137, 157). Hepatitis B antigen was found in a previously unstudied child at 19 weeks of age when she developed acute hepatitis which subsequently became chronic with cirrhosis; the mother, who gave a history of jaundice in late pregnancy, was also antigen-positive (162). Some infants who became antigen-positive have been noted to develop a prolonged carrier state, the duration and significance of which is not known. The case reported by Turner et al. (157) was still antigen-positive 22 months after the first positive test at 8 weeks of age.

Recent observations by Smithwick et al. (141) suggested a possible link between antigenemia of mothers at delivery and the incidence of prematurity among their offspring. Four of 5 mothers with antigen-positive hepatitis and 4 of 7 antigen-carriers without hepatitis delivered at or before the 36th week of gestation. This may be significant in addicts, who have been noted to have a high frequency of the hepatitis B antigen carrier state (4.2 percent, compared to 0.1 percent in the general population (153)) as well as of hepatitis.

In summary, present evidence suggests that hepatitis B antigen may be transmitted across the placenta, but is only rarely recoverable from the infant at birth. Infants of mothers with antigen-positive hepatitis late in pregnancy sometimes develop antigenemia and hepatitis, which is usually subclinical, following an interval that suggests transmission at or near the time of delivery. In some infants a prolonged carrier state follows, the significance of which is not known. In addition, hepatitis B antigenemia in a pregnant woman may predispose her to deliver prematurely.

Syphilis

Female addicts, who commonly support their drug habits by prostitution, can be expected to have a high incidence of syphilitic infection. Various reports have confirmed that this is so, and, in addition, have demonstrated that biologic false positive reactions (BFP) occur with remarkable frequency among addicts.

Harris and Andrei(72) found lipoidal tests for syphilis (VDRL and Kolmer) positive in 28 percent of 520 addicts and in 9.3 percent of 294 non-addicts arrested for prostitution. When treponemal tests were performed on the positive sera, 58 percent in the addict group were found to represent BFP reactions compared to only 14.3 percent in the non-addict group. Other authors have found BFP reactions accounting for 50–95 percent of the positive serologic tests for syphilis in groups of addicts(21,71,128,156). Attempts to correlate BFP reactions in addicts with immunologic abnormalities or with chronic liver dysfunction have been unsuccessful(72,156) and the phenomenon remains unexplained.

Both syphilitic infection and the proteins responsible for BFP reactions can be transmitted to the fetus. Consequently, it is important to differentiate infants with congenital syphilis from uninfected infants with passively transmitted maternal antibody. Determination of specific IgM fluorescent treponemal antibody in the infant's serum is a useful test for the diagnosis of active infection shortly after birth(100).

Tetanus

Tetanus, now rarely seen in urban areas of the United States except among addicts, occurs almost twice as often in females as in males. Female addicts are more likely to use subcutaneous injections ("skin popping"), thus introducing contaminated material into puncture wounds which favor the growth of clostridia(23). Tetanus in addicts has been associated with a mortality rate of approximately 90 percent(138). Tetanus occurring during pregnancy would be a serious threat to the fetus even if the mother survived. Because of the particular risk of tetanus among addicts, it is advisable to provide them with tetanus immunization when the opportunity arises.

Malaria

The first report of malaria among narcotic addicts in the United States appeared in 1932(65), followed by a review of 200 cases in 1940(110). Over the next few years, however, malaria virtually disappeared among addicts in the United States. Whether this was secondary to increasing adulteration of heroin with quinine, or to eradication of the mosquito-borne form of the disease is uncertain(128).

Recently several thousand servicemen have returned from Vietnam with malaria, and some of these have been implicated as the source of transfusion-induced cases(60). A recent report describes a case of P. falciparum malaria acquired by a drug user who shared needles with servicemen who had been in Vietnam(47). It is quite likely that more cases will be appearing in the United States, and that some of them may be seen in pregnant drug abusers, with the consequent possibility of fetal infection. It is well established that intrauterine transmission of malaria may occur, sometimes even in the absence of active disease symptoms in the mother(39,43,73,99).

Congenital malaria has been extremely rare in the United States in the past 50 years and, with only one exception, the mothers of the few reported cases had acquired their infection abroad. Keitel *et al.*(89) reported a case of congenital quartan malaria in an infant of a women who had always lived in the Washington, D.C. area, and who had been using shared needles for several months to administer intravenous heroin. The infant was apparently well until 15 months of age when spiking fever appeared, followed by development of the nephrotic syndrome, diagnosed as due to P. malariae. Treatment with chloroquine phosphate was followed by prompt resolution of nephrosis and all other clinical and laboratory evidence of the disease, with no recurrence noted in over a year of follow-up.

Bacterial Infections

Addicts commonly experience episodes of bacteremia from direct intravenous injection of contaminated material or from foci of infection, such as abscesses or endocarditis. Thus, the possibility exists that bacteria in the blood stream of a pregnant addict can gain access to and infect her fetus. However, Blanc(15) and Benirschke(12) have stressed the rarity with which bacteria can be incriminated in transplacental infections, in contrast to some viruses, spirochetes, and protozoa. Bacterial infections in infants of addicts are, as in other infants, usually acquired by the ascending route from the birth canal, or by exposure during or following birth.

THE INFANT OF THE NARCOTIC ADDICTED MOTHER

The Neonatal Narcotic Withdrawal Syndrome

The infant who has been chronically exposed to narcotics taken by his mother during pregnancy is suddenly cut off from his source of drugs at the time of delivery. If he has developed a physiologic dependence on these drugs, abstinence symptoms may be expected to ensue. In two recently reported series, 85 percent(124) and 67.4 percent(164) of infants born to mothers with a history of narcotic abuse showed signs of withdrawal. Symptoms, if they occur, are usually seen in both mother and infant, unless they are modified by a continued intake of narcotic drugs or by other medication. However, some infants may become symptomatic while their mothers remain symptom-free and, more rarely, an infant may remain asymptomatic while his mother develops withdrawal(152). The infant whose mother has been drug-free for a week or more prior to delivery generally does not show signs of withdrawal(69, 147). The absence of symptoms in some infants of mothers said to have a heavy drug intake may be accounted for by the unreliability of maternal drug histories. Some women deliberately exaggerate the extent of their "habit" in the hope of being given generous substitution therapy in the hospital. More often, the addicts themselves have little knowledge of the potency of the drugs they have been taking. Louria(97) stated that heroin currently being sold to street addicts is generally more diluted than it was several years ago and cited a study by the office of the Chief Medical Examiner of the City of New York in which wide variations (0–77 percent) in heroin content were found on analysis of 132 confiscated "bags," with 10 percent of these packets containing no heroin at all. Cobrinik(25) attempted to correlate severity of withdrawal in the infant with maternal drug dose. He noted mild symptoms in infants of mothers taking 6 mg or less of heroin daily, and moderate or severe symptoms when the daily maternal dose exceeded 12 mg.

Withdrawal symptoms usually begin during the first 24 hours of life. Occasionally, symptoms may be observed at birth, or delayed for as long as 4 days. Adult addicts withdrawn from heroin become symptomatic within 12–14 hours after the last dose of narcotic(84). The more gradual onset in some infants is perhaps related to a short interval between the mothers' last dose and delivery, to the effect of medications administered during labor, and to relatively slower drug metabolism and excretion by the immature infant.

The neonatal narcotic withdrawal syndrome has been described by several authors(25, 69, 75, 88, 93). There is general agreement that the cardinal symptoms are coarse tremors, hyperactivity, and irritability, and that a number of other symptoms frequently occur, including vomiting, poor feeding, greedy sucking, increased muscle tone, nasal stuffiness, sneezing, yawning, skin abrasions secondary to hyperactivity, persistent angry crying, sweating, and loose stools. Tachypnea, which may result in respiratory alkalosis, has only recently been appreciated as a frequent component of the syndrome(68, 115).

High fever, and vascular collapse are mentioned in some publications (75, 106, 134), but have not been encountered in the author's experience with more than 300 infants of heroin users over a 12-year period at Bellevue Hospital(115). It is possible that early recognition and treatment of severely affected infants prevents progression of the withdrawal syndrome and the development of such potentially serious complications. While loose stools occur along with other withdrawal symptoms in some babies, severe diarrhea is unusual in the absence of some other cause such as enteric infection(88, 164). Convulsions have been listed among the symptoms of neonatal narcotic withdrawal by a number of authors

(69,120,147,152). However, experience at 3 large municipal hospitals in New York City has shown them to be a rare complication(88,124). Severe tremors, or myoclonic jerks, which are often exhibited by infants in withdrawal, may sometimes be misinterpreted as seizure activity by inexperienced observers. True convulsions should always raise the suspicion of another etiology, such as hypoglycemia, hypocalcemia, or meningitis, or of withdrawal from drugs other than narcotics. In adults, convulsions are not a part of the morphine or heroin abstinence syndrome. However, it is well known that they may occur following abrupt withdrawal of barbiturates, alcohol, or any of several tranquilizers(54,82,83).

Symptoms of neonatal narcotic withdrawal have been said by some authors to subside within a week or two(88,92,93,147), and by others to persist for as long as several weeks(25,75,127). A number of published reports indicate duration only in terms of the length of the treatment course, but provide little information as to the criteria used for continuing or discontinuing therapy. It is not clear whether the wide variations in length of courses of treatment truly represent variations in duration of the original withdrawal symptomatology, development of dependence on the treatment drug resulting in recurrence of symptoms when dosage is reduced, or differences in interpretation of symptoms by different observers.

Most authors describing narcotic withdrawal in infants have made no attempt to distinguish between the acute and subacute phases of the disorder that have been described in adults and in experimental animals. In adults, the morphine or heroin abstinence syndrome follows a characteristic pattern in which symptoms are at peak intensity between 48 and 72 hours after the last dose, then diminish so that objective signs are virtually gone by 7–10 days. However, patients often continue to complain of sleep difficulties, myalgias, weakness, and malaise for several weeks(84), and autonomic imbalance, as evidenced by an abnormal cold pressor response, may persist up to 6 months(76,77). Similarly, in morphine addicted rats, two distinct phases are seen: "primary abstinence," with acute symptoms persisting approximately 72 hours, and "secondary abstinence" in which minor differences between addicted and control rats are seen for as long as 4–6 months following withdrawal(103).

Observations by Desmond *et al.*(42) suggest that heroin withdrawn infants similarly have a relatively short period of acute symptomatology, which may be followed by a period of disturbed behavior manifested by sleeplessness and crying for 2–3 months, and hyperphagia, hyperacusis, and outbursts of screaming for as long as 6 months. It may be that some of the prolonged treatment courses reported represent attempts to abolish completely such persisting subacute symptoms.

Diagnosis of the neonatal narcotic withdrawal syndrome is not difficult when the history of maternal drug abuse is known and characteristic signs are observed in the infant. If the diagnosis is suspected but drug abuse is denied, examination of the mother for stigmata such as needle marks and thrombosed veins or withdrawal signs may reveal the source of the infant's difficulties. It must be kept in mind that the legitimate medical use of narcotics by the mother(58,159) may also give rise to withdrawal symptoms in her infant.

Useful confirmatory evidence of the use of drugs can be obtained from analysis of urine by rapid chromatographic techniques which detect the presence of a number of drugs including morphine,* methadone, barbiturates, amphetamines, quinine, phenothiazines, and various other tranquilizers(40,45,59,102). The presence of quinine, a common adulterant of heroin, is strongly suggestive of illicit drug use, but not pathognomonic because an individual may excrete quinine after ingesting it in medication or in tonic drinks. It has been reported that quinine may be detectable in urine up to 3 days beyond the last point of morphine recovery(38).

The narcotic withdrawal syndrome is a self-limited condition, and, in milder cases, subsides in a few days with no specific therapy. A quiet, warm environment, gentle handling, swaddling, and frequent small feedings are helpful, as are measures to minimize skin abrasions, such as placing the infant on a sheepskin or in a diaper "hammock" tied in his crib. Prophylactic therapy based solely upon a history of maternal drug intake, as suggested by some(119), would result in unnecessarily treating the many infants who remain asymptomatic or whose symptoms respond to simple supportive measures. No harm is done by a period of observation to determine whether or not treatment is indicated.

Infants who cry continuously, have difficulty feeding, or show marked tremors and irritability even when undisturbed, deserve some form of sedation to relieve their evident discomfort and to prevent the possible development of more serious disturbances, such as dehydration, excessive weight loss, hyperpyrexia, or vascular collapse.

A number of treatment regimens have been used for the management of infant narcotic withdrawal (*see* Table 1), and most have been successful to some degree in controlling symptoms. Of historical interest only are treatment by allowing the still addicted mother to breastfeed her baby (123), or by blowing opium smoke in the infant's face(155). Morphine is very effective in controlling acute symptoms, as one might predict, but

---

*Heroin (diacetyl-morphine) is excreted as morphine following de-acetylation in the body.

Table 1 Treatment of neonatal narcotic withdrawal.

Medication	Recommended Dosage
Phenobarbital(88)	8–10 mg/kg/24 hrs., 4 divided doses
Chlorpromazine(25,88)	2.5–4.5 mg/kg/24 hrs., 4 divided doses
Paregoric(25,124) (camphorated tincture of opium)	1–3 drops/kg q 3–6 hrs. (may be increased if necessary)
Morphine	0.1–0.2 mg/kg/dose (recommended only for emergency use – see text)

only prolongs the narcotic-dependent state. Its use should be reserved for the extremely rare situation of shock that develops in an infant in whom severe symptoms have progressed unrecognized and untreated.

Diazepam has recently been suggested for the treatment of neonatal narcotic withdrawal(113). However, judging from the reported results in a preliminary trial in 18 infants(113), diazepam does not appear to be more effective in controlling symptoms than other agents now used in many centers(88). Furthermore, there is in vitro evidence that the benzoic acid and sodium benzoate present as buffer preservatives in the injectable preparation of diazepam exert a potent displacing effect on bilirubin from its binding sites on albumin(31,130). This raises the possibility that use of this preparation in infants could result in brain damage produced by bilirubin displaced from its intravascular binding sites. The use of parenteral diazepam is, therefore, not recommended for management of withdrawal symptoms in the newborn period.

Methadone has been used with apparent success for the management of neonatal narcotic withdrawal, but experience with this drug has been limited(92).

The most widely used drugs have been paregoric (camphorated tincture of opium), phenobarbital, and chlorpromazine. Phenobarbital and chlorpromazine were compared in a group of 38 infants with moderate or severe withdrawal symptoms(88). Medication was either stopped abruptly after 4 days, or given in full dosage for 10 days and discontinued by stepwise reduction of the dose over the succeeding 6 days. All infants showed a significant decrease in the severity of symptoms within the first day after starting therapy with either drug, often within 1 or 2 hours following the first dose. Symptoms persisted beyond 4 days in only 8 of the 38 patients, and in none of these was it deemed indicated to reinstitute therapy following completion of the assigned course. This study revealed no clear-cut superiority of either phenobarbital or chlorpromazine, and suggested that the majority of infants with narcotic withdrawal can be managed satisfactorily with a short course of less than a week of drug therapy. Similar comparative trials have not been carried out with paregoric or other drugs.

The management of infants with a history of chronic narcotic exposure before birth should be individualized. Careful observation will determine which infants require no special treatment, which will respond to simple supportive measures, and which are in need of medication to control symptoms. Sedation should be sufficient to permit the infant to rest between feedings and to control hyperactivity so that the infant does not abrade the skin of his face and extremities against the bedclothes, but not so deep as to interfere with normal activity and feeding behavior. It is not necessary to obliterate all tremulous movements.

Medication should be discontinued or reduced after a few days and the infant observed. In many infants, acute withdrawal symptoms will not recur or, if they do, will be mild enough to be managed with only gentle handling and careful feeding. If an infant shows recurrent symptoms which do not allow him to feed and gain weight normally or to rest between feedings, the original dose of medication should be resumed, followed by gradual reduction of the dose at intervals of 2–3 days as the infant's condition permits. Once acute symptoms have subsided so that the child is eating well and gaining weight, further drug therapy is rarely indicated. Continued attention to avoiding excessive stimuli in the child's environment and support of the parents or other caretakers in their handling of what may be a "difficult" baby for several weeks may be helpful.

Effects of Maternal Narcotic Addiction on Fetal Development

A high incidence of low birth weight has been noted in most series of infants of addicted mothers, with up to 55 percent of infants weighing less than 2500 g(25,88,124,127,152,164). Examination of infants using clinical techniques of gestational age assessment(90,158) reveals that intrauterine growth retardation and prematurity contribute about equally to the low birth weight rate(88,124,164).

It is not known to what extent the addicted mothers' poor health and environmental circumstances, exposure to narcotic drugs, or some combination of factors, are responsible for intrauterine growth retardation and premature delivery of their infants.

The inverse relationship between the incidence of low birth weight and socioeconomic status is well known, although the reasons for this relationship are complex and not well understood. Addicted mothers living in the most disadvantaged segments of our communities deliver low birth weight infants with over three times the frequency observed among all mothers in the same areas. This is perhaps not surprising, in view of the severely disorganized life-style of most addicts, but raises the possibility that factors in addition to those generally associated with an impoverished environment are responsible for some of the prematurity and fetal growth retardation among infants of addicts.

In addition to poor nutrition and overall health status among addicts, it is well known that there is a high incidence of hepatitis in this group. The suggested role of hepatitis or hepatitis B antigenemia in the etiology of prematurity has been discussed above.

Some possible mechanisms through which the administration or withdrawal of narcotics might affect fetal growth are suggested by experimental data. Prolonged exposure of cells in tissue culture to various concentrations of morphine sulfate is compatible with unimpaired, and at some concentrations even enhanced, cell growth. However, tissue cultures thus made morphine-dependent show prompt cessation of growth, degenerative changes, and sometimes cell death when the supply of narcotic is interrupted, with withdrawal effects noted for periods lasting up to 7 days (36,67). It is conceivable that intermittent periods of maternal drug withdrawal during pregnancy may have a similar adverse effect on the growth of fetal tissues.

Fetal growth can be compromised by impaired placental circulation. *In vitro* experiments with perfused human placentas demonstrate that morphine and meperidine and, to a lesser extent, codeine, produce a marked constrictor effect on placental vessels(63). It is not known whether any of these drugs significantly affects placental perfusion *in vivo*.

Further investigation may identify other factors responsible for low birth weight among infants of addicts.

Claman and Strang(24) found the average birth weight in a group of 12 infants born to addict mothers who had been incarcerated for a period of a month or more prior to delivery to be more than a pound greater than the average birth weight of 25 infants born to active addicts. They ascribed this difference to the voracious appetite and rapid weight gain seen in addicts following withdrawal. Whether a similar beneficial effect on birth weight will be observed in infants of mothers whose nutrition and environmental circumstances are improved in a treatment program but who continue on high doses of an alternative narcotic (methadone) remains to be determined. Blatman(17) found the average birth weight (2700) of infants in his methadone maintenance series was not significantly different from that of infants born to addicts not on methadone maintenance (2600). On the other hand, preliminary findings of a group in Philadelphia suggest that mothers in their maintenance program do not give birth to premature or low birth weight infants as frequently as do untreated addicts(57).

Some writers have implied that congenital anomalies occur with increased frequency among infants of addicts(119,127). There is no documentation of such a relationship. Major malformations were found in only 4 of 384 infants(164), 0 of 40 infants(124), and 2 of 249 infants(17) in 3 recently reported series, an incidence not significantly different from that in the general population. The experience at Bellevue Hospital has also suggested that congenital anomalies are not more common among infants of addicts(115). No particular recurring pattern of malformation is apparent in the several cases scattered throughout the literature.

The question of possible teratogenic effects of hallucinogenic drugs is discussed below.

Other Effects of Maternal Narcotic Addiction

Evidence was presented in a recent report of a reduced incidence and severity of hyperbilirubinemia in infants of heroin addicts(26). The authors proposed that bilirubin metabolism in these infants had been enhanced by an inducing effect of narcotics on hepatic enzyme activity. They cited as supporting evidence for this mechanism their finding that a course of morphine sulfate produced a marked rise in glucuronyl transferase activity in hepatic tissue of adult Swiss-Webster mice. However, it cannot be assumed on the basis of these data that morphine produces induction of transferase activity in the human because of the marked species differences in the phenomenon of enzyme induction by various drugs and chemicals(35). It is of interest that morphine has failed to induce hepatic enzymes when studied in the rat(101).

Another report documents the relative rarity of the idiopathic respiratory distress syndrome (RDS) in a series of premature infants with symptoms of heroin withdrawal as compared to control infants of similar gestational age(68). The authors speculate on the possibility that opiates, by inducing enzymes in lung tissue, may stimulate accelerated production of surfactant, whose deficiency in the lungs of immature infants has been linked to the development of RDS. Although RDS has been mentioned by other authors as occurring in some infants of addicted mothers, sometimes with autopsy confirmation, no previous statistical analyses of incidence correlated with gestational age have been published. This interesting observation deserves further study.

Infants of narcotic addicted mothers do not have an unusual incidence of respiratory depression at birth(17,124). This is of note since addicted women often give themselves a large dose of narcotic just before entering the hospital late in labor, and narcotics given to mothers between 1 and 3 hours before delivery are known to produce depression of their newborn infants(32). The suggestion has been made that the lack of depression is related to the development of tolerance to narcotics by the fetus who is chronically exposed to them *in utero* (124).

Prognosis, Disposition, and Follow-up

In the past, infants with narcotic withdrawal were given an exceptionally poor prognosis for survival. In 1913, Pettey(123) wrote that ". . . high mortality among the infants of such mothers is not unavoidable, but managed as they usually are, a large majority of children born to such mothers die on the second or third day after birth." Goodfriend *et al.* (69), who reviewed the 216 cases reported between 1892 and the time of their report in 1956, found the overall mortality rate to be 34 percent and that of untreated cases 94 percent. However, Hill and Desmond(75) reported that only 9 percent of the 93 cases reported between 1947 and 1963 died in the neonatal period. Many fatalities in the earlier literature were attributable to dehydration or inanition. Causes of death, when specified, in more recent reports are varied, including multiple congenital anomalies, pneumonia or atelectasis, massive aspiration, hyaline membrane disease, and sepsis. The recent experience of 3 groups, reporting on a total of 462 infants of addicted mothers seen in 4 New York municipal hospitals(88, 124,164), indicates that the neonatal mortality rate among these babies is not significantly higher than in other infants at the same institutions, and that withdrawal symptoms *per se*, given appropriate management, cannot be considered an important direct cause of death.

The disposition and further care of the infant of an addict mother represent a greater challenge to the clinician than the management of the child's withdrawal symptoms. Many addicted women express strong maternal feelings and a desire to keep their babies, but have an unrealistic view of their own ability to provide for a child's emotional and physical needs. A drug-oriented life is incompatible with meeting the constant demands imposed by a young infant. Furthermore, the personality structure of many addicts contains elements which have been shown to predispose to child abuse. Thus, an abusing parent often places unrealistic demands on an infant to fill some parental need, and may express resentment of the infant's inability to fill this need by overtly hostile behavior(145). It is not unusual for a pregnant addict to look forward to the arrival of her baby as the source of new motivation that will at last enable her to free herself of her drug habit. Unfortunately, in most cases the mother soon resumes her intake of drugs, and may displace her sense of failure onto the infant whose arrival did not bring the desired result. Investigation of cases of child abuse has also revealed that a fussy, crying child who is difficult to soothe may be seen as rejecting his mother, who is looking to her baby for love and comfort she does not find elsewhere(146). Since the subacute phase of neonatal narcotic withdrawal may last for several weeks and be characterized by irritable behavior and crying outbursts, the infant showing these symptoms may be at particular risk if his mother's emotional makeup predisposes her to child abuse. Therefore, the child's safety must be a primary concern in deciding whether he should be discharged in his mother's care.

The office of the Chief Medical Examiner of the City of New York has found that in more than half of the 40 deaths due to child abuse or neglect during the first 6 months of 1971, investigation revealed one or both parents to be narcotic addicts(8). While there is no way to assess the percentage of infants living with addicted parents who meet such a fate, or what role the parents' use of drugs has played in these deaths, this information illustrates the possible danger of discharging a baby to an addict parent without assurance of adequate supervision.

In practice, the decision to send a child home has usually been based on the presence of some non-addicted adult in the household capable of assuming responsibility for care of the child. At Bellevue Hospital and some other large New York municipal hospitals approximately half of the infants of addicted mothers are sent home, and the remainder spend extended periods of time in the hospitals or other institutions awaiting placement in foster or adoptive homes.

A few new comprehensive care programs for pregnant addicts and their infants are attempting to provide alternative solutions to the difficult problems posed by these patients. Encouraging preliminary results are reported from a methadone maintenance program in which women are brought into treatment during pregnancy. Infants of women remaining on methadone maintenance have been discharged to the mothers' care with the continuing support of social and psychiatric services. In almost all instances, the homes have been found to be adequate and it has been possible to maintain continuing follow-up contact with the mothers and their babies for periods as long as 5 or 6 years (16, 17).

Another approach is now being tried in a small pilot program at New York's Odyssey House (41). Pregnant addicts are admitted to a residential setting and slowly withdrawn on methadone, while being given necessary medical and psychiatric treatment. Following delivery, the mothers remain with their babies in the drug-free residential environment for as long as is necessary. It is too early to know what the success rate of this type of program will be. Even if it is shown to be highly successful in rehabilitating some addicts, the large investment of money and personnel required for long-term residential treatment makes it unlikely that this approach will be able to serve the needs of the majority of pregnant addicts.

A major concern of those who care for infants of addict mothers has been the possibility of sequellae which could interfere with the infants' future development or health. Little information is available at the present time on which to base predictions of the outcome of these children. Difficulties of follow-up have thus far precluded systematic study of any sizable group, although there are a number of scattered reports of infants with withdrawal symptoms in the newborn period who have appeared to be developing normally when seen several months to several years later (25, 75, 120, 123, 126, 152).

Comprehensive care programs for addict mothers and their infants are demonstrating for the first time that it is possible to keep these babies in follow-up, thus providing the opportunity to evaluate their physical and mental development. Fourteen infants of mothers in a methadone maintenance program have been studied at intervals for periods of from $4\frac{1}{2}$ to 42 months following birth (17). Physical development was said to be normal in all instances. Psychometric testing using the Knobloch-modified Gesell Test or the Bayley Scales of Infant Development, showed normal or average results in 11 of 14 infants, a high normal intelligence in 1 infant, below average intelligence in 1 infant, and poor language development in 1 infant who was otherwise normal. These preliminary results are encouraging. However, the small size of the sample and the lack of normal controls and infants whose addict mothers were not on methadone maintenance in this study prevent one from drawing conclusions from these data concerning either eventual outcome of infants of addicts or the possible influence of treatment regimens for the addict mother.

Further information on the long-term prognosis for infants born to addicts is badly needed. Such information would be of great value when counseling the addict concerning her pregnancy. It would also facilitate the efforts of adoption agencies, since these babies currently carry an unknown risk and may therefore be rejected by prospective adoptive parents.

EFFECTS OF ANTENATAL EXPOSURE TO NON-NARCOTIC DRUGS OF ABUSE

Little has been established to date concerning the effects on infants of antenatal exposure to several of the commonly abused drugs. Until better information is available, we are forced to draw on experience in adults to provide some clues as to possible effects in infants born to mothers who have been taking amphetamines, barbiturates, hallucinogens, or tranquilizers.

Amphetamines and Cocaine

The abrupt discontinuance of prolonged amphetamine use in adults leads to lethargy and psychological depression, but not to a true abstinence syndrome(34), and it is assumed that infants whose mothers have been chronically using amphetamines during pregnancy will not develop typical withdrawal signs. Thus, when Sussman(152) noted irritability and other symptoms in 2 of 4 infants of methamphetamine abusers, he suggested that there was probably hidden narcotic addiction as well. Neuberg (114) described 4 infants born to women taking methamphetamine. Three were symptom-free, but the fourth was markedly drowsy for 4 days, possibly representing a parallel to the lethargy seen in adults who discontinue amphetamine intake. The only known hazard of abrupt withdrawal of amphetamines is severe and sometimes suicidal depression, which should not be a problem in the neonate, but should be looked for in the mother with a history of amphetamine abuse. Cocaine abuse similarly does not produce true addiction, and would not be expected to cause abstinence symptoms in infants.

Hallucinogens

Interest in the effects of exposure to lysergic acid diethylamide (LSD) on the fetus was greatly stimulated by the report of Cohen et al.(29) in 1967 that chromosomal damage was observed in tissue culture and in one patient following exposure to LSD. Wide publicity which followed in the lay press raised sufficient concern about the possibility of malformed offspring and genetic damage for future generations that there was at least a temporary decrease in experimentation with LSD and other psychedelic drugs among the members of the drug culture. Meanwhile, several investigations of the possible genetic or teratogenic hazards of LSD were undertaken, with results which were often conflicting.

While the induction of chromosome breaks in cultured human leukocytes by the addition of LSD to the medium was confirmed by Jarvik *et al.*(86), these authors found that similar effects could be produced by aspirin or ergonovine maleate. Chromosome damage has been described in some reports in leukocytes from adults previously exposed to LSD (27,51,81), but others have found no increase in the incidence of chromosome abnormalities over that observed in controls(96,142,154). Administration of LSD in early pregnancy was reported to result in increased abortions, stunting, or fetal abnormalities in studies carried out in rats(3), mice(7), and hamsters(64), but no teratogenic effect was found by other investigators in studies of rats(161), and of rabbits(55). Damage to meiotic chromosomes of mice due to LSD was reported in two studies(30,136), but not confirmed by a third(85).

There is a similar lack of agreement among reported studies of leukocyte cultures taken from human infants exposed to LSD *in utero*. Cohen *et al.*(28) studied 9 such infants and found each of them to have an increased incidence of chromosomal damage. On the other hand, Dumars (48) reported no significant increase in chromosome abnormalities over that found in controls in studies of 30 children whose mothers had used LSD before and during pregnancy.

There are several accounts of congenital anomalies in infants whose mothers gave a history of ingestion of LSD (and often other drugs as well) in early pregnancy. Limb deformities were described in 4 infants(5,22, 74,163), and exstrophy of the bladder in 1(66). Berlin and Jacobson(14) reported on a prospective study of 124 pregnancies with a history of LSD use by the mother. Among 59 live born infants, 3 had myelomeningocele and hydrocephalus, 1 had hydrocephalus only, and 1 had congenital amputation of both feet and multiple hemangiomata. Of 14 abortuses studied, 4 had severe midline fusion defects of the central nervous system.

While these reports of malformed infants are sufficient to maintain suspicion of LSD as a possible teratogen, the relationship is far from conclusive and considerably more information is needed in this area.

Studies of the teratogenic potential of marijuana are sparse indeed. Cannabis resin given to female rats for 5 months produced a decrease in reproductive activity and increased maternal deaths, but no fetal abnormalities(107). The intraperitoneal administration of cannabis produced an increased rate of fetal resorptions and malformations in rats(121). Little is known of the effects, if any, on the human fetus.

An extensive review of studies of the genetic effects of drugs of abuse has recently been published by Moorhead, Jarvik, and Cohen(109).

There are, as yet, no reports in the literature of newborn infants who showed acute effects of hallucinogenic drugs. However, it is reasonable to presume that the infant of a mother who delivered while under the influence of LSD might show some form of altered behavior.

Adverse reactions to LSD have been reported to persist or recur for months following ingestion in some patients(56,139). A previously normal 5-year-old girl was carefully studied following a single accidental toxic episode due to LSD. Abnormalities of her EEG, depressed intelligence quotient, distorted body image, and disorganized visual-motor functions improved only gradually over several months(105). It is not known whether *in utero* exposure to LSD has an adverse effect on future neurologic, personality, or intellectual development.

Barbiturates

A severe abstinence syndrome following abrupt withdrawal of barbiturates has been described in adults(61,82). Symptoms of tremors, anxiety, vomiting, abdominal cramps, and sleeplessness resemble those in narcotic withdrawal, but, in addition, there is frequently delirium, as well as a risk of grand mal seizures and occasionally, sudden death. Withdrawal symptoms are treated with barbiturates in gradually tapered doses. Narcotics are ineffective in controlling barbiturate withdrawal.

A series of 15 infants born to mothers who had been taking barbiturates during pregnancy was recently described by Desmond et al.(42). Withdrawal symptoms were observed which closely resembled those in a group of infants of heroin addicts, except that they were frequently later in onset in the barbiturate group, with half of the infants developing symptoms between the 6th and 14th days of life. The diagnosis may be easily overlooked in infants whose symptoms do not develop until after routine discharge from the hospital nursery.

It is interesting that none of Desmond's cases of neonatal barbiturate withdrawal developed seizures. Perhaps the relatively slower metabolism and excretion rate of the newborn results in a more gradual decrease in barbiturate levels, and thus serves to protect him against some of the consequences of abrupt withdrawal in the adult.

Barbiturates are known to be potent inducers of enzyme activity. For a discussion of the effects of phenobarbital enzyme induction in infants on the metabolism of bilirubin and other substances the reader is referred to the commentary by Behrman and Fisher(11).

Minor Tranquilizers and Alcohol

Chronic use of alcohol(83) or any of the so-called minor tranquilizers is known to produce physical dependence in adults, and an abstinence syndrome of the barbiturate type, with a similar risk of seizures and occasional fatalities(54). The drugs reported to have produced withdrawal symptoms in adults are meprobamate(70), glutethimide(87), methyprylon(13), ethchlorvynol(20), ethinamate(53), oxazepam(133), chlordiazepoxide(78), and diazepam(125). Withdrawal symptoms related to any of these agents respond to treatment with barbiturates or with the drug which the patient has been taking, but not to narcotics or phenothiazines(132).

Alcohol withdrawal, manifested by tremors, irritability, and sleeplessness, has been described in 2 infants of alcoholic mothers(117,129). While cases of neonatal withdrawal from minor tranquilizers have not appeared in the literature, suggestive symptoms have been observed in infants whose mothers had been taking glutethimide(144) or meprobamate (94). It is probable that the other drugs known to affect adults can similarly produce withdrawal in chronically exposed infants and a history of their use should be sought in mothers of infants who show characteristic signs of withdrawal without other explanation.

CONCLUDING REMARKS

The first description of the neonatal narcotic withdrawal syndrome appeared in the medical literature almost a century ago. Many articles on the subject have been published since that time, most of them during the past 15 years. Early recognition and therapy of affected infants have been shown to result in prompt control of symptoms and a good prognosis for survival in a condition which was previously thought to be associated with a major risk of serious complications or death.

In spite of gains in the management of these infants, many problems related to drug abuse in pregnancy remain to be solved. We still know very little about the causes or significance of the remarkably high incidence of intrauterine growth retardation and prematurity among infants of addicts. We know still less about the long-range prognosis for growth and development of infants exposed to narcotics before birth. As abuse of multiple drugs becomes more widespread, we are badly in need not only of more information on the actions of each individual drug, but also on the effects of interactions between these drugs in various combinations on the infant *in utero*.

New complexities have been introduced by changes in the prevailing patterns of drug abuse in our culture over the past several decades. Of particular significance to pregnant addicts and their infants are changes which have occurred in the socioeconomic milieu of drug addiction in the United States.

At the turn of the century, narcotics were widely available without legal restriction. Approximately half of the nation's addicts were women, who often became addicted unwittingly through the habitual use of popular patent medicines with a high content of opium. Addiction was more likely to occur among the middle or upper classes than among the poor. Federal regulation of narcotic distribution, which began with the passage of the Harrison Act in 1914, succeeded in reducing the numbers of addicts, particularly among women, in the years which followed. During World War II, wartime conditions sharply curtailed the flow of narcotics into the United States. Since the mid-1940s, when illegal shipments of heroin began to reappear, addiction in this country has occurred predominantly among residents of the most economically depressed areas of our large urban centers. Laws restricting the distribution of narcotics and the high prices exacted by dealers in illegal drugs result in the necessity for most addicts to engage in criminal activity of various sorts to support their drug habits.

The pregnant addict of 75 years ago was likely to be a middle-class housewife without major complicating social pathology. While her infant might have been jeopardized because most physicians at that time were unaware of the significance of neonatal narcotic withdrawal or its management, if he recovered he was probably cared for by his mother in a reasonably normal home environment. In contrast, the pregnant addict today is more often living a life characterized by inadequate food and housing, neglected health, prostitution, frequent arrests, and an unstable or nonexistent family life. The greatest risks faced by the infant of the present-day addict are not those of acute neonatal withdrawal, but those related to the adverse conditions which accompany his mother's drug habit.

Until our society finds more effective deterrents to the abuse of drugs than now exist, we will be faced with the problems of infants exposed to the double jeopardy of drug exposure in fetal life and severely deprived environmental circumstances before and after birth. Successful management of neonatal drug withdrawal effects accomplishes very little for the affected infant if all that awaits him is prolonged institutional care or an uncertain and possibly hazardous future with his addicted mother.

Efforts now underway to provide better alternatives by involving pregnant addicts in programs of comprehensive care for themselves and their infants show encouraging early results. It has been demonstrated that addicts who enter such programs can be enabled to stabilize their own lives, to avail themselves of regular prenatal care along with treatment for their addiction, and, with the help of supporting services, to provide adequate mothering for their children. Continuing research is needed into the effectiveness, safety, and feasibility of various treatment methods such as those using methadone maintenance, narcotic antagonists, or a drug-free residential environment.

While it is unlikely that treatment programs will ever reach all pregnant addicts, pregnancy provides a new motivation for many addicted women to rid themselves of their drug habits. The development of more programs which will capitalize on this period of motivation to engage pregnant addicts in treatment of their addiction can be expected to pay dual dividends in improving prospects for normal lives for these young women as well as for their newborn infants.

Acknowledgments   The author is indebted to Dr. Sanford N. Cohen for his help and encouragement, to Dr. Saul Krugman for his critical review and comments, and to Miss Lucille Rung for her patience in preparation of the manuscript.

REFERENCES

1. Adriani, J. and Morton, R. C. Drug dependence: Important considerations from the anesthesiologist's viewpoint. *Anesth. Analg.*, 1968, **47**: 472.
2. Akamatsu, T. J. and McDonald, J. S. Other non-obstetric disorders. In Bonica, J. J.: *Principles and practice of obstetric analgesia and anesthesia*, Davis, Philadelphia, 1969. P. 1121.
3. Alexander, G. J., Miles, B. E., Gold, G. M., and Alexander, R. B. LSD: Injection early in pregnancy produces abnormalities in offspring of rats. *Science*, 1967, **157**: 459.
4. Asling, J. and Way, E. L. Placental transfer of drugs. In *Fundamentals of drug metabolism and disposition*. LaDu, B. N., Mandel, H. G., and Way, E. L. (Eds.) Williams and Wilkins, Baltimore, Md., 1971. Pp. 99–102.
5. Assemany, S. R., Neu, R. L., and Gardner, L. I. Deformities in a child whose mother took LSD. *Lancet*, 1970, **1**: 1290.
6. Aterman, K. Neonatal hepatitis and its relation to viral hepatitis of mother. *Amer. J. Dis. Child*, 1963, **105**: 395.
7. Auerbach, R. and Rugowski, J. A. Lysergic acid diethylamide: Effect on embryos. *Science*, 1967, **157**: 1325.
8. Baden, M. M. Personal communication.

9. Baker, J. B. E. The effects of drugs on the foetus. *Pharmacol. Rev.*, 1960, **12**: 37.
10. Beard, A. G. Hepatitis in three siblings: Possibility of intrauterine transmission. *J. Pediat*, 1956, **49**: 454.
11. Behrman, R. E. and Fisher, D. E. Phenobarbital for neonatal jaundice. *J. Pediat*, 1970, **76**: 945.
12. Benirschke, K. Routes and types of infection in the fetus and the newborn. *Amer. J. Dis. Child*, 1960, **99**: 714.
13. Berger, H. Addiction to methyprylon: Report of a case of 24-year-old nurse with possible synergism with phenothiazine. *JAMA*, 1961, **177**: 63.
14. Berlin, C. M. and Jacobson, C. B. Congenital anomalies associated with parental LSD ingestion. Society for Pediatric Research, Atlantic City, N. J., April 29–May 2, 1970.
15. Blanc, W. A. Pathways of fetal and early neonatal infection. *J. Pediat.*, 1961, **59**: 473.
16. Blatman, S. Personal communication.
17. Blatman, S. and Lipsitz, P. Infants born to heroin addicts maintained on methadone: Neonatal observations and follow-up. *Proceedings of the Third National Conference on Methadone Treatment*, New York, N.Y., Nov. 14–16, 1970, NIMH.
18. Blinick, G., Wallach, R. C., and Jerez, E. Pregnancy in narcotics addicts treated by medical withdrawal. The methadone detoxification program. *Amer. J. Obstet. Gynec.*, 1969, **105**: 997.
19. Bloom, W. A. from Third National Conference on Methadone Treatment New York, N.Y., Nov. 14–16, 1970, NIMH as reported in "Medical News" *JAMA*, 1970, **214**: 1977.
20. Blumenthal, M. D. and Reinhart, M. J. Psychosis and convulsions following withdrawal from ethchlorvynol. *JAMA*, 1964, **190**: 154.
21. Boak, R. A., Carpenter, C. M., and Miller, J. N. Biologic false-positive reactions for syphilis among narcotic addicts. *JAMA*, 1961, **175**: 326.
22. Carakushansky, G., Neu, R. L., and Gardner, L. I. Lysergide and cannabis as possible teratogens in man. *Lancet*, 1969, **1**: 150.
23. Cherubin, C. E. Infectious disease problems of narcotic addicts. *Arch. Intern. Med.*, 1971, **128**: 309.
24. Claman, A. D. and Strang, R. I. Obstetric and gynecologic aspects of heroin addiction. *Amer. J. Obstet. Gynec.*, 1962, **83**: 252.
25. Cobrinik, R. W., Hood, R. T. Jr, and Chusid, E. The effect of maternal narcotic addiction on the newborn infant. *Pediatrics*, 1959, **24**: 288.
26. Cohen, M. I., Nathenson, G., McNamara, H., and Litt, I. F. The mitigating effect of addiction to heroin on neonatal jaundice. American Pediatric Society, Atlantic City, April 28–May 1, 1971.
27. Cohen, M. M., Hirschhorn, K., and Frosch, W. A. *In vivo* and *in vitro* chromosomal damage induced by LSD-25. *New Eng. J. Med.*, 1967, **277**: 1043.
28. Cohen, M. M., Hirschhorn, K., Verbo, S., Frosch, W. A., and Groeschel, M. M. The effects of LSD-25 on the chromosomes of children exposed in utero. *Pediat. Res.*, 1968, **2**: 486.
29. Cohen, M. M., Marinello, M. J., and Back, N. Chromosomal damage in human leukocytes induced by lysergic acid-diethylamide. *Science*, 1967, **155**: 1417.
30. Cohen, M. M. and Mukherjee, A. B. Meiotic chromosome damage induced by LSD-25. *Nature*, 1968, **219**: 1072.
31. Cohen, S. N., Neumann, L. L., and Ganapathy, S. Diazepam (Valium) for neonatal narcotic withdrawal: A question of safety. (letter) *Pediatrics*. 1972, **49**: 928.

32. Cohen, S. N. and Olson, W. A. Drugs that depress the newborn infant. *Pediat. Clin. N. Amer.*, 1970, **17**: 835.
33. Connaughton, J. F. Jr., Finnegan, L., Wieland, W. Q., and Polin, J. I. Jr. Current concepts in management of pregnant narcotic addicts. Abstract of Report to Nineteenth Annual Clinical Meeting of the American College of Obstetrics and Gynecology. *Obstet. Gynec.*, 1971, **37**: 631.
34. Connell, P. H. Clinical manifestations and treatment of amphetamine type of dependence. *JAMA*, 1966, **196**: 718.
35. Conney, A. H. Pharmacological implications of microsomal enzyme induction. *Pharmacol. Rev.*, 1967, **19**: 317.
36. Corssen, G. and Skora, I. A. "Addiction" reactions in cultured human cells. *JAMA*, 1964, **187**: 328.
37. Cossart, Y. E., Hargreaves, D., and March, S. P. Australia antigen and the human foetus. *Amer. J. Dis. Child*, 1972, **123**: 376.
38. Coumbis, R. J., Albano, E. H., and Lyons, M. Drug detection in urines of commercial blood bank donors. *JAMA*, 1970, **214**: 596.
39. Covell, G. Congenital malaria. *Trop. Dis. Bull.*, 1950, **47**: 1147.
40. Davidow, B., LiPetri, N., and Quame, B. A thin-layer chromatographic screening procedure for detecting drug abuse. *Amer. J. Clin. Pathol.*, 1968, **50**: 714.
41. Densen-Gerber, J. Personal communication.
42. Desmond, M. M., Schwanecke, R. P., Wilson, G. S., Yasunga, S., and Burgdorff, I. Maternal barbiturate utilization and neonatal withdrawal symptomatology. *J. Pediat.* 1972, **80**: 190.
43. Dimson, S. B. Congenital malaria in England. *Brit. Med. J.*, 1954, **2**: 1083.
44. Dole, V. P. "Blockade with methadone" in Clouet, D. H., *Narcotic drugs: Biochemical pharmacology*, Plenum Press, New York, 1971. Pp. 478–483.
45. Dole, V. P., Kim, W. K., and Eglitis, I. Detection of narcotic drugs, tranquilizers, amphetamines and barbiturates in urine. *JAMA*, 1966, **198**: 349.
46. Dole, V. P. and Nyswander, M. A medical treatment for diacetylmorphine (heroin) addiction: A clinical trial with methadone hydrochloride. *JAMA*, 1965, **193**: 646.
47. Dover, A. S. Malaria in a heroin user. *JAMA*, 1971, **215**: 1987.
48. Dumars, K. W. Jr. Parental drug usage: Effect upon chromosomes of progeny. *Pediatrics*, 1971, **47**: 1037.
49. Earle, L. B. Maternal opium habit and infant mortality. *Med. Standard*, Chicago, 1888, **3**: 2.
50. Edgar, J. C. *Practice of obstetrics*, 5th Edition, P. Blakiston's, 1916.
51. Egozcue, J., Irwin, S., and Maruffo, C. A. Chromosomal damage in LSD users. *JAMA*, 1968, **204**: 214.
52. Eiseman, B., Lam, R. C., and Rush B. Surgery on the narcotic addict. *Ann. Surg.*, 1964, **159**: 748.
53. Ellinwood, E. H. Jr, Ewing, J. A., and Hoaken, P. C. S. Habituation to ethinamate. *New Eng. J. Med.*, 1962, **266**: 185.
54. Essig, C. F. Newer sedative drugs that can cause states of intoxication and dependence of barbiturate type. *JAMA*, 1966, **196**: 714.
55. Fabro, S. and Sieber, S. M. Is lysergide a teratogen? *Lancet*, 1968, **1**: 639.
56. Fink, M., Simeon, J., Hague, W., and Itil, T. Prolonged adverse reactions to LSD in psychotic subjects. *Arch. Gen. Psychiat.*, 1966, **15**: 450.
57. Finnegan, L. Personal communication.

58. Fisch, G. R. and Henley, W. L. Symptoms of narcotic withdrawal in a newborn infant secondary to medical therapy of the mother. *Pediatrics*, 1961, **28**: 852.
59. Fish, F. Analysis for drugs of abuse: Some applications and limitations. *J. Forens. Sci. Soc.*, 1969, **9**: 48.
60. Fisher, G. U. and Schultz, M. G. Unusual host-parasite relationship in blood-donors responsible for transfusion-induced falciparum malaria. *Lancet*, 1969, **2**: 716.
61. Fraser, H. F., Isbell, H., Eisenman, A. J., Wikler, A., and Pescor, F. T. Chronic barbiturate intoxication: Further studies. *Arch. Intern. Med.*, 1954, **94**: 34.
61a. Gartner, L. Personal communication.
62. Gaulden, E. C., Littlefield, D. C., Putoff, O. E., and Seivert, A. L. Menstrual abnormalities associated with heroin addiction. *Amer. J. Obstet. Gynec.*, 1964, **90**: 155.
63. Gautieri, R. F. and Ciuchta, H. P. Effect of certain drugs on perfused human placenta: I. Narcotic analgesics, serotonin, and relaxin. *J. Pharm. Sci.*, 1962, **51**: 55.
64. Geber, W. F. Congenital malformations induced by mescaline, lysergic acid diethylamide and bromolysergic acid in the hamster. *Science*, 1967, **158**: 265.
65. Geiger, J. C. Malaria in narcotic addicts. *JAMA*, 1932, **98**: 1494.
66. Gelehrter, T. D. Lysergic acid diethylamide (LSD) and exstrophy of the bladder. *J. Pediat.* 1970, **77**: 1065.
67. Ghadirian, A. A tissue culture study of morphine dependence on the mammalian CNS. *Canad. Psychiat. Ass. J.*, 1969, **14**: 607.
68. Glass, L., Rajegowda, B. K., and Evans, H. E. Absence of respiratory distress syndrome in premature infants of heroin-addicted mothers. *Lancet*, 1971, **2**: 685.
69. Goodfriend, M. J., Shey, I. A., and Klein, M. D. The effects of maternal narcotic addiction on the newborn. *Amer. J. Obstet. Gynec.*, 1956, **71**: 29.
70. Haizlip, T. M. and Ewing, J. A. Meprobamate habituation: A controlled clinical study. *New Eng. J. Med.*, 1958, **258**: 1181.
71. Harris, A., Brown, L., Portnoy, J., and Price, E. V. Narcotic addiction and BFP reactions in tests for syphilis. *Public Health Rep.*, 1962, **77**: 537.
72. Harris, W. D. M. and Andrei, J. Serologic tests for syphilis among narcotic addicts. *New York J. Med.*, 1967, **67**: 2967.
73. Harvey, B., Remington, J. S., and Sulzer, A. J. IgM malaria antibodies in a case of congenital malaria in the United States. *Lancet*, 1969, **1**: 333.
74. Hecht, F., Beals, R. K., Lees, M. H., Jolly, H., and Roberts, P. Lysergic-acid-diethylamide and cannabis as possible teratogens in man. *Lancet*, 1968, **2**: 1087.
75. Hill, R. M. and Desmond, M. M. Management of the narcotic withdrawal syndrome in the neonate. *Pediat. Clin. N. Amer.*, 1963, **10**: 67.
76. Himmelsbach, C. K. Studies on the relation of drug addiction to the autonomic nervous system: Results of cold pressor tests. *J. Pharmacol. Exp. Ther.*, 1941, **73**: 91.
77. Himmelsbach, C. K. Clinical studies of drug addiction: Physical dependence, withdrawal and recovery. *Arch. Intern. Med.*, 1942, **69**: 766.
78. Hollister, L. E., Motzenbecker, F. P., and Degan, R. D. Withdrawal reactions from chlordiazepoxide ("Librium"). *Psychopharmacologia*, 1961, **2**: 62.
79. Hsia, D. Y.-Y. and Porto, S. Detoxification mechanisms in the liver. In *Physiology of the perinatal period*, Stave, U., (Ed.), Appleton-Century-Crofts, Educational Div., Meredith Corp., New York, 1970. Vol. 1, pp. 629–632.
80. Hsia, D. Y-Y., Taylor, R. G., and Gellis, S. S. A long-term follow-up study on infectious hepatitis during pregnancy. *J. Pediat.*, 1952, **41**: 13.
81. Hungerford, D. A., Taylor, K. M., Shagass, C., LaBadie, G. U., Balaban, G. B., and Paton, G. R. Cytogenetic effects of LSD 25 therapy in man. *JAMA*, 1968, **206**: 2287.

82. Isbell, H. Addiction to barbiturates and the barbiturate abstinence syndrome. *Ann. Intern. Med.*, 1950, **33**: 108.
83. Isbell, H., Fraser, H. F., Wikler, A., Belleville, R. E., and Eisenman, A. J. An experimental study of the etiology of "rum fits" and delirium tremens. *Quart. J. Stud. Alcohol*, 1955, **16**: 1.
84. Isbell, H. and White, W. M. Clinical characteristics of addictions. *Amer. J. Med.*, 1953, **14**: 558.
85. Jagiello, G. and Polani, P. E. Mouse germ cells and LSD-25. *Cytogenetics*, 1969, **8**: 136.
86. Jarvik, L. F., Kato, T., Saunders, B., and Moralishvili, E. LSD and human chromosomes. In *Psychopharmacology: A review of progress*, Efron, D. A. (Ed.), U.S. Dept. of HEW, Public Health Service Publ. # 1836, Washington, D.C., 1968. Pp. 1247–1252.
87. Johnson, F. A. and VanBuren, H. C. Abstinence syndrome following glutethimide intoxication. *JAMA*, 1962, **180**: 1024.
88. Kahn, E. J., Neumann, L. L., and Polk, G.-A. The course of the heroin withdrawal syndrome in newborn infants treated with phenobarbital or chlorpromazine. *J. Pediat.*, 1969, **75**: 495.
89. Keitel, H. G., Goodman, H. C., Havel, R. J., Gordon, R. S., and Baxter, J. H. Nephrotic syndrome in congenital quartan malaria. *JAMA*, 1956, **161**: 520.
90. Koenigsberger, M. R. Judgement of fetal age. I. Neurologic evaluation. *Pediat. Clin. N. Amer.*, 1966, **13**: 823.
91. Koval, M. *Differential estimates of opiate use in New York City*. New York State Narcotic Addiction Control Commission, Albany, N.Y., April 1971.
92. Krause, S. O., Murray, P. M., Holmes, J. B., and Burch, R. E. Heroin addiction among pregnant women and their newborn babies. *Amer. J. Obst. Gynec.*, 1958, **75**: 754.
93. Kunstadter, R. H., Klein, R. I., Lundeen, E. C., Witz, W., and Morrison, M. Narcotic withdrawal symptoms in newborn infants. *JAMA*, 1958, **168**: 1008.
94. Lawrence, R. Personal communication.
95. London, W. T., DiFiglia, M., and Rodgers, J. Failure of tranplacental transmission of Australia antigen. *Lancet*, 1969, **3**: 900.
96. Loughman, W. D., Sargent, T. W., and Israelstam, D. M. Leukocytes of humans exposed to lysergic acid diethylamide: Lack of chromosomal damage. *Science*, 1967, **158**: 508.
97. Louria, D. B., Hensle, T. Jr, and Rose, J. Major medical complications of heroin addiction. *Ann. Intern. Med.*, 1967, **67**: 1.
98. McCollum, R. W. Report of a conference: Serum antigens in viral hepatitis. *J. Infect. Dis.*, 1969, **120**: 641.
99. McQuay, R. M., Silberman, S., Mudrik, P., and Keith, L. E. Congenital malaria in Chicago; A case report and a review of published reports (U.S.A.) *Amer. J. Trop. Med.*, 1967, **16**: 258.
100. Mamunes, P., Cave, V. G., Budell, J. W., Andersen, J. A., and Steward, R. E. Early diagnosis of neonatal syphilis. *Amer. J. Dis. Child.*, 1970, **120**: 17.
101. Mannering, G. J. Microsomal enzyme systems which catalyze drug metabolism. In LaDu, B. N., Mandel, H. G., and Way, E. L., (Eds.) *Fundamentals of drug metabolism and drug disposition*. Williams and Wilkins, Baltimore, 1971. P. 219.
102. Marks, V., Fry, D., Chapple, P. A. L., and Gray, G. Application of urine analysis to diagnosis and treatment of heroin addiction. *Brit. Med. J.*, 1969, **2**: 153.

103. Martin, W. R., Wikler, A., Eades, C. G., and Pescor, F. T. Tolerance to and physical dependence on morphine in rats. *Psychopharmacologia*, 1963, **4**: 247.
104. Marx, L. C. (Chairman). Clinical Anesthesia Conference: Hypotension during anesthesia in narcotic addicts. *New York J. Med.*, 1966, **66**: 2685.
105. Milman, D. H. An untoward reaction to accidental ingestion of LSD in a 5-year-old girl. *JAMA*, 1967, **201**: 821.
106. Mims, L. C. and Riley, H. D. Jr. The narcotic withdrawal syndrome in the newborn infant. *Oklahoma State Med. Assoc. J.*, 1969, **62**: 411.
107. Miras, C. J. Some aspects of cannabis action in hashish: Its chemistry and pharmacology. Ciba Foundation Study Group, No. 21, 1965. Pp. 37–53.
108. Monif, G. R. G. *Viral infections of the human fetus*. Macmillan, Collier-Macmillan Limited, London, 1969. Pp. 133–143.
109. Moorhead, P. S., Jarvik, L. F., and Cohen, M. M. Cytogenetic method for mutagenicity testing. In Epstein, S. S. (Ed.) *Drugs of abuse: Their genetic and other chronic nonpsychiatric hazards*. MIT Press, Cambridge, Mass., 1971.
110. Most, H. Falciparum malaria in drug addicts: Clinical aspects. *Amer. J. Trop. Med.*, 1940, **20**: 551.
111. Moya, F. Uptake, distribution and placental transfer of drugs. In Shnider, S. M. (Ed.) *Obstetrical Anesthesia*. Williams & Wilkins, Baltimore, 1970. Pp. 21–27.
112. Moya, F. and Thorndike, V. Passage of drugs across the placenta. *Amer. J. Obstet. Gynec.*, 1962, **84**: 1778.
113. Nathenson, G., Golden, G. S., and Litt, I. F. Diazepam in the management of the neonatal narcotic withdrawal syndrome. *Pediatrics*, 1971, **48**: 523.
114. Neuberg, R. Drug dependence and pregnancy: A review of the problems and their management. *J. obstet. Gynaec. Brit. Comm.*, 1970, **77**: 1117.
115. Neumann, L. L. Unpublished observations.
116. Newman, S. J., Madden, D. L., Gitnick, G. L., and Sever, J. L. A serological survey for Australia antigen and antibody. *Amer. J. Dis. Child.*, 1971, **122**: 129.
117. Nichols, M. M. Acute alcohol withdrawal syndrome in a newborn. *Amer. J. Dis. Child.*, 1967, **113**: 714.
118. Novak, E. R., Jones, G. S., and Jones, H. W. Jr. *Novak's textbook of gynecology*, 8th Edition, Williams & Wilkins, Baltimore, 1970. Pp. 595–596.
119. Perlmutter, J. F. Drug addiction in pregnant women. *Amer. J. Obstet. Gynec.*, 1967, **99**: 569.
120. Perlstein, M. A. Congenital morphinism: A rare cause of convulsions in the newborn. *JAMA*, 1947, **135**: 633.
121. Persaud, T. V. N. and Ellington, A. C. Teratogenic activity of cannabis resin. *Lancet*, 1968, **2**: 406.
122. Pettey, G. E. Congenital morphinism, with report of cases. In *The narcotic drug diseases and allied ailments; Pathology, pathogenesis and treatment*. F. A. Davis, Philadelphia, 1913. P. 128.
123. *Ibid.* Pp. 324–335.
123a. Pierson, P. S., Howard, P., and Kleber, H. D. Sudden deaths in infants born to methadone-maintained addicts. *JAMA*, 1972, **220**: 1733.
123b. Rajegowda, B. K., Glass, L., Evans, H. E., Masó, G., Swartz, D. P., and Leblanc, W. Methadone withdrawal in newborn infants. *J. Pediat.*, 1972, **81**: 532.
124. Reddy, A. M., Harper, R. G., and Stern, G. Observations on heroin and methadone withdrawal in the newborn. *Pediatrics*, 1971, **48**: 353.
125. Relkin, R. Death following withdrawal of diazepam: *New York J. Med.*, 1966, **66**: 1770.

126. Roman, L. P. and Middelkamp, J. N. Narcotic addiction in a newborn infant. *J. Pediat.*, 1958, **53**: 231.
127. Rosenthal, T., Patrick, S. W., and Krug, D. C. Congenital neonatal narcotics addiction: A natural history. *Amer. J. Public Health*, 1964, **54**: 1252.
128. Sapira, J. S. The narcotic addict as a medical patient. *Amer. J. Med.*, 1968, **45**: 555.
129. Schaefer, O. Alcohol withdrawal syndrome in a newborn infant of a Yukon Indian mother. *Canad. Med. Ass. J.*, 1962, **87**: 1333.
130. Schiff, D., Chan, G., and Stern, L. Fixed drug combinations and the displacement of bilirubin from albumin. *Pediatrics*, 1971, **48**: 139.
131. Schweitzer, I. L. and Spears, R. L. Hepatitis-associated antigen (Australia antigen) in mother and infant. *New Eng. J. Med.*, 1970, **283**: 570.
132. Seevers, M. H. Psychopharmacological elements of drug dependence. *JAMA*, 1968, **206**: 1263.
133. Selig, J. W. A possible oxazepam abstinence syndrome. *JAMA*, 1966, **198**: 951.
134. Semoff, M. C. F. Narcotic addiction of the newborn. *Arizona Med.*, 1967, **24**: 933.
135. Shute, E. and Davis, M. E. The effect on the infant of morphine administered in labor. *Surg. Gynec. Obstet*, 1933, **57**: 727.
136. Skakkebaek, N. E., Philip, J., and Rafaelson, O. J. LSD in mice: Abnormalities in meiotic chromosomes. *Science*, 1968, **160**: 1246.
137. Skinhøj, P., Sardeman, H., Cohn, J., Mikkelsen, M., and Olesen, H. Hepatitis associated antigen (HAA) in pregnant women and their newborn infants. *Amer. J. Dis. Child.*, 1972, **123**: 380.
138. Skudder, P. A., Inglis, A. E., and McCarroll, J. R. Tetanus in New York City. *New York J. Med.*, 1962, **62**: 2793.
139. Smart, R. G. and Bateman, K. Unfavourable reactions to LSD: A review and analysis of the available case reports. *Canad. Med. Ass. J.*, 1967, **97**: 1214.
140. Smithwick, E. M. and Go, S. G. Hepatitis-associated antigen in cord and maternal sera. *Lancet*, 1970, **2**: 1080.
141. Smithwick, E. M., Pascual, E., and Go, S. G. Hepatitis-associated antigen: A possible relationship with premature delivery. Society for Pediatric Research and American Pediatric Society, Atlantic City, April 28–May 1, 1971.
142. Sparkes, R. S., Melnyk, I., and Bozzetti, L. P. Chromosomal effect *in vivo* of exposure to lysergic acid diethylamide. *Science*, 1968, **160**: 1343.
143. Splaver, T. E. and Williams, A. C. Management of the narcotic-addicted surgical patient: Concepts of medical and surgical care. *J. Oral Surg.*, 1970, **28**: 346.
144. Staub, W. A. Personal communication.
145. Steele, B. F. and Pollock, C. B. A psychiatric study of parents who abuse infants and small children. In Helfer, R. E. and Kempe, C. H., *The battered child*. Univ. of Chicago Press, 1968, Pp. 109–110.
146. *Ibid.* Pp. 128–129.
147. Steg, N. Narcotic withdrawal reactions in the newborn. *Amer. J. Dis. Child*, 1957, **94**: 286.
148. Stern, R. The pregnant addict: A study of 66 case histories, 1950–1959. *Amer. J. Obstet. Gynec.*, 1966, **94**: 253.
149. Stoffer, S. S. A gynecological study of drug addicts. *Amer. J. Obstet. Gynec.*, 1968, **101**: 779.
150. Stokes, J. Jr., Wolman, J. J., Blanchard, M. C., and Farquhar, J. D., Viral hepatitis in the newborn: Clinical features, epidemiology, and pathology. *Amer. J. Dis. Child.*, 1951, **82**: 213.

151. Stone, M. L., Salerno, M. L., Salerno, L. J., Green, M., and Zelson, C. Narcotic addiction in pregnancy. *Amer. J. Obstet. Gynec.*, 1971, **109**: 716.

152. Sussman, S. Narcotic and methamphetamine use during pregnancy. *Amer. J. Dis. Child.*, 1963, **106**: 325.

153. Sutnick, A. I., Cerda, J. J., Toskes, P. P., London, W. T., and Blumberg, B. S. Australia antigen and viral hepatitis in drug abusers. *Arch. Intern. Med.*, 1971, **127**: 939.

154. Tjio, J.-H., Pahnke, W. N., and Kurland, A. A. LSD and chromosomes: A controlled experiment. *JAMA*, 1968, **210**: 849.

155. To, S. and Oh, J. Über die Vergiftungen de von der neugeborenen Zeit an Opium gewöhnten menschen. *Jap. J. M. Sc. Tr., IV Pharmacol.*, 1934, **8**: 100. Cited in Cobrinik, R. W., Hood, R. T. Jr, and Chusid, E. *Op. cit.*

156. Tuffanelli, D. L. and Wuepper, K. D. False-positive reaction for syphilis in narcotic addicts: Immunologic studies. *Clin. Res*, 1967, **15**: 255.

157. Turner, G. C., Field, A. M., Lasheen, R. M., Todd, R. M., White, G. B. B., and Porter, A. A. SH (Australia) antigen in early life. *Arch. Dis. Child*, 1971, **46**: 616.

158. Usher, R., McLean, F., and Scott, K. E. Judgement of fetal age. II. Clinical significance of gestational age and an objective method for its assessment. *Pediat. Clin. N. Amer.*, 1966, **13**: 835.

159. Van Leeuwen, G., Guthrie, R., and Stange, F. Narcotic withdrawal reaction in a newborn infant due to codeine. *Pediatrics*, 1965, **36**: 635.

160. Wallach, R. C., Jerez, E., and Blinick, G. Pregnancy and menstrual function in narcotics addicts treated with methadone; the methadone maintenance program. *Amer. J. Obstet. Gynec.*, 1969, **105**: 1226.

161. Warkany, J. and Takacs, E. Lysergic acid diethylamide (LSD): No teratogenicity in rats. *Science*, 1968, **159**: 731.

162. Wright, R., Perkins, J. R., Bower, B. D., and Jerrome, D. W. Cirrhosis associated with the Australia antigen in an infant who acquired hepatitis from her mother. *Brit. Med. J.*, 1970, **4**: 719.

163. Zellweger, H., McDonald, J. S., and Abbo, G. Is lysergic acid diethylamide a teratogen? *Lancet*, 1967, **2**: 1066.

164. Zelson, C., Rubio, E., and Wasserman, E. Neonatal narcotic addiction: 10 year observation. *Pediatrics*, 1971, **48**: 178.

The Major Drugs of Use Among Adolescents and Young Adults

ERICH GOODE

INTRODUCTION

Like the image in the fun house mirror, the public's conception of adolescent drug use is severely distorted, and in a variety of ways. To begin with, most people have no idea *which* drugs adolescents are using; second, *how often* they use them — what is a typical level of involvement or use; third, *how many* young people are using and becoming involved with drugs; fourth, *what motivates* the young adult to try or use drugs; and fifth, *what changes* take place in a youth's life after using drugs. In this essay, I will attempt to deal with these issues.

However, before these questions can possibly be dealt with, an even more *basic* question must be asked and answered: *what is a drug?* This might seem like an extremely silly and superfluous question; everybody knows what a drug is. Actually this is not so; in fact, different people have different definitions, different ideas as to what a drug is. There are many different kinds of drugs, different reasons for calling some substance a drug. Defining a drug is something like having imperfectly overlapping circles: by one definition, one set of chemicals may be included within the circle; by another definition, a somewhat different, but to some degree overlapping, set of chemicals may be included. But no single definition can cover all drugs, all chemical substances which would be defined as a drug within all definitions. Most people think of only the *legal* definition: chemical substances whose possession is against the law, or whose use without a medical prescription is illegal. By this definition, marijuana, cocaine, and heroin would be drugs, as would the non-medical use of amphetamines, barbiturates, and codeine. But the legal definition is only one relevant definition—there are many others. There is also a *medical* definition: chemicals used in medical therapy. Penicillin is a drug according to a medical definition, and so are steroids, insulin, digitalis, thyroid, estrogens—even vitamins could be considered drugs according to a medical definition. If we were interested in drugs from the perspective of *ethnobotany*, or the use of plants by tribal people to induce mentally altered states, then we would call peyote, marijuana, opium, the "magic mushroom" (or *psilocybe mexicana*), morning-glory seeds, kava-kava, and alcohol, drugs—but almost none of the substances which fall into the medical definition would be included. We might also define drugs according to whether they are *psychoactive*—whether they influence the processes of the mind, how people think, their mood, emotions, their feelings, their psychic and mental processes. But, as with the other definitions, some chemical substances will be included and some will be excluded. Marijuana and LSD are certainly psychoactive—they influence the human mind—but many therapeutic drugs do not have this effect, aside from making someone feel better. Someone who has just taken an oral dose of methadone does not think radically differently from "normally." In other words, according to a criterion of the psychoactive effects of a drug, methadone is not really a drug. However, it *is* a drug according to a medical, or therapeutic definition, and it is used, to some degree, illegally, on the street—and by that definition it is also a drug.

The point is, there is no single, universal, uniform, standard definition that covers all substances that everyone would consider drugs. No single definition is completely adequate. Different definitions are useful for different purposes. It is important to realize this, because most people think that it is possible to describe someone who uses drugs in very simple terms—the drug user is sick; or he has a death-wish; he deserves to be punished; he conforms to some psychological or social type, and so on. Most people wish to think of illegal substances as "drugs," and legal substances as *beverages* (like liquor), or as *medicine* (like barbiturate pills), or simply as a "nasty habit" (like cigarettes). The more that users of many different types of drugs are studied, the more that we realize that the division between users of legal and illegal drugs is somewhat arbitrary and artificial; drug users turn out to be almost everybody. Because someone uses a chemical which society has declared to be illegal does not magically make him radically different from the person who uses a chemical which might have very similar effects, but which society has decided to keep legally available.

My own definition of what drugs would include are the following elements: (1) they are psychoactive—they influence mood and thinking processes; (2) they are used specifically to achieve euphoria, or to "get high"; (3) their use and possession are against the law. There are other possible definitions, but this one is useful to me.

Our next job is to *classify* different kinds of drugs. Even those chemical substances which are included within our characteristics may be very different from one another. Pharmacologists categorize drugs according to their effects, but, in reality, this is somewhat misleading, and for at least two reasons. First, *all drugs have a wide range of different effects.* It is misleading to say that a drug is *a* stimulant, or *a* depressant, or *a* narcotic, because these describe only *one effect at a time*, and a drug may also be many other things as well, and have many other effects. For instance, morphine is a narcotic—that is, it is a pain-killer. However, it also has an antidiarrheal effect—it is effective in offsetting diarrhea—and it is also excellent as a cough medicine. It has many other effects as well. In other words, drugs are classified according to a category, but that does not mean that the specific action that puts them into one or another category is the *only* action they have. In fact, *no* drug has a single action, and which of the many actions of different drugs we choose to use to *put* them into categories is dependent on what we, what society, thinks of the action—what uses we can find for one or another effect. It is not nature that classifies, but men who classify nature.

There is a second reason why it is a little arbitrary (but also necessary) to put drugs into compartments, to classify them according to some scheme. It is that the "effects" of drugs are dependent on forces *outside* the drug, as well as *within* the drug itself. In other words, a drug has certain effects not *only* because of what it is as a chemical, but *also* because of many social and psychological reasons. Drug *expectations* influence drug effects—what people think they are taking, and what they think the effects are going to be—may actually influence what effects occur. The social *situations* in which drug use takes place will influence what effects a drug has. The same drug, taken in two different situations, will actually have two different "effects." People who take morphine in a hospital setting will not usually get high from it, euphoria will not necessarily be one of morphine's "effects." Nevertheless, if the same drug is stolen from the hospital and is used illegally, on the street, the user will nearly always experience euphoria from it—because that is the reason he will be taking it, to get high. So *social definitions* and *attitudes toward drugs* have a great deal to do with their actual effects, with how people experience the effects of drugs. Social beliefs about drugs and their effects can have an independent impact on what drugs do to people. The social belief that heroin has the fantastic power to enslave the addict actually does give it even greater power to enslave; if this belief were absent, it would really be easier to kick the heroin habit. The fact that it is, or was a few years ago, widely believed that LSD would make people "go crazy" contributes, to a great degree, to actual incidents of people experiencing psychotic outbreaks. The fact that it is less widely and less strongly believed today that LSD produces madness means that fewer people become psychotic under the influence of LSD. Social norms and beliefs concerning drug effects will exert a powerful influence on what effects drugs actually have. Societies do not believe that a drug has certain effects simply because it does. Once they believe something about a drug, however wrong to begin with, that belief will exert an independent effect, regardless of what its "actual" effects are. In fact, what its *believed* effects are can become its *actual* effects. This is not to say that the social definition is the whole story, but it is a large part of the drug picture, of the drug equation. It is also important to realize *who* is taking a drug. Effects will vary from one person to another. The personality and mental health of a person will influence, to some extent, his drug reactions. How he feels about himself, as well as about the people with whom he is taking a drug, will have an impact on what he experiences under the influence of a drug. His past drug experiences will partly determine drug "effects." The point is, drug effects do not grow solely out of a chemical reaction, but out of many different factors, only one of which is the chemical. This is why it is misleading to put drugs into simple airtight categories. The same drug can have different effects on different people—and even on the same person, at different times.

There are also a number of other factors that pharmacologists study which influence variability in effects, even in animals. *Dose* or *potency* is the most obvious one; generally, the more of a drug you administer, the more extreme the reaction. But sometimes, effects will be contradictory. A moderate dose of an amphetamine will almost always produce stimulation, alertness, intense activity, but a very large dose may sometimes produce sedation, lethargy, even sleep. So dose is crucial, and any discussion which leaves this out is necessarily incomplete. The same is true of *route of administration*. For instance, methadone given orally produces no (or a very small degree of) euphoria and lethargy, but, if it is injected intravenously, it is possible to get high from it. The same drug produces two different effects, varying simply according to route of administration. Most users of marijuana enjoy the drug when they *smoke* it; but, if it is taken *orally* by eating, they experience more unpleasant, and fewer pleasant—and more extreme—reactions. So route of administration is important, and it should be kept in mind when considering drug effects and drug categories.

Still, it is useful to apply some sort of categorical scheme to drugs. Drugs do have effects that can be classified; and people using drugs think of them as belonging to certain categories, certain groups. Almost no one pops *anything* into his mouth, as long as it is a "drug." Most people want to take *certain kinds* of drugs, but not others. What are these categories of drugs? Pharmacologists agree that the following types of drugs should be classified, each within its own type: *stimulants, depressants, narcotics,* and *hallucinogens.* They are not quite sure what to do with marijuana. Some scientists think that it belongs in the hallucinogenic category; many think that it belongs in a separate category altogether. I will follow the latter custom. Now, when a drug is put into a class, this does not mean that its effects are identical to all other drugs in that class. It does mean that the drugs in that class share some important characteristics, that their effects are broadly similar. Also, that there is a degree of *cross-tolerance* from one drug to another in that category. Tolerance means two things: one, that the user generally needs a higher and higher dose to achieve the same effect (this has its limits, though); and two, the body is able to "tolerate," without serious ill-effect, a larger and larger dose (and this, too, has its limits.) Cross-tolerance means that different drugs within the same class can be substituted, and the same thing will happen. If you take LSD every day for a few days, the effects will wear off; it will eventually become impossible to get high unless you stop for a while. This will also be true if you take LSD for a few days, and then switch to mescaline, or psilocybin—you still will not be able to get high. There is a cross-tolerance between LSD, mescaline, and psilocybin; they are all hallucinogens. There is also a cross-tolerance between drugs classified as stimulants, between drugs classified as depressants, between drugs classified as narcotics. However, you cannot produce a cross-tolerance from stimulants to depressants, from narcotics to hallucinogens, and so on; also you cannot produce a cross-tolerance from marijuana to any of the other drug classes, including hallucinogens. This is why many pharmacologists think that marijuana probably belongs in a group of its own.

STIMULANTS AND DEPRESSANTS

The biggest drug problem in America is with the depressants, and with one depressant drug in particular: *alcohol*. Since most states in the United States have a legal drinking age of 21, and others set it at 18, 19, and 20, alcohol is the drug most commonly used illegally by adolescents and young adults in this country. It is also the most commonly used drug by adults. There are more alcohol addicts, or alcoholics, than addicts of all of the other drugs combined. In fact, alcohol addicts comprise over three-fourths of all drug addicts. If we ignore cigarettes for the moment, alcohol unquestionably causes more problems for society than *all other drugs combined*. It certainly causes more deaths. It certainly drains more money from the economy. It certainly is the biggest medical problem. There are more arrests in America every year for public drunkenness than for any other offense. More than half of all homicides take place when the killer is drunk. In almost half of all rapes of adult women, and two-thirds of all sexual attacks on young girls, the sex offender was drunk. Recent estimates claim that there are almost ten million alcoholics in this country. Alcoholism is, in fact, an epidemic disease. The other addictions, especially to heroin, cannot compare in extent with alcohol addiction. There are about *forty times* as many alcoholics in the United States as heroin addicts; heroin addiction is a miniscule disease problem compared with alcoholism. Without doubt alcoholism is the number one drug problem in America.

However, adolescents and young adults are less commonly addicted to alcohol than adults are. Alcoholism is most typically a disease of middle age, and not of young adulthood. It generally takes many years to become addicted to alcohol. On the other hand, it is possible to become a heroin addict within weeks. This is one of the reasons why heroin is felt to be a bigger drug problem among young people than alcohol. At the same time, more adolescents use alcohol *than any other drug*. In all the excitement over the "generation gap," it should not be forgotten that liquor is still the drug most often used by all age groups, including the young. It is true that marijuana is crowding alcohol out in some areas, and it is true that older people use *more* alcohol than young people do—but alcohol is still the drug of choice among the youth of America.

Barbiturates are also depressant drugs. Until a few years ago, very few young people used barbiturates to get high; the few that did, had stolen a few pills from their mothers. Now there is a vigorous black market sale of barbiturates to young people, and now it is not uncommon to see high school and even college students stoned on "downs." In two studies I conducted on the college student body of a large state university, barbiturate use jumped over *four times* in only the 1970–1971 period! Barbiturates are very similar in effect to alcohol. Both are addicting in a physical sense — one's body becomes physically dependent on these drugs upon long-term heavy use. This means that if someone who is physically dependent suddenly discontinues the use of the drug, he will undergo *withdrawal* symptoms. He will become very, very sick for several days. Nausea, vomiting, cramps, aches and pains all about the body, muscular twitching (this is where the term "kicking" the habit comes from), convulsions, and sometimes even coma, are common symptoms which occur when someone is withdrawn from a depressant, from alcohol or barbiturate drugs, and heroin as well. (It is known as the "DT's" when the alcoholic tries to "kick" — or *delerium tremens*.) If physical dependence is severe, and use has taken place over a long period of time, death has been known to occur. Withdrawal from alcohol and barbiturates is much more severe than withdrawal from narcotics such as heroin. In fact, a narcotic withdrawal is probably never fatal in and of itself, but an alcoholic or a barbiturate withdrawal sometimes is. Young people who take barbiturates rarely do so in addicting quantities. There are probably about a million addicts of sedatives and hypnotics (which include both barbiturates and tranquilizers, which are similar in many respects) in the United States, but very few of them are youths; most are middle-aged women with psychiatric problems. Adolescents will "drop" barbiturates on weekends to get high, as a kind of recreation, but it rarely becomes a routine, day-to-day habit, the way that heroin addiction sometimes does. Secobarbital (known as "sekkies," or "seggies" on the street), Nembutal ("nemmies," or "nimbies"), amytal, and tuinal (a combination of amytal and secobarbital, called "tooies" in the jargon of users), are commonly used. (The names often also follow the colors and patterns of the capsules the drugs are put into: rainbows, red birds, yellow jackets, reds, etc.)

Alcohol and barbiturates are similar in their effects (although not identical, of course). The reflexes are slowed down; coordination is impaired; a feeling of anxiety and tension is reduced; sedation occurs; the speech is somewhat slurred; the mind tends to be "clouded" — that is, one's ability to perform intellectual tasks is reduced. At higher doses, sleep is induced. (Barbiturates are typically used either for sedation, or calming, or for hypnosis, or sleep; these are degrees of the same function.) Both alcohol and barbiturates inhibit respiration. In fact, death from an "overdose" of depressant drugs is caused by paralysis of the breathing mechanisms. (The same is true for heroin.) The user will go into a coma before he dies, so that he will not be able to take any more drugs. It takes about ten to fifteen times the amount to kill a person as to get him high; thus, the "lethal dose" is not too far from the "effective dose," and overdoses can be very common with these drugs. There are quite a few more overdoses from barbiturates than from heroin in the United States.

A great many common household substances contain *stimulants* — which are relatively weak in the doses typically taken. Nicotine is contained in the ordinary tobacco cigarette. Caffeine is in cola, tea, coffee, and cocoa. We have come to accept these substances in our everyday life and do not think of them as "drugs." At one time, governments made valiant attempts to stamp out cigarette smoking, but it was to no avail; the habit spread like wildfire. In the seventeenth century tobacco was smoked in Russia in precisely the same way that marijuana is today—with much the same effect. This underscores our contention that the "effects" of drugs depend on conventions surrounding use, as well as modes of administering them. By holding inhaled tobacco smoke for a long time, and exhaling it slowly, it is possible to become "stoned"—and probably unconscious and very sick as well. Public health experts estimate that cigarettes probably account for the premature deaths of about 125,000 Americans each year, which puts nicotine next to alcohol as the second most lethal drug in use in the United States today. Since no deaths have been directly attributable to marijuana, the disproportionate attention paid to the two drugs should be puzzling. The Chief Medical Officer of Health for Great Britain has said that *"the abolition of cigarette smoking would be the greatest contribution to public health now open to us."* The Royal College of Physicians said that the present health situation in relation to smoking is a "holocaust."

Moreover, cigarettes are involved in drug use by the young in other than direct ways. A number of legal drugs actually provide the *introduction* to the taking of mind-altering drugs—which, in a certain proportion of the cases, *leads to the use of illegal drugs.* Since most of us have been bombarded with the idea that marijuana "leads to heroin," we have lost sight of many other processes which occur as well. In at least two ways, legal drugs lead to the use of illegal drugs. The first is that *parents who use legal drugs* (mostly alcohol, stimulants, cigarettes, and depressants such as barbiturates) *raise children who are likely to use illegal drugs*, such as marijuana, heroin, and LSD. The adolescent or young adult's likelihood of using *any* illegal drug is increased considerably if his parents use these legal drugs. A number of studies have been conducted on this relationship, and the findings are remarkably consistent with one another. A study conducted by the Addiction Research Foundation of Toronto showed that mothers who used tranquilizers nearly every day were *three times* as likely to raise children who would use marijuana, *six times* as likely to raise children who would use an opiate drug (such as heroin), and *eight times* as likely to raise children who would use barbiturates illegally, than was true of mothers who never used tranquilizers. A second study, done independently in a Long Island high school and conducted by two high school students, corroborated this finding. Mothers who drank alcohol were significantly more likely to have children who would use marijuana, LSD, or any other illegal drug. Mothers whose children had *seen* them drunk were more likely to raise illegal drug-using children. The more that parents drank, the greater the likelihood that their children would use illegal drugs. A third study, done by the New Jersey College of Medicine, revealed that children whose parents (either the father or the mother, but especially the mother) smoked a pack or more of cigarettes a day were *four to five times* as likely to use dangerous drugs such as heroin or methedrine. Obviously, therefore, the parental example is a powerful one, and the separation between legal and illegal drugs is not as great as has been assumed in the past.

In a second way, too, legal drug use influences the use of illegal drugs. This is that any young person who uses alcohol and cigarettes, even if he is of a legal age to do so, has a higher chance of eventually using illegal substances later on—*any* illegal drugs—than the young person who never drinks alcohol or smokes cigarettes. In other words, legal drugs actually provide the *introduction* to drug use. In one study I did on a college campus, cigarette smokers were about *twice* as likely to use any and all illegal drugs as non-smokers were. This held true for heroin as well as for marijuana—although, obviously, the use of marijuana was far greater for everyone than the use of heroin. About half of the non-smokers said that they never smoked marijuana, but only 13 percent of the pack-a-day smokers also had never smoked marijuana. Only 2 percent of the non-smokers had ever tried heroin, but 6 percent of the heavy smokers had. The use of *all* illegal drugs doubled for smokers of ordinary tobacco cigarettes when compared with non-smokers. A study conducted by the Columbia University School of Public Health of a national probability sample of adolescents age 12–17 found that only 3 percent of the non-smokers of cigarettes had ever tried marijuana, but this jumped nearly *seventeen times*, to approximately *half*, for the smokers. Studies in various settings and locales have demonstrated that precisely the same generalization holds for young liquor drinkers as well; the adolescent who drinks alcohol has a significantly higher likelihood of eventually using illegal drugs than his peer who does not drink liquor. Thus, to make the distinction between legal and illegal drugs is misleading. In a very real sense, alcohol and cigarettes "lead to" the use of illegal drugs.

Prescription drugs also lend an air of tolerance to drug use. Most adolescents typically do not gain access to drugs via prescription, since physicians are acutely aware of the dangers of drugs administered to young people. But the tolerant attitude toward prescribing drugs to older people *does* have a considerable impact on drug taking of young people, in the following ways: (1) prescription drugs are often stolen by adolescents from their parents; (2) producing prescription drugs on an extremely high-volume basis means that a good deal of the volume produced will find its way into the hands of those who have no medical reason for using the drugs; (3) prescribing and using drugs legally sets in motion the drug-using cycle which produces the correlation between legal and illegal drug use mentioned above. A cultural climate of drug use is encouraged and stimulated by prescription drugs on a mass basis.

Roughly a million pounds of the barbiturates, plus another million pounds of only one tranquilizer (Equanil, or Miltown) were produced and consumed in the United States each year in the late 1960s. In a study of a nationally-representative sample of the American population, it was found that about half of all Americans in 1967 had taken mood-altering drugs such as amphetamines, barbiturates, or tranquilizers at least once in their life-times and about a quarter had done so in the year previous to the interview. This percentage is considerably higher than that for the use of marijuana: in a Harris Poll conducted in 1968, only 4 percent of a cross-section of all Americans over age 21 had smoked marijuana at least once. And the rise in prescription drugs over the past decade or so has been astronomical. There are probably roughly a million sedative (barbiturate and tranquilizer) addicts in the United States who would undergo painful withdrawal symptoms if they discontinued the use of their legal drugs. The sedative addict contrasts markedly socially with the heroin addict, although pharmacologically there is little difference between the two. The barbiturate and sedative addict takes his drug for quasi-medical and therapeutic reasons. He enjoys the stamp of approval from the medical profession. He seldom has anything to do with crime in the conventional sense. He is able to secure his "fix" without having to steal or prostitute himself. He is almost never arrested. He has to spend only about $3 per day for his supply. Society does not frown on his use of drugs. He belongs to the group that has been called the "hidden addicts." In fact, the "pill junkie's" addiction is often hidden from himself, he rarely thinks of himself as an addict in the same way that a street heroin addict does. He is enshrouded in a cloak of respectability.

An examination of the voluminous pages of advertising by the pharmaceutical industry in medical journals illustrates the intense penetration of "legitimate" drug-taking into American social life. The American Medical Association receives half of its revenue from the pharmaceutical industry. A page of advertising in *The Journal of the American Medical Association* costs more than a page in any other non-commercial weekly in America (with one exception). Medical journals receive far more revenue from drug advertising than from any other source. For instance, *The New England Journal of Medicine* in 1968 received about $660,000 in subscription revenue, but two and a quarter million dollars from advertising, about three-fourths of which came from drug companies. The pharmaceutical industry is a multi-billion dollar business, and has one of the very highest margins of profit in existence. (Another is the cosmetic industry.) There is no question whatsoever that the drug industry's expansionist policies have resulted in drug use in this country far beyond what is necessary — and has created a climate of tolerance for drugs that has extended into the use of illegal drugs, and has therefore contributed to the drug "problem" among the young.

There are two fairly distinct patterns of amphetamine use in the United States. Small to moderate doses are taken in quasi-legitimate, although sometimes illegal, circumstances by individuals not defined by society as criminal or deviant: the depressed housewife, the harried businessman, the long-haul truckdriver, the ambitious athlete, the anxious student cramming for an exam. These individuals will use amphetamine more or less instrumentally, to attain a mental or physical state conducive to some practical end of which society approves. Amphetamine is used instrumentally or therapeutically in tablet or capsule form; Dexedrine, Benzedrine, Desoxyn, Biphetamine, and Diphetamine are common trade names. Between $2\frac{1}{2}$ and 10 mg would constitute a typical dosage. In such low doses, the typical bodily and mental effects of the amphetamines would be: (1) an increased alertness and a diminution of fatigue, (2) heightened competence in simple motor skills and intellectual acuity, (3) the feeling of increased energy, (4) the stimulation for the need for increased motor activity, particularly walking about and talking, (5) a feeling of euphoria, an inhibition of depression, (6) a feeling of confidence and even grandeur, (7) an inhibition of appetite, (8) dryness of the mouth, (9) increased heartbeat.

The second social segment which uses amphetamine on a more than occasional basis is the denizen of the street "speed" scene. This subculture of methedrine (methedrine is a powerful form of amphetamine) users probably attained its greatest extent during the period around 1967, and then declined after that; many former methedrine "freaks" switched to heroin and became narcotic addicts. The switch probably had two sources. First, amphetamine had to be used in a kind of "up-down" cycle. The speed freak will inject methedrine intravenously for 2–5 days at a stretch (called a "run") and then sleep for a day or so; but often sleep was possible only after taking a depressant drug of some kind — often barbiturates, or heroin. In addition, methedrine was a much more "demanding" and unique drug than heroin; it was to a far greater degree all-encompassing, and more physically debilitating. Thus, although there are still tens of thousands of young Americans injecting amphetamines, the number is considerably less than it was a few years ago. Most ex-methedrine freaks are now heroin addicts.

Instead of taking 10 mg, as the housewife might, the speed freak might take 100 mg or even a gram (or 1000 mg) a day. One methedrine user was observed injecting 15 g into his system during a 24-hour period! The speed freak specifically seeks the euphoria associated with the methedrine high. By injecting the drug directly into his bloodstream, he achieves a "rush" which is likened to a sexual orgasm. Methedrine comes to completely dominate the lives of those using it; it is said on the drug scene that only a speed freak can tolerate another speed freak. The constant wakefulness, incessant babbling, the volcanic nervous energy, the paranoia, the arrogant parasitism, are extremely difficult to tolerate if one does not oneself share that particular way of life. Thus, friendships within the methedrine subculture tend to be almost exclusively with other users of amphetamines.

Medically, methedrine is among the most toxic and debilitating drugs when taken in immense quantities, as do many users. Methedrine contrasts with heroin in that few users overdose on methedrine, since the difference between "effective" dose (or the amount required to get someone high) is very far from the "lethal dose," or the amount necessary to kill someone. With heroin, however, the dosages are very close; thus, in an "overdose" sense, heroin is extremely dangerous and methedrine is "safe." In terms of long-term toxicity to the body, aside from overdosing, it is exactly the reverse: heroin is extremely "safe," and methedrine is extremely toxic. An amazing range of medical pathologies is associated with heavy, long-term intravenous use of the amphetamine drugs. Recent observers have begun to feel that, in contrast with prior generalizations, perhaps heavy methedrine use is actually physically addicting, in the classical sense, in that withdrawal pangs appear upon a discontinuance of its use. Psychosis, especially paranoia, is felt to be a fixture of heavy amphetamine usage. David Smith, a physician who treats the population of the Haight-Ashbury, a heavy amphetamine using community, has written: "The amphetamine psychosis *almost always occurs* after pro-longed high dose usage." Certain compulsive fixations appear, such as picking at imaginary bugs crawling under one's skin. Other psychic reactions attendant upon heavy long-term amphetamine use commonly reported which are admitted and undesired even by users themselves are: a memory loss, an inability to concentrate, emotional lability, and a tendency toward violence.

MARIJUANA

Among young people marijuana is the second most commonly used illegal drug after alcohol. Estimates as to the number of marijuana smokers in high school and college are often wildly distorted, ranging in some cases up to 90 percent. Actually, it is a good deal less than this. In a nation-wide representative Gallup Poll taken in December 1970, 42 percent of the college students in the sample said that they had at least tried marijuana. This was approximately a doubling since the previous Gallup Poll, taken in Spring 1969, when only 22 percent of American college students said that they had smoked marijuana once or more. Different surveys at different colleges and universities across the country indicate a rise since 1967 or so of about *one percent every month or two*. Thus, by Spring 1972, probably about half of all college students have illegally smoked marijuana, and the figure will continue to rise. In addition, a recent Harris Poll indicated that a majority of all college students (53 percent) favor the legalization of marijuana. Most observers would say that the use of marijuana, and the sentiment favoring use and legalization, in high schools is not quite as great as in colleges. In a study sponsored by the Addiction Research Foundation in Toronto in 1970, just under one student in five (or 18.3 percent to be exact) in grades seven through thirteen had used marijuana one or more times; this was nearly a tripling from 1968 when only 6.7 percent had done so. The age of turning on is dropping all the time — marijuana smokers are using the drug for the first time at a younger and younger age — but it is still not the norm for school children to do so. (Although in many urban centers, such as New York, the typical teen-ager has probably tried marijuana.)

If we forget about alcohol for the moment and consider only those drugs that are illegal for everyone, adults and adolescents alike, then marijuana is by far the most commonly-used illegal drug. In fact, in two studies I did on one campus in 1970 and 1971, more marijuana was used than *all* of the other drugs *added together.* More than 80 percent of *all* instances of illegal drug use (excepting alcohol) were with marijuana alone. There is no close competitor. No other illegal drug is used with anywhere near the frequency of marijuana. No other drug is "replacing" marijuana. Thus, to discuss all drugs used among adolescents with equal weight, as if they were all used with equal frequency, is extremely misleading. The issue of illegal drug use among young people is, aside from the use of alcohol, largely an issue of marijuana use. A second point should be made about marijuana: the *average* level of use is, roughly, weekly. In my own 1970 and 1971 campus studies, the mid-point for all students who had tried marijuana once or more was almost exactly once per week. In a different study, a very large survey of 7500 residents of New York State, conducted by the Narcotic Addiction Control Commission, about a third of all those who had tried marijuana used it six times a month or more. It is easy to think that everyone who has tried marijuana is a chronic daily user; this image turns out to be false. In fact, only roughly 1 marijuana user in 10 seems to be a daily smoker, and even he will confine its use, typically, to the night-time. About 1 or 2 percent of all users are high during all of their waking hours. The *typical* marijuana smoker is under the influence of his drug only about 4 percent of his waking hours. Many observers of the drug scene lose sight of this fact. Too often, commentators will slide from talking about marijuana use in general to talking about the impact of heavy, daily, chronic use, which is a minority phenomenon. It is too easy to attribute a wide range of negative influences to something which is a far more marginal and superficial part of the lives of the young people we are observing.

Marijuana is a generic term covering any and all psychoactive products from the *Cannabis sativa* plant. The specific product which is called marijuana in the United States is most often simply the leaf of the plant. The street name most commonly used is "grass"; a few years ago, "pot" was the most common slang term. "Dope" is also commonly used, especially among heavier users. At a certain time of the year, *Cannabis sativa* coats itself with a sticky resin; it is this resin which contains most of the psychoactive chemical which gets people high. The higher up on the plant, the more concentrated and potent this resin is. Pure resin is dried and hardened, and called hashish in the Middle East and in America. In 1964, the chemical contained in grass and in hashish which is probably the psychoactive ingredient, tetrahydrocannabinol, or THC for short, was synthesized. Hashish contains about 5 percent THC, and fairly potent Mexican grass will be about 1 percent THC. Different grades and shipments and batches of grass will contain very, very different potencies. Vietnamese marijuana may be as high as 5 or 10 percent THC. Some home-grown or self-harvested varieties may contain a tiny fraction of 1 percent, or even mere traces, and will almost not be psychoactive at all. Also, grass loses potency with age; the longer it sits on the shelf, the weaker it becomes. A given batch will lose about 2 percent of its THC per month. Now, when one batch is, let us say, twice as potent as another, this does not mean that someone can get twice as high—it just takes twice as much of the stuff to get just as high. Recent analysis has shown that the male plant contains the *same* potency as the female. Up until a year or so ago, it was believed by nearly everyone that the female plant contained most of the potency of THC; this turned out to be false.

Marijuana, whether in its leaf form or in its dried resin, or hashish, form, is nearly always smoked in the United States. The leaf variety comes in the form of a loose, fine, dried herb. It will be sprinkled into cigarette papers and then rolled into a "joint," a small, thin marijuana cigarette. Hashish is much more often smoked in a pipe; it comes to the customer most of the time in a hard block, which must be chipped or cut off in tiny pieces which are lit. The technique for smoking hashish and grass is the same, however: the smoker will take deep drags, hold the smoke in his lungs for as long as possible, and then the smoke will be exhaled slowly. This is an efficient method of getting the drug into the bloodstream. The effects will be felt within minutes of smoking high-quality marijuana, and, within about 10 or 15 minutes, the user will be "stoned." This will last for several hours, and by four hours or so later, the smoker will no longer be under the influence. (Although traces of THC will remain in his bloodstream for about 72 hours or so afterward.)

It is important to distinguish between those effects of marijuana (remembering the qualifications I mentioned before about how effects will vary by external factors) which are "*objective*," or which can be seen by an outside observer—the scientist—and those effects which are "*subjective*," or those which can be felt only by someone who is high, and which must be explained to the external observer who cannot "see" them himself. What are the "objective" effects of marijuana? It is amazing that there are so few. Marijuana does not dilate the pupils, as was thought a few years ago. It is nearly impossible for a human being to "overdose" on marijuana; there have been no reliable, undisputable deaths of humans from an "overdose" of marijuana. Alcohol is between 500 and 1000 times more lethal than marijuana. With marijuana, the quantity that can get the user high, and the quantity that will kill him are very, very far apart; with alcohol, they are much closer together. (With heroin, they are closer still.) In the strictly lethal sense, marijuana is one of the safest drugs known to man. It requires gigantic doses of marijuana to kill laboratory animals — such high doses that men never take them, or could possibly ever take them. Nearly everyone agrees that an actual *physical* dependence does not occur with marijuana; it is impossible to become "addicted" to grass or hashish, regardless of how much one uses. There are, of course, daily smokers of marijuana, but they are in the minority; the smoker who is high all of his waking hours is an even smaller minority still. Thus, whatever a "psychological dependence" may mean (and I am inclined to think that it is really quite meaningless), marijuana does not *typically* develop in the user anything like a "psychological dependence." Different experiments with pregnant animals have produced no consistent results regarding birth defects. The evidence on long-term adverse effects are simply not available; no one really knows for sure what the impact of heavy marijuana use over many years will be. About the only physical effects which we know for sure are a reddening of the whites of the eyes, a slight dryness of the mouth, and a slight increase in heartbeat rate.

Experimental effects on performance have also produced mixed results. The classic experiment by Andrew Weil and Norman Zinberg showed that *experienced* marijuana users could perform motor and intellectual tasks about as well stoned as normally. However, marijuana-naive subjects (those that had never before been high) did show a deterioration in performance, and especially so the greater the dosage. The well-known Washington State driving experiments, likewise, did not show any serious deterioration of motor performance under the influence of marijuana, but they did show a severe impairment under the influence of alcohol. The drunk driver (everyone was tested on a driver simulator, not in actual driving conditions) was a significantly worse driver, but the driver stoned was no worse at all. This held true even at high doses, and it held true even for marijuana novices. Although this study has come under considerable attack, it is still the best one that relates directly to driving performance.

A completely different result was obtained by a team of researchers at

Indianapolis, who are affiliated with the Indiana University Medical School and the Lilly drug laboratories. The conclusion from these tests was that there was a striking and significant deterioration of motor and intellectual performance under the influence of marijuana, much more so than for alcohol which was much closer to performance while normal. At this point, it is impossible to reconcile these two sets of experiments; they would appear to be contradictory. About all that can be said about marijuana's impact on motor skills is that the evidence does not point in any specific direction, and final conclusions will have to await further research.

A number of different surveys have been done on the *subjective* effects of marijuana. When I asked a broad cross-section of marijuana smokers in New York City to describe the effects of the drug on them, I got a wide range of responses. The most common was that the drug made them more relaxed, more peaceful, calmer; not quite half, or 46 percent, said this spontaneously. About a third, or 36 percent, said that all of their senses were more "turned on," more receptive to stimuli, more perceptive, more sensitive. Another third, or 31 percent, said that they thought deeper thoughts, that their minds were more "profound" when high. And about 3 users in 10, or 29 percent, said that they laughed more, that everything seemed funnier when high. A quarter, 25 percent, felt that everything they felt and thought was exaggerated, that it all took on much greater emotional significance. And not quite a quarter, 23 percent, said that time seemed elongated, stretched out, they felt that much more time had passed by than the clock had said. I received many other responses, but these were the most common. Other interview studies on the "subjective" effects of marijuana have been done. Most of them agree with these findings. Two physicians at the University of California at Los Angeles administered a check-list questionnaire to 1 student in 10 at UCLA. Naturally, a check-list will elicit more people agreeing to any single effect, but the same effects did turn up, and in about the same order. Hunger appeared to be the most common response. Eighty-five percent of the heavy (or "chronic") users said that they felt hunger "often" or "always;" 83 percent said that they felt increased sexual pleasure often or always; 82 percent felt more relaxed, a decreased tension; 80 percent felt a heightened sense of taste; 79 percent said that their hearing was intensified; 78 percent felt a kind of "mellowness." Like my own study, there were lots of other responses, but what emerges from these two studies, as well as from many others, is that *most users, most of the time, describe the subjective effects of their marijuana experience in overwhelmingly favorable and pleasurable terms.* In short, they seem to like what they feel. This is not to say that they never experience negative effects — it is just that they are far less common than the positive ones. Most users enjoy their marijuana experiences. Moreover, this feature of marijuana use — simple hedonism — appears to be unquestionably the principal reason for its continued use. Marijuana becomes woven into recreational activities for the young user, during listening to music, a party or any social gathering, watching television, and so on. In other words, the classic image of the lonely, desperate, frightened teen-ager seeking solace in drugs, seeking a punishing, self-flagellating activity, does not appear to have any validity with regard to marijuana use. The drug is used most of the time by most young people for simple socializing enjoyment. Marijuana users do not turn to the drug because they feel themselves to be lonely; they turn on the first time specifically because they have friends, and continue to use it in intimate gatherings among friends, largely out of pleasure-seeking motives.

Marijuana use has aroused a storm of controversy. Much of the debate centers around the following questions: (1) Does marijuana cause "psychotic episodes"? (2) Does it lead to adverse long-range effects in behavior, such as a deterioration in motivation? (3) Does marijuana lead to heroin use? It would be impossible to answer any one of these questions to the satisfaction of most observers, even in an entire book-length discussion, but they are important questions, and should be dealt with, even if sketchily.

It has sometimes been stated that marijuana, or cannabis generally, including hashish as well as THC, is a *psychotomimetic* drug — that among its important effects is its impact on producing in the user a madness-like (or madness "mimicking") state, a "marijuana psychosis." Some observers believe that this has not occurred to a great extent in America simply because the potencies of the grass available here are too low to cause this effect, but that if they were more powerful, such adverse psychic reactions would be observed in greater profusion. Marijuana, this line of reasoning goes, is a *dilute form* of a *very powerful* drug, a drug which at a sufficiently high dosage actually produces a temporary psychosis in all users. This is the contention of a group of researchers at the Addiction Research Center at Lexington. These researchers attempted to demonstrate their contention by giving former narcotic addicts at the government's prison-hospital high doses of THC. They then administered a battery of questions to them, questions such as: "Is your skin sensitive?", "Do you feel strange, as if you were in a dream?", "Are you having a lot of thoughts?", "My thoughts seem to come and go," "My appetite is increased", "Are you happy?" "I couldn't get mad at anyone right now," "Time passes slowly", "Are colors brighter?", and so on. When the researchers got a lot of "yes" answers to these questions, as they did when LSD was administered, they decided that THC (and hence, marijuana) is a *psychotomimetic* drug—that it produced a madness-like state in all users at a sufficiently high dose.

In other words, these researchers did not say that marijuana just *produces* a madness-like state, but that the marijuana high *is, in and of itself,* a psychotic state. When we have an image of a psychotic reaction, we think of someone who is in danger of harming himself or others, perhaps huddled in a corner cowering with fear, perhaps paranoid at any and all around him, perhaps running about raving. This was not observed. What was labeled as a madness-like state by the Lexington researchers was simply the state that characterizes the marijuana high. Many users find this state pleasurable; a few do not. *No one* finds a true psychotic reaction pleasurable. It is only through a semantic word game that the Lexington research can be used to label marijuana as a psychotomimetic—a drug which typically produces in the user a psychotic reaction. The items which were supposed to test whether the subject is undergoing a psychotic reaction were simply reactions which were different from the "normal," everyday sensations. Naturally, marijuana is a *psychoactive* drug; it influences mood, emotion, sensations, feelings, perceptions. This is a somewhat different experience from the everyday, from what most people consider "normal." This is why some users enjoy smoking marijuana; they delight in the departure from the ordinary. But is this madness? It is nothing more than the researchers' prejudices that these sensations were labeled a temporary psychosis. The Lexington experiments definitely do not demonstrate that marijuana, or cannabis, or THC, produces anything like a true psychotic reaction—only that users experience sensations different from normal. We will have to search elsewhere for evidence on psychotic reactions.

No one questions the fact that marijuana is capable of producing in someone, at some time, a negative psychic reaction. Some people are going to "freak out" over something—even an examination, or losing an athletic contest, or (a famous case a few years ago) finding out that one's parents once had sexual intercourse. The question is, *how common* are these reactions?—not simply, do they *ever* occur? (It is possible to discover *some* examples of some very weird events "ever" occurring; but the question is, how *typical* are they?) Two very careful clinical studies of adverse psychotic reactions to cannabis have been done by Andrew Weil, who co-authored the first truly controlled experiment on performance effects of marijuana, and by David E. Smith, the physician administering to the "hippie" population of the Haight-Ashbury district of San Francisco, a very heavy drug-using population. Dr. Weil states that "adverse acute reactions to marijuana are infrequent." In fact, one of Weil's purposes in writing his report, originally published in *The New England Journal of Medicine*, was to argue that most negative reactions to marijuana are "panic reactions," plain and simple, and not true temporary psychoses. In fact, Weil states the physician who attempts to treat the panic case will often make it worse by, through ignorance, regarding it as a case of a full-blown psychosis. In most cases, simple but firm assurance is sufficient to calm the user.

David Smith's conclusions are virtually the same as Weil's. In one article, Smith states that in the first 15 months of the Haight-Ashbury Clinic, about 30,000 patients were treated, about 95 percent of whom had used marijuana—and yet no cases of what Smith called a "primary psychosis" was seen. Outside the Clinic, the few cases of marijuana-induced psychotic episodes Smith has seen have been panic reactions by "up tight" novices who were in what was, for them, bizarre and far-out and unfamiliar surroundings. They exhibited "extreme paranoid reactions characterized by fear of arrest and discovery." Both Smith and Weil emphasize that the personality of the user, the setting he is in, especially his feelings about his companions, his feelings about smoking marijuana, especially its illegality, his self-confidence, his fears about "letting go," about losing control (or seeming to), and the user's experience with the drug in the past, all have a great deal to do with panic reactions—in fact, probably more than the biochemical reactions of the drug itself. Weil and Smith also stress the fact that route of administration can have its impact; if the drug is smoked, panic reactions will be less common, since the user can stop when he is sufficiently high, or feels uncomfortable. But if the drug is ingested orally, a larger quantity can be consumed, and continue to have its impact long after the user has stopped ingesting the drug, since absorption is much slower orally. Oral ingestion of cannabis produces more extreme, negative, psychotic and "LSD-like" reactions in the user.

What about the adverse long-range effects of marijuana? Dr. Edward Bloomquist, in his book, *Marijuana*, mentions the "insidious devastation" of the marijuana user's mind as a result of prolonged use. William McGlothlin, a psychologist, and Louis Jolyon West, a psychiatrist, mention the possibility that marijuana may develop in the user over the long run an "amotivational syndrome," a lack of interest in achievement, the long-term loss of ambition, the development of a life characterized by lethargy, sloth, apathy, languor. What is the evidence for this?

Two physicians, Harold Kolansky and William Moore, in an article entitled "Effects of Marijuana on Adolescents and Young Adults," published in April 1971 in *The Journal of the American Medical Association*, state that their young marijuana-smoking patients "consistently showed very poor social judgment, poor attention span, poor concentration, confusion, anxiety, depression, apathy, passivity, indifference, and, often, slowed or slurred speech ... a paranoid suspiciousness of others, and a regression to a more infantile state ...." The authors claim that it was specifically smoking marijuana which lead to these symptoms: "In no instance were these symptoms in evidence prior to the use of marijuana." For instance, they claim that the paranoid reactions they observe "*is a direct result* of the toxic effects of cannabis upon the ego organization of those patients described in this study." The imagery which dominates the Kolansky and Moore article is that of a *chemical assault on the brain*. They appear to be convinced that there is *neurological damage* to moderate and heavy users of cannabis. (They did not seem to have done any neurological examinations, however.)

The American Medical Association regarded the report so significant that it issued advance copies to the media, claiming that it was the first study which provided "substantiation by sound medical research" of the harm of prolonged marijuana use. If the study were a solid contribution to the research literature on marijuana effects, this would be news, indeed. Unfortunately, the Kolansky–Moore study is hopelessly and completely worthless as a piece of adequate research. When Kolansky and Moore appeared as expert witnesses before the National Commission on Marihuana and Drug Abuse, six marijuana researchers also submitted their critiques of the report. All six of these researchers were physicians. They all, in the course of their work, treated patients with drug-related problems. All six dealt with the same material and data as Kolansky and Moore — dredged up in clinical interviews — and yet, all six were struck by precisely the same fallacy; the main point raised in all of these critiques was of "*making a temporal sequence into a causal sequence*," to quote Dr. Leon Wurmser's critique. Dr. Solomon Snyder, author of the book, *Uses of Marijuana*, elaborates on the point: "From the case descriptions provided it seems highly unlikely that these individuals could possibly have been 'normal' prior to their use of marijuana .... Thus, all Drs. Kolansky and Moore have shown is that some marijuana users have mental illness. From their study it is not at all possible to ascribe a cause and effect relationship." Dr. Lester Grinspoon, author of *Marijuana Reconsidered*, summarizes his critique in the following words: "All in all, this paper [by Kolansky and Moore] is, from a scientific point of view, so unsound as to be all but meaningless. Unfortunately, from a social point of view it will have great significance in that it confirms for those people who have a hyperemotional bias against marijuana all the things they would like to believe happen as a consequence of the use of marijuana . . . I am convinced that if the AMA were less interested in the imposition of a moral hegemony with respect to this issue and more concerned with the scientific aspects of this drug, this paper would not have been accepted for publication."

What appears obvious is that the biases of Drs. Kolansky and Moore lead them to seek out pathologies in their patients, and then *attribute* them to smoking marijuana. Many of the "effects" which they claim are the consequence of cannabis use can be located within the process of marijuana users becoming gradually absorbed into a drug-using subculture, and gradually changing their values and life-style as they acquire more and more drug-using friends. For instance, Kolansky and Moore claim that "promiscuity" (a quaint and archaic Victorian term) is one "effect" of smoking marijuana. To attribute this to marijuana use is to display a narrowness of vision which limits what one sees. It happens that the sexually permissive are most likely to turn on and that the marijuana users are most likely to be sexually permissive. Neither is the "cause" of the other, but both are part of a permissive subculture. Anyone who uses marijuana is going to be exposed to companions who are more liberal sexually, just as anyone who is liberal sexually stands a high likelihood of becoming friends with other young people who use marijuana, and who have a tolerant attitude toward marijuana use. To say that marijuana "causes" the sexual permissiveness is as silly and narrow as the reverse. It is possible to demonstrate almost any contention if the cases are selected carefully enough. A wide range of marijuana users would reveal a "normal" cross-section of young people. If the polls are correct—and it would require extremely solid reasons to claim that they are not—something like 20 million young Americans have tried marijuana, and about half that number are more or less regular users. When something like half of the American college population uses grass, it is extremely difficult to believe that they are destroying themselves to the extent that Kolansky and Moore believe them to be.

Studies which examine a cross-section of all marijuana users (as opposed to a narrow biased segment, as with Kolansky and Moore's report) have demonstrated that the drug appears to have relatively little impact on the lives of the young people using it. Recall that, typically, the marijuana user is under the influence of the drug 4 percent of his waking hours. Now, if an observer were to witness activity during this 4 percent period, it would be certain that it would be more languid than normally. Stoned, few people want to do very much that is vigorous. Most will lie about, dream, engage in senseless conversation, listen to music, watch television, perhaps make love, and so on. There is a kind of necessary assumption built into the "amotivational syndrome" position that marijuana intoxication will form a very high proportion of the user's temporal life, but this turns out, upon examination, to be atypical. When we look at various measures of achievement, and compare users with non-users, the two actually turn out to be not very different. Take grades as an example. A great number of college studies have been done (including one of my own) comparing the grade point average of marijuana smokers with students who do not smoke marijuana. At the college level, no differences at all have emerged. The *average* level of marijuana use does not seem to be associated with a loss in motivation. However, I also found that *heavy* marijuana users tended to do somewhat less well than infrequent users. In fact, it was the *infrequent* user who tended to have the *highest* grades, the *abstainer* who had *intermediate* grades, while the *heavy* user had the *lowest* grades. Thus, it is possible that a lack of interest in achievement may well be associated with frequent marijuana use, but as to whether this is the marijuana use itself, or the style of life associated with marijuana use — with the subculture of marijuana users, and not the drug — cannot be answered at this point. My feeling is that it is the subculture. It is likely that heavy drug involvement is simply an indicator of involvement with other young people who use drugs, which tends to be correlated with values that include a disdain for hard work and conventional achievement. It is unlikely that the biochemistry of marijuana has anything to do with it in the typical case. In any case, the average marijuana user seems to have the same will to achieve as the average non-user of marijuana.

Many studies of *pre-college* youths, however, have yielded differences in various measures of achievement, including grades, between marijuana users and non-users — with the non-user often turning out to be more achievement-oriented, often having higher grades than the user. Why should no differences emerge among the young in college on most studies, and significant differences in most high school and especially grade school studies? At least two explanations offer themselves: (1) The hormonal and biochemical processes occurring in the adolescent are basically

different from those of the post-18-year-old young adult and, consequently, the body's reactions with any drug will also be basically different.
(2) The young person who turns on before college is basically different
and far more unconventional from the one who turns on first in college —
just as it would be true that participation in any unconventional activity,
such as premarital intercourse, would produce similar differences. At
this point, it is not possible to verify either explanation, but I would lean
heavily toward (2), and be highly skeptical about (1).

Does marijuana lead to heroin? Before a satisfactory answer can be
given to the question it would be necessary to unravel what it means.
Different observers have quite different conceptions of what marijuana
"leading to" heroin actually means. And unless its precise meaning is
specified, the whole question is absurd. Here are a few *different* meanings
of the marijuana-to-heroin debate:

(1) *Most* young people who smoke marijuana "progress" to the use of,
and addiction to, heroin. Now, there is no doubt that this is completely
false. Only a very small proportion of all marijuana smokers so progress.
In one study I did, this was 13 percent; in another, it was 6 percent. It has
been estimated that 20 million Americans have tried marijuana; estimates
as to the number of addicts run around a quarter of a million. No observer
of the drug scene claims that in the *typical* case the marijuana smoker
"goes on" to the use of or addiction to heroin. (2) A majority of all heroin
addicts once used marijuana. This is a true statement. In some studies,
this is about 7 addicts in 10; in other studies, it is over 90 percent. It is
also true that most addicts did a lot of things and smoked, ate, ingested,
tried, a wide range of substances. What this proves is not clear. (3) A
majority of all addicts "started with" marijuana — marijuana was the first
psychoactive drug they ever tried or used. This is not true. Most addicts
"started with" alcohol, and not grass. In fact, as adolescents, addicts are
more likely to drink, especially to excess, than is true of their young peers
who do not become addicts later on. In other words, there is a "progression" from liquor to heroin.

(4) For a majority of all heroin addicts, marijuana was the first experience with using an *illegal* drug. Again, not quite true. The first illegal drug
most heroin users ever used was alcohol; that is, underage drinking was
generally their first experience with breaking the law in connection with
drug use. (5) Marijuana users have a higher statistical likelihood of using
and becoming involved with heroin than do comparable non-users; moreover, the more that someone smokes marijuana, the greater is this likelihood. These two generalizations are true. No study of any group or

population has failed to find a statistical relationship between marijuana use and heroin use. As the use of marijuana goes up, so does the likelihood of trying, using, and becoming addicted to, heroin. In two studies I did, the difference between the infrequent, or less than monthly, marijuana user, and the frequent, or daily, marijuana user to the proportion trying heroin was on the order of about *ten times.*

(6) The chemical substance itself, the drug, marijuana, in and of itself, is *causally* related to the taking of, and the eventual addiction to, heroin. This is the most important proposition of all – and the most difficult to decide. It is the contention of the Attorney General of the United States, John Mitchell, that there is something in the chemistry of getting high on marijuana that impels the user toward heroin addiction; in fact, Mitchell has stated that "we have got to get proof" that marijuana creates this kind of dependency. Recent research makes this contention extremely dubious. It is highly unlikely that in and of itself, marijuana "effects" have anything to do with the "escalation" which is sometimes observed. A recent study by sociologist Bruce Johnson pinpoints precisely where the escalation which does take place is likely to be. In a survey of the drug use patterns of 20 different campuses in the New York area, Johnson shows that *even heavy marijuana users do not try heroin if they do not have heroin-using friends.* Heavy cannabis use (or the "effects" hypothesis of Attorney General Mitchell) is not, in and of itself, sufficient to "lead to" heroin use; the biochemistry of getting high on marijuana cannot account for the progression, because by itself it is not sufficient to "cause" the escalation. *Having heroin users as friends is several times more powerful in "causing" one's own use of heroin than is one's own use of marijuana* – even the heavy use of marijuana. How does one acquire heroin-using friends? Johnson's study shows that no matter how frequently or infrequently one smokes grass, *selling* marijuana and especially selling other drugs increases the likelihood of having heroin-using friends – and, consequently, of using heroin oneself. In other words, the really crucial relationship between marijuana and heroin is not marijuana use, *per se,* but selling marijuana, and, even more so, selling other drugs. The marijuana smoker who does not sell the stuff has only a slightly higher chance of trying and using heroin than the complete abstainer, the non-user of grass. But the seller of marijuana and other drugs has the highest chance of all. This very strongly suggests that *it is the very illegality of marijuana* that provides the impulse toward escalation – and not the use of the drug itself, not any biochemical compulsion built into marijuana use, and getting high on marijuana.

58 Erich Goode

HALLUCINOGENS

Although LSD is the most popular and well known of hallucinogens, or psychedelics, used today, it is the one with the shortest history. Peyote, another psychedelic drug, is a cactus which grows in Mexico and the American Southwest, and was used in religious ceremonies by the Indians of that region long before the coming of the European. Peyote contains eight mind-altering chemicals, the best known of which is mescaline. Peyote was used to a very tiny degree among a few European intellectuals at the turn of the century, and by some "beats" of the 1950s, but since it has a bitter taste and induces vomiting, it never really was used on a wide-spread basis. Indians still use it — the Native American Church, in which peyote is taken as a sacrament (peyote represents the body of Jesus), has spread from the Southwest into the Plains states, and into Canada. A great deal of what is called mescaline is sold and used on the black market among drug users today, but most of it turns out to be something else when analyzed in a laboratory — mostly LSD, mixed with amphetamine. (Mescaline is much more difficult to synthesize than LSD, which is why genuine mescaline is rarely sold.) In other words, many young people taking drugs today think that they have taken "mescaline," and report experiences with that drug, but, in fact, they have usually ingested a different drug. Other psychedelics used include: DMT, or dimethyltript-amine, STP (or known to chemists as DOM), and psilocybin; these drugs, however, are used with far less frequency by young people today than LSD. There are no other hallucinogens which are in current widespread use. (Although in many articles about the drug use of young people, long rosters of drugs will be presented, as if all on the list were commonly used.) The possibility of any number of new drugs appearing and becoming widely used is high, however.

What are the effects of the hallucinogens, or psychedelics? It should be noted that these two names convey misleading and slanted meanings. "Psychedelic" has a pro-drug bias; it implies that these drugs allow the mind to "manifest" itself most truly and clearly under the influence — that the human mind works best while high on a psychedelic drug. "Hallu-cinogenic" implies that actual full-blown hallucinations are a common effect of these drugs; this meaning is clearly an anti-drug bias. Both these terms are inaccurate as descriptions of what actually happens while some-one is under the influence of one of these drugs. However, no completely neutral term exists, so we will use both psychedelic and hallucinogen, without implying that their connotations are necessarily valid.

The effect most clearly ingrained in the public mind of the hallucinogenic drugs is the *psychotic episode*, or outbreaks of temporary insanity. Although such an effect would be cause for serious concern when it did occur, an actual outbreak so serious as to require hospitalization is relatively rare under the influence of LSD-type drugs. Joel Fort, a drug researcher, has estimated that such temporary psychotic outbreaks occur in about one "trip" every thousand to ten thousand or so. Also, whether they do occur or not depends not only on the simple fact of taking the drug, but also is strongly influenced by the psychological health and the personality of the individual taking the drug. Certainly someone taking LSD in a setting in which he feels comfortable, with others whose company he enjoys, is more likely to have a good "trip" than if he took it in a situation he sensed to be hostile and threatening. However, these are not guarantees; some veterans of hundreds of good trips can have an occasional frightening "bummer." Moreover, most LSD available on the street is contaminated with various impurities; pure LSD is rare. Thus, many of the negative experiences with this drug can be partly attributed to chemicals mixed in with the LSD — sometimes, for instance, strychnine.

LSD and the other psychedelics, or hallucinogens, have a wide range of effects, most of which are highly variable according to surrounding, mood, personality, and experiences of the user, and so on. To think that they occur simply out of a chemical reaction from the drug would be erroneous. I have interviewed hundreds of young people (and some not so young) who have taken hallucinogenic drugs, and who have described their experiences to me. One common experience, or "effect," of psychedelics was what scientists call *eidetic imagery* (and what users sometimes call "eyeball movies"). This is the perception of closed-eye visions and images of extreme richness and dramatic intensity. They will sometimes resemble cartoons, moving, waving patterns, often of great beauty and interest. Typically, these images will be changing very rapidly, often too rapidly to be able to describe at the time, as they occur. The user will often be dazzled by the onslaught of color and motion — all with his eyes closed. The closest thing to this phenomenon in the non-drug world would be a number of contemporary animated cartoons, such as *Yellow Submarine*.

Another common experience on hallucinogenic drugs is what is technically known as *synesthesia*, or the simultaneous perception of two or more senses being "translated" one into another. Thus, users will report being able to "see" sounds, or "hear" color. The emotional equivalent of one sense will be conveyed by another sense. Bursts of color might be seen as the user is listening to, and watching, the clapping of hands.

Notes might be seen bouncing around in time to music, or music might be felt physically, as an almost sexual experience.

Another perception commonly experienced under the influence of psychedelic drugs, particularly LSD, is that the world appears to be in constant motion, fluid and dynamic. Some descriptions I have heard from users of this sensation were: "Things were oozing as if they were made of jelly." "Paint ran off the walls." "I saw wriggling, writhing images." "A brick wall wobbled and moved." "Every physical thing seemed to be swimming in a fluid as if a whole wall had been set in liquid, and was standing there before me, shimmering slightly."

A fourth common element of the psychedelic experience was that everything took on greater *emotional significance*; things appeared to be subjectively exaggerated in importance. Related to this feeling was the experience of tremendous *mood swings*. Subjective affect was much more *intense* than normally—both in a positive and in a negative direction. What would appear as normal, what would be accepted without thought or emotion, suddenly took on epic proportions when under the influence. A mild sadness would turn into the deepest pit of hell. Pleasure became ecstasy. These emotions would intermingle, would follow one upon the other with great rapidity. Everything seemed new and exciting—a world of wonderment, and sometimes terror. Laughing and crying might take place within a 5-minute period. In fact, one of the most outstanding evaluations of the psychedelic experience by users is a feeling of *ambivalence*— of liking it intensely, but, at the same time, intensely disliking it. There was a strong feeling afterward that what had occurred, what was perceived and experienced was both good and bad, and *extremely* so. Psychedelic trips tend to be colored by a very intense feeling of extremes, fantastic shifts in mood.

LSD does not literally make the senses more acute, as many users will claim, but it does open up the psyche to receive the senses. Psychedelic drugs allow a kind of "sensory overloading." The inhibitions we are trained to exercise appear to have less authority while under the influence of hallucinogenic drugs. We normally block out most of what comes to us as sensory stimuli. We limit and filter out most of what would otherwise bombard our senses. We "attend" to a very narrow range of sensations. Otherwise, our day-to-day and even minute-to-minute experience would be impossibly complicated and exhausting. The human mind can handle a limited quantity of input, a small proportion of what is potentially an almost infinitude of information and stimuli, but under the influence of LSD-type drugs, we suddenly become assaulted, flooded with sensory input—which we would normally be unable to handle. We marvel at everything, even the most banal phenomena. Our customary blocking and screening mechanisms seem to be inhibited, and everything comes rushing in on us.

The full-blown authentic hallucination, the perception of materially non-existent physical objects, thinking that something is "there" when it "isn't," is relatively rare under the influence of LSD or other psychedelics. Usually the user knows that what he is seeing isn't "real." So it might be proper to call what users "see" pseudo-hallucinations, or "virtual" hallucinations. Often, some sort of actually existing object provides a kind of "raw material" for a flight of fantasy. Many of these are of two types: the perception of one's own body, distorted, and the perception of the bodies and faces of others, distorted. A high school teacher explained the latter to me. Walking outside his apartment under the influence of LSD, he said that he saw the following: "The people outside, on the street, were horrible freaks. I never saw such twisted, distorted monsters in my life. Everyone was old, fat, or pathologically skinny, with twisted arms, hunchbacks, bloated bellies, turnip-like tubers of flesh, flesh run rampant, a grotesque travesty of human flesh, the Gothic artist's ideal." These perceptions, although they could be thought of as distortions of "reality," were not always thought of as horrible. A young artist told me: "The first thing that I noticed was that my arm was made of gold. This held my attention for a long time. It was beautiful." A young woman who worked for a market research firm explained, "I saw myself in the mirror with one eye. It was disturbing, but not horrible." A third sort of "virtual" hallucination perceived by the LSD users I interviewed was perceiving *animals*. Some were transmutations of humans into animals, while others were completely original creations, seen out of whole cloth. A young woman said that she saw a "man with a frog's head walking down the street." A high school teacher told me of the following experience under the influence of a large dose of LSD: "Several friends came by and tried to coax me to go to the Bronx Zoo. When they asked me, it sounded as if I was in a jungle with a vegetable canopy above me, and their pleas were like little gremlins squeaking. One of my friends said we can see the reptiles, and, man, I really *saw* a reptile, right there in my living room, a silver, green, and black snake, slithering across the floor."

The last effect I will mention is not a subjective one, but is removed from sensory perceptions; it is an "objective" effect. This is the issue of genetic damage. In March 1967, an article was published in the prestigious scientific journal, *Science*, authored by geneticist and physician

Maimon Cohen and two of his colleagues, whose findings indicated that chromosomal damage occurred when human blood cells were placed in a culture containing LSD. In addition, one schizophrenic mental patient who was treated with LSD 15 times in a therapeutic setting was found to have a higher percentage of chromosome breaks than was typical or normal. Within 24 hours of the paper's publication, the news swept across the country. These findings from an improperly controlled study were immediately translated into the incontrovertible "fact" that taking LSD could produce monster-children as a consequence of genetic damage to users of the drug. The recent memory of the thalidomide tragedy was invoked as a parallel. An article appeared in *The Saturday Evening Post* which declared: "If you take LSD, even once, your children may be born malformed or retarded. New research finds it's causing genetic damage that poses a threat of havoc now and appalling abnormalities for generations yet unborn." In the propaganda against the use of LSD by the young, genetic damage became a standard fixture.

Unfortunately for the propagandists, the very latest research does not bear out the 1967 findings. Apparently the original studies were improperly conducted and controlled. Most black market LSD is impure. The question which cannot be answered in the earliest studies showing damage was whether the effects described were due to the LSD or to the impurities contained in most street LSD. Second, many users of LSD—in fact, the majority—also use other drugs. Were the breakages due to the LSD, or to nicotine, marijuana, alcohol, barbiturates, amphetamines, etc.? It was impossible to tell, as no controls were applied. How can we isolate the specific role of LSD? Third, the potency of street LSD is almost never known, and this was not considered in the original research. Fourth, breaks in chromosomes do not automatically mean malformed children, even when such breaks occur. Fifth, a certain proportion of birth defects are born in children each year—about 5 percent, or about a quarter of a million births in the United States yearly, with or without LSD. A controlled study is needed, and not merely of isolated examples of babies who are born with congenital abnormalities from mothers who took LSD. The question is: Is the *rate* of birth defects of children of LSD-ingesting mothers any different from the rate of birth defects in children born to mothers not taking LSD?

After an exhaustive summary of the available findings reported in nearly 100 scientific papers, four researchers, Dishotsky, Loughman, Mogar, and Lipscomb, concluded that individuals who have taken pure LSD showed no increases in the rate of chromosome breakages beyond normal, but that the breaks in those who have taken impure black market LSD are about three times what is typical. The researchers conclude that: "We believe that pure LSD ingested in moderate dosages does not produce chromosome damage detected by available methods." Their conclusion on the ability of LSD to cause mutagenesis and birth defects in man at "trip" doses is that the available evidence points very strongly in the direction that the drug "is unlikely to be mutagenic in any concentration used by human subjects." They also say: "There is no evidence of a malformed child born to a woman who ingested pure LSD."

Even many experts believe that the use of LSD and other psychedelics has waned since the days of Timothy Leary's proselytizing. What is true is that the media coverage of the use of LSD has waned considerably, and users are taking the drug with much less ostentatious fanfare. There is much less of a mystique to taking LSD today than was true in the middle 1960s. There are, it is also true, far fewer hospitalizations as a consequence of psychotic episodes under the influence of LSD today compared with the 1965–1969 period. But the use of LSD is rising. A study done in the public schools of Toronto, grades seven through thirteen, revealed that the percentage of students who had ever tried LSD at least once or more in their lives was 3 percent in 1968, but it was *three times* this in 1970, or 9 per cent. A nation-wide Gallup Poll of American college students taken in 1967 showed that only 1 percent had ever tried LSD. By 1969, another Gallup Poll showed this had increased to 4 percent, and in December 1970 this figure had risen to 14 percent – a stupendous rise in LSD experimentation.

However, this "ever used" statistic is of limited utility. Not all those who are part of this figure are committed "acid heads." Continued use is far less frequent and common than mere experimentation. More than almost any other drug in current use, LSD is discontinued very, very rapidly. The drop-off in use after the experimental first few trials is extremely sharp. Of the total population of everyone who has ever used LSD, possibly a minority has used it more than a dozen times or so. In my own study of marijuana smokers, about half (or 99 out of 204) had taken LSD at least once, but a quarter of this half had tried it exactly once, and another 19 subjects took it only twice. Only 4 out of the 99 had taken LSD 100 times or more, and not one had used it 150 times or more. In other words, LSD is not a drug which is used with much frequency at all in the usual case although, naturally, it will be possible to find frequent users. Most people who use it are curious about it, want to try it, but are rarely motivated to continue using it after their curiosity is satisfied. Thus, it is not typically a drug for which users develop a "habit." The term "psychological dependence" means less for the use of LSD than it does for any drug currently used if, indeed, it has any meaning at all.

NARCOTICS

Heroin addiction in youth has a kind of *crisis quality* to it—that is, in spite of its relative rarity, and in spite of greater objective harm from other sources and other drugs, more adults become more hysterical concerning narcotics than almost anything else. Heroin is the best known of the narcotics, known medically as narcotic analgesics, or pain-killers. Man has not yet discovered a really potent pain-killer which is not addicting. A number of narcotics are derived from the opium poppy, and are called "opiates": morphine, heroin, dilaudid, codeine, and a few weaker preparations, such as paregoric, an alcohol-based "tincture" of opium. Heroin is derived from morphine on a roughly one-to-five basis; morphine was derived directly from opium—which is about 10 percent crude morphine. There are also a number of synthetic narcotics, usually called "opioids." They include meperidine (or Demerol), and methadone (or Dolophine), the two best-known synthetic narcotics. Heroin is probably the most potent of the narcotics, by weight, when pure, but it is almost never pure when purchased on the street; typically, packets of heroin are 95–98 percent or so composed of some filler such as quinine, mannitol, and milk sugar. However, one of the greatest sources of overdosing is presented in the completely *unknown* potency of street heroin. An addict may be able to physically handle or tolerate doses of a certain strength—say, 3 percent heroin. One day a new shipment may arrive, and the addict may receive a packet (or "bag") of 20 percent heroin. Since the difference between getting high (or the "effective dose") and getting killed (the "lethal dose") is extremely narrow, this greater-strength heroin may actually kill the addict. The greatest threat to the user of narcotics is overdosing, and it is largely because of the great variability in the potency of black market heroin that the narcotic addict will overdose.

In spite of increases in the use of, and probably addiction to, narcotics, and especially heroin, in the past several years, heroin is still one of the *least* often used drugs among adolescents and young adults. There are a half-dozen or so drugs which are used illegally with much greater frequency than heroin. Alcohol is still the number one illegal drug used by the young in this country. Marijuana is in a strong second place—and first, if we discount alcohol, as most people do, not thinking of alcohol as a "drug." Running in a not-so-strong third place is amphetamine; LSD is used with a frequency just behind amphetamines. After that, and in roughly decreasing order of "popularity," are barbiturates, cocaine, opium, and heroin. (If methedrine is counted as a separate drug from the amphetamines, it would be just after opium.) Of course, which specific drugs are the most often used will depend almost entirely on the social, economic, racial, sexual, regional, and age composition of the young people in question. Glue is sniffed by the very young, and its use declines sharply with increasing age. Marijuana is more likely to be used among middle-class and affluent youths today—although working-class young people smoke marijuana as well, just with a bit less frequency. Hundreds of studies have demonstrated this positive relationship between social class characteristics of the parents of young people and the likelihood of using marijuana. This relationship is especially strong when we use education to measure social class, children of the most educated parents have the *highest* rates of smoking marijuana. College students today try and use a wide range of illegal psychoactive drugs; colleges can be thought of as "hotbeds" of drug use, at least when compared with the non-college young adults today. Some drugs, such as tranquilizers, are more likely to be used among women. Heroin is used, in contrast, by males far more than by females. The use of some drugs is associated with race. Whites are much more likely to use methedrine, LSD, and the amphetamines. Blacks, on the other hand, have a higher likelihood of trying cocaine and heroin. (Marijuana appears to be equally used by the two racial groups.) In other words, the ranking of the relative "popularity" of the various drugs depends on the social characteristics of those we are talking about.

Nevertheless, taking an overall view, heroin is, in comparison with the other drugs, relatively infrequently used. In my two surveys on a college campus conducted in 1970 and 1971, only 3 and 4 percent had used heroin in the 6 months prior to the study. For both years, experimental use was far more frequent than continued use, although regular use of all of the drugs, including heroin, increased from 1970 to 1971. In the 1970 Toronto study conducted by the Addiction Research Foundation, only 4 percent of the students in grades seven through thirteen had ever tried *any* opiate—and opium was the most commonly used opiate, not heroin. Among all those who try heroin, most discontinue its use rather rapidly. The myth of "one shot and you're hooked for life" is just that—a myth. It has become daring and foolhardy to try heroin. To have "made" heroin once or twice has become the sign of being sophisticated, wild, and "hip." But few young people are so committed to this inverted ideology that their whole lives become dominated by the thirst for the next shot. In fact, this tendency to discontinue use appears to be true of all illegal drugs, with the exception of marijuana. Marijuana seems to have far more *persistence* than any currently-used illegal drug. In my 1971 college survey, only 14 percent of all the heroin users in the sample had used the drug weekly or more; this was true of 8 percent of those who had tried cocaine, 2 percent for opium, and 6 percent for methedrine. But it was over 50 percent for marijuana. Thus, with heroin, as with most dangerous drugs, the continued user, and, hence, the addict almost invariably is in a minority among all those who have tried this drug. Now, it is possible to overdose with just one shot — and anyone "just" experimenting with heroin is flirting with death; this is true. Any, *any* percentage who continue to use, and become addicted to, heroin, is too high. But these concerns should not blind us to the fact that with heroin, experimentation *usually* leads to a discontinuation of use, and, much less commonly, to addiction.

Heroin in the 1950s and the early 1960s was a drug whose use was almost exclusively confined to the slum, and mostly used among young ghetto dwellers. This pattern has largely broken down. Now a much wider range of young people are trying, and even becoming addicted to, heroin. Sociologists and public health experts are not quite sure why this trend has occurred, but far more use is taking place in the suburbs and the colleges than ever before. It is a sad commentary, however, on our society's values and concerns that drug addiction became a major crisis only after this trend toward addiction among middle-class youths occurred. Before that, when it was confined largely to the working-class slums, neither the public nor officials were as upset about it as is true today. It was only after the sons and daughters of the affluent got into trouble from drug use that programs designed to alleviate the situation were launched.

All of the narcotics, as with alcohol and barbiturates, are physically addicting. This means that withdrawal symptoms appear in the user when heavy, long-term use is discontinued. The similarities between the narcotic withdrawal and the withdrawal after barbiturate and alcohol addiction are basically the same; the similarities are far greater than the differences. (One difference which has been observed is that withdrawal subsequent to alcoholism and barbiturate dependency sometimes results in death, whereas no deaths have been directly traceable to a narcotics withdrawal, *per se*.) Most observers feel that addiction is not a simple function of biochemical reactions. A certain proportion of street addicts — that is, who use heroin regularly, who think of themselves as addicts, and who are so regarded by others, both addicts and non-addicts alike — are not "addicted" in the literal sense. Much of their compulsive and continued drug taking does not arise from a physical need, strictly speaking, but out of social expectations and demands, and various aspects of a particular type of personality. Many "addicts" experience little more than the symptoms of a bad cold when they have to "kick." Thinking that they are addicted, of course, makes it worse; their withdrawal will be more severe than if they were not aware of their addiction, as sometimes happens with some "hospital addicts." Much street heroin available today is so weak that even these expectations are not sufficient to bring on an extreme withdrawal reaction. What addicts experience when they "kick" is a variable, and not a constant. It is dependent on many things. The variability of black market heroin is one. A good deal of it is sufficiently potent to cause a true physiological addiction in users; some of it is not. Another variable is how often it is used. Many addicts will escalate from a "nickel bag" (a packet costing five dollars) a day to 2 or 3, or 10 or 20, packets a day—and this is usually sufficient to bring about a true addiction. However, the point is, ironically, not all "addicts" are addicted.

The life of the typical street "junkie" has been described at length and in detail by many observers. One of the most common fallacies is to assume that all or even most of the features of the heroin scene can be directly causally traced to the biochemical effects of the drug itself. Even so hard and so biological a fact as death from an overdose can be traced, in large part, to social, legal, economic, and psychological "causes." Contrast the life of the average street junkie with that of the physician narcotic addict. Estimates place the proportion of all physicians in America who are addicted to a narcotic drug at about 1 percent or so, an extremely high rate when compared with the general population. (In fact, physicians tend to use drugs at a significantly higher rate than do their age and economic peers.) Physician addicts almost never overdose, because they are aware of the strength of their doses and they are able to administer standardized doses, unlike the street junkie. They almost never contract any of the various secondary diseases that street addicts suffer, such as hepatitis, pneumonia, or malnutrition, because they take precautions to avoid them, and because they do not have to search and scramble in the deadly game of "copping" drugs on the street. The medical pathologies associated with street addiction (overdosing aside) can be traced predominantly to conditions external to the drug itself. The heavy long-term addiction to narcotics, including heroin, does not damage or destroy human bodily tissue, in direct contrast with alcohol, nicotine, barbiturates, and amphetamines. In fact, ironically enough, in strictly organic terms, heroin is an extremely "safe" drug. The organs are not damaged, destroyed, or threatened by even a lifetime of narcotic addiction. There are no malfunctions of the body, no tissue damage, no physical deterioration, directly traceable to the use of any narcotic, including heroin. (Again, overdosing aside.)

"Opiate addiction *per se* causes no anatomical changes in the body," writes Harris Isbell, a physician working at Lexington's Addiction Research Center for narcotic addicts. Abraham Wikler, another medical expert at Lexington's Center, puts it this way: "No irreversible organic damage to the nervous system or viscera is known to occur as a result of opioids *per se*." At the same time, it must be realized that an "artificially" created and sustained reality – the largely man-made realities and dangers of heroin addiction, given the present legal and logistical entanglements – is every bit as real and as powerful as a "naturally" occurring reality, that is, the direct biochemical reaction of the drug itself, contained directly within the drug and its action of biological tissue.

Given the high death rate of addicts – caused, as I said, not by the destructive action of heroin, but by overdosing, and by secondary diseases commonly contracted by addicts – the question which comes to mind to all observers is: "Why should anyone *want* to become an addict?" *Regardless of the cause*, anyone who becomes addicted to heroin in America today stands an extremely high chance of destroying himself. An addict is a very poor risk as far as living is concerned, regardless of whether or not the drug itself destroys human tissue, or whether it is the narcotics scene itself which is deadly. Why, then, would any young person take this sort of risk with his or her life? By applying moral judgments, it becomes impossible to understand the point of view of the participants, and, therefore, it is easy to miss the motivation entirely. Too often we dismiss what the participant feels and experiences; we fail to take the view of the narcotic user or the addict toward his situation into account, and apply our own standards to an evaluation of his activity. By eliciting descriptions from users themselves of their drug experiences, we will come closer to an understanding of this puzzling phenomenon. If everything that an addict says about his experiences becomes labeled a "rationalization," we will never be able to learn the causes of addiction. Current studies have attempted to penetrate the world of the heroin scene. From these recent descriptions, some of the following points become clear to the perceptive student of the heroin scene. First of all, "turning on" – trying a drug for the first time – is nearly always a *group* activity; friends and acquaintances turn one another on. Second, drug use has become a kind of symbol of belonging to a special subculture, a group that considers itself an underground and kind of elite collectivity. Drug taking has become a prestige item among some of today's young people. Competition emerges — users within this subculture (it does not encompass even a majority of today's youth, however) want to be able to say that they have experimented with, or "made," a certain drug which is exotic and dangerous in the eyes of their peers. Third, excitement and rebellion have become a part of the motivation for trying and using certain drugs among some segments of the young. (This is not necessarily true of all drugs; moreover, this reason cannot explain continued use, although it might very well explain experimental use.)

Another important point is that everything connected with narcotics use involves an important dimension of the *learning* process. One learns that taking one or another drug is an exciting thing to do; one learns how to secure the drug, to administer it, and one even learns how to recognize its effects, as well as enjoy these effects. These processes do not occur "naturally"; they do not emerge organically out of the drug itself. This lore is transmitted by groups of intimates. Many first trials with heroin are extremely unpleasant. It is only after a number of experiences that the neophyte will be able to enjoy its effects. One college heroin user told me that for her the "rush" sensation after injecting heroin into her vein was even more pleasurable than a sexual orgasm. But it is here that a fifth important point comes into play: the pleasure of administering the drug gradually diminishes over time. Addicts eventually have to increase the dose in order to keep experiencing the same amount of pleasure from administering heroin. Eventually, a point is reached when this orgasm-like pleasure becomes dissipated. Eventually, the quantity taken to achieve this increasingly fleeting pleasure reaches such a level that addiction itself is either a likelihood or a certainty. Every addict says, during his "honeymoon" phase of using sporadically: "I can handle it. I can take it or leave it alone." Almost no addict started out to become hooked, but the rapid tolerance which builds with heroin moves the user in that direction. Euphoria diminishes; doses increase; eventually, an addict is born — or at the very least, someone who is taking heroin several times a day, day in and day out.

The typical life of the street junkie is — *by his own admission* — dismal at best. A heroin habit will cost anywhere from $15 to $100 per day. This is out of the reach of all but the most affluent in our society. A life of crime is almost inevitable. Descriptions by addicts of their daily rounds show that nearly all have to resort to crime to support their habits.

"Boosting," or stealing from stores, is extremely common. Burglary becomes routine for many. Most women addicts resort to prostitution to support their habit. Selling drugs to the less centrally-placed drug user who does not have access to inexpensive, high-volume drugs will bring in revenue for a certain proportion of addicts. In other words, life for the addict is typically an incessant and dangerous scramble for cash, a kind of grotesque travesty of conventional business life. The popular image of the addict "nodding out" after a shot, in a sense, "retreating" from life's problems, describes only a tiny segment of the addict's world – and for some, this experience has ceased to occur. In fact, the constant "hustle" more accurately characterizes the addict's life than somnolence and sedation.

Many addicts talk of kicking. Very few are able to do so on their own. Nearly all have tried a few times. During abstention, especially among other ex-addicts, heroin forms a major topic of conversation and concern. Prisons and prison-hospitals have been an almost unmitigated failure in "treating" narcotic addiction; the overwhelming majority of all addicts coming out of federally-sponsored prison-hospitals and jails become re-addicted within a matter of months, and some do so within a few hours. Some hopeful signs can be seen in two recent developments in medical therapy: chemicals that both substitute for and block the action of heroin – methadone and cyclazocine being the most well known – and, second, the therapeutic community, such as Synanon and Phoenix House. An over-reliance in the past on punitive police methods to solve the addiction problem has resulted in nothing but a bigger and more serious problem, and has given support to organized crime. Perhaps the future will witness an abandonment of this tragic blunder, and a significant movement in the direction of relying on more rational and effective solutions.

REFERENCES

Angel, K. No marijuana for adolescents. *The New York Times Magazine*, Nov. 30, 1969.
Barber, B. *Drugs and society*. New York, Russell Sage Foundation, 1967.
Becker, H. S. *Outsiders*. New York, Free Press, 1963.
Becker, H. S. History, culture, and subjective experience. *J. of Health and Social Behavior*, Sept. 1967, **8**: 163–176.
Becker, H. S. Ending campus drug incidents. *Trans-action*, April 1968.
Bloomquist, E. R. *Marijuana*. Beverly Hills, Calif., Glencoe Press, 1968.
Bloomquist, E. R. *Marijuana: The second trip*. Beverly Hills, Calif., Glencoe Press, 1971.
Blum, R. H. *Students and drugs*. San Francisco, Jossey-Bass, 1969.
Blum, R. H. *Society and drugs*. San Francisco, Jossey-Bass, 1969.

Blumer, H., *et al. The world of youthful drug use.* Berkeley, School of Criminology, University of California, Jan. 1971.

Bogg, R. A., *et al. Drugs and Michigan high school students.* Lansing, Michigan House of Representatives, Special Committee on Narcotics, Dec. 1968.

Carey, J. T. and Mandel, J. A San Francisco Bay Area speed scene. *J. of Health and Social Behavior,* June 1968, **9**: 164–174.

Chambers, C. D. *An assessment of drug use in the general population.* New York, Narcotic Addiction Control Commission, May 1971.

Cheek, F. E. and Newell, S. Deceptions in the drug market. *Science,* Jan. 19, 1970, **167**: 1276.

Cohen, M. M. Chromosomal damage in human leukocytes induced by lysergic acid diethylamide. *Science,* March 17, 1967, **155**: 1417–1419.

Crancer, A. Jr., *et al.* Comparison of the effects of marihuana and alcohol on simulated driving performance. *Science,* May 16, 1969, **164**: 851–854.

Dishotsky, N. I., *et al.* LSD and genetic damage. *Science,* April 30, 1971, **172**: 431–440.

Duster, T. *The legislation of morality.* New York, Free Press, 1970.

Faltermayer, E. What we know about marijuana— So far. *Fortune,* March 1971.

Fiddle, S. *Portraits from a shooting gallery.* New York, Harper & Row, 1967.

Fort, J. *The pleasure seekers.* Indianapolis, Bobbs-Merrill, 1969.

Glaser, D., *et al.* Later heroin use by marijuana-using, heroin-using, and non-drug-using adolescent offenders in New York City. *The Intern. J. Addict.,* June 1969, **4**: 145–155.

Goode, E. *The marijuana smokers.* New York, Basic Books, 1970.

Goode, E. *Drugs in American society.* New York, Alfred Knopf, 1972.

Goode, E. (Ed.) *Marijuana.* 1st edition. New York, Atherton Press, 1969.

Goode, E. (Ed.) *Marijuana.* 2nd edition. New York, Lieber/Atherton, 1973.

Grinspoon, L. *Marijuana reconsidered.* Cambridge, Mass., Harvard University Press, 1971.

Isbell, H. and Jasinski, D. R. A comparison of LSD-25 with (−)Δ^9 trans-tetrahydrocannabinol (THC) and attempted cross-tolerance between LSD and THC. *Psychopharmacologia,* 1969, **14**: 115–123.

Jaffe, J. H. Drug addiction and drug abuse. In Louis S. Goodman and Alfred Gilman (Eds.), *The pharmacological basis of therapeutics,* 3rd edition. New York, Macmillan, 1970. Pp. 276–313.

Johnson, B. D. *Social determinants of the use of dangerous drugs by college students.* New York, Wiley, 1972.

Jones, R. T. and Stone, G. C. Psychological studies of marijuana and alcohol in man. *Psychopharmacologia,* 1970, **18**: 108–117.

Josephson, E., *et al.* Adolescent marijuana use: Report on a national survey. Paper presented at the First International Conference on Student Drug Surveys, Newark, N.J., Sept. 14, 1971.

Kolansky, H. and Moore, W. T. Effects of marijuana on adolescents and young adults. *JAMA,* April 19, 1971, **216**: 486–492.

Krippner, S. Drug deceptions. *Science,* May 8, 1970, **168**, 654–655.

Larner, J. and Tefferteller, R. (Eds.) *The addict in the street.* New York, Grove Press, 1964.

Lawrence, T. and Velleman, J. Drugs/Teens—Alcohol/Parents. *Science Digest,* Oct. 1970.

Lennard, H. L., *et al. Mystification and drug misuse.* San Francisco, Jossey-Bass, 1971.

Lindesmith, A. R. *Addiction and opiates.* Chicago, Aldine, 1968.

Lindesmith, A. R. *The addict and the law.* Bloomington, Ind., Indiana University Press, 1965.

Louria, D. B. *Overcoming drugs.* New York, McGraw-Hill, 1971.

Manno, J. E., *et al.* The influence of alcohol and marijuana on motor and mental performance. *Clinical Pharmacology and Therapeutics*, March–April 1971, **12**: 202–211.

McGlothlin, W. and West, L. J. The marijuana problem: An overview. *Amer. J. Psych.*, Sept. 1968, **125**: 370–378.

Milman, D. H. The role of marijuana in patterns of drug abuse by adolescents. *J. Pediat.*, Feb. 1969, **74**: 283–290.

Moffett, A. D. and Chambers, C. D. The hidden addiction. *Social Work*, July 1970, **15**: 54–59.

Pearlman, S. Drugs on the campus – An annotated guide to the literature. *Intern. J. Addict.*, June 1969, **4**: 249–300.

Scher, J. The marijuana habit. *J. Amer. Med. Assoc.*, Nov. 9, 1970, **214**: 1120.

Smart, R. G. Relationships between parental and adolescent drug use. Paper presented at the Fifteenth Annual Meeting of the Eastern Psychiatric Association, New York City, Nov. 7, 1970.

Smart, R. G., Fejer, D., and White, W. J. The extent of drug use in metropolitan Toronto schools: A study of changes from 1968 to 1970. *Addictions*, Spring 1971, **18**: 3–19.

Smith, D. E. Acute and chronic toxicity of marijuana. *J. of Psychedelic Drugs*, Fall 1968, **2**: 37–47.

Smith, D. E. (Ed.) *The new social drug.* Englewood Cliffs, N.J., Prentice-Hall, 1970.

Smith, D. E. (Ed.) Speed kills: A review of amphetamine abuse. *J. of Psychedelic Drugs*, Spring 1969, **2**: whole issue.

Smith, D. E. and Mehl, C. An analysis of marijuana toxicity. In David E. Smith (Ed.), *The new social drug.* Englewood Cliffs, N.J., Prentice-Hall, 1970. Pp. 63–77.

Snyder, S. H. *Uses of marijuana.* New York, Oxford University Press, 1971.

Sutter, A. G. Worlds of drug use on the street scene. In Donald R. Cressey and David A. Ward (Eds.), *Delinquency, crime and social process.* New York, Harper & Row, 1969. Pp. 802–829.

Sutter, A. G. The world of the righteous dope fiend. *Issues in Criminology*, Fall 1966, **2**: 177–222.

Tart, C. T. *On being stoned: A psychological study of marijuana intoxication.* Palo Alto, Calif., Science and Behavior Books, 1971.

United States Department of Health, Education, and Welfare, National Institute of Mental Health, *Marijuana and Health.* Washington, D.C., U.S. Government Printing Office, Jan. 31, 1971.

Weil, A. T. Adverse reactions to marijuana: Classification and suggested treatment. *The New Eng. J. Med.*, April 30, 1970, **282**: 997–1000.

Weil, A. T., Zinberg, N. E., and Nelsen, J. M. Clinical and psychological effects of marijuana in man. *Science*, Dec. 13, 1968, **162**: 1234–1242.

Wikler, A. Drugs: Addiction, organic and psychological aspects. In *The International Encyclopaedia of the Social Sciences.* New York, Macmillan, 1968. Pp. 290–298.

Wikler, A. Clinical and social aspects of marijuana intoxication. *Arch. Gen. Psychiatry*, Oct. 1970, **23**: 320–325.

Winick, C. Physician narcotic addicts. *Social Problems*, Fall 1961, **9**: 174–186.

Wittenborn, J. R., *et al.* (Eds.) *Drugs and youth.* Springfield, Ill., Charles C Thomas, 1969.

Young, J. *The drugtakers.* London, MacGibbon and Kee, 1971.

A Survey of the Inhaling of
Solvents Among Teen-agers

JACOB SOKOL

Juveniles rebel against adults but are conformists among themselves. Some conformities come and go as harmless fads; however, when the motive of imitative behavior is to acquire status, antisocial acts or acts resulting in personal harm may be performed. Among the latter are inhalation of lighter fluids, gasoline, Freon-aerosol mixtures, spray finishes (gold, Builders Emporium), Carbona, and Pam.

GLUE SNIFFING

The practice of glue sniffing among juveniles first came to the attention of law enforcement personnel in 1961. At times, glue sniffing reached epidemic proportions. The glue sniffer is still a problem today(1,2,3,6, 10,37,41,42).

The Hawaii State Medical Association conducted a survey of physicians in 1971 regarding drug abuse among youth. Of 393 who replied, 143 reported having seen drug abuse problems within the preceding 60 days, and of those seen 68 sniffed paint and glue(111).

The results of the National Household Based Survey conducted by the Columbia University School of Public Health revealed, among other data, that 37 percent of those interviewed were frequent or occasional glue sniffers(112).

The Los Angeles County Sheriff's Department made the following arrests during the period from July 1, 1970 to July 1, 1971: 180 juveniles under the age of 18 years arrested for sniffing solvents and glue, 60 arrests of youths over the age of 18 years.

The East Los Angeles Station of the Sheriff's Department arrested 79 juveniles and 17 adults.

During the month of July 1971, the Los Angeles County Sheriff's Department arrested 34 juveniles and 17 adults. The East Los Angeles Station of the Sheriff's Department arrested 17 juveniles (Personal Communication).

A very popular practice among youngsters, especially in the East Los Angeles area, is to sniff the spray finishes (gold), manufactured by the Builders Emporium, which contain toluene and xylene. These have the same effect as sniffing glue and may cause the same pathological conditions(69).

Unfortunately, due to the increased focus on LSD and marijuana, the incidence of glue sniffing is overshadowed. Up to June 1966, I investigated over 1000 cases of glue sniffing while serving as Chief Physician of the Central Juvenile Hall of the Los Angeles County Probation Department.

The procedure for glue sniffing is as follows: The teen-ager squeezes glue from a tube onto a piece of cloth or rag, or even an old sock. Ordinarily, the cloth is brought to the open mouth and the fumes deeply inhaled. Occasionally a glue sniffer will inhale through the nostrils. Instead of a cloth, a plastic bag may be used(1,2,3,6,8,10,12,18,33,41,42,46).

Toluene (methyl benzene) is the common solvent found in plastic cements. Toluene acts as a depressant on the central nervous system. Other solvents are xylene, methyl isobutyl ketone (isopropyl acetone), other ketones, isopropyl alcohol, ethyl acetate, methyl cellosolve acetate, tri-chlor-ethylene, and benzaldehyde(1, 2, 3, 4, 12, 13, 18, 35, 37, 38, 39, 40,41,42,43,66,67).

While under the influence of glue, and especially in the euphoric state, glue sniffers are dangerous to society and to themselves(1,2,3,8,10,11, 29,36,37,42,43). A 16-year-old boy assaulted his 9-year-old brother, held glue rags to the faces of his infant brother and toddler niece, and at one time held lighted matches over the mouth of his infant brother(16,17). A 15-year-old boy, along with four of his friends, raided a neighborhood and fired 15 shots into an inhabited building. A 16-year-old boy tried to beat his parents and younger brother with a heavy steel knife-sharpening tool(20). A teen-age youth pleaded guilty to kidnapping a newly-wed couple, then fatally shot the husband and raped the wife(80). An 18-year-old youth was alleged to have fatally stabbed a friend with whom he reportedly was sniffing glue(80). A 16-year-old youth while under the combined influence of alcohol (from drinking ale) and toluene-containing plastic cement fumes exhibited wild, nearly maniacal, behavior which culminated in his fatally shooting a special (railroad) police officer(80). A youngster who was admitted to Juvenile Hall under the influence of glue had, according to the police report, climbed on roofs (Personal Communication).

While under the influence of glue, many sniffers have hallucinations (8,10,11,13,18). One boy heard barking dogs late at night and developed a fear that "the Devil is coming in the window to take me away." The boy was screaming "Help me!" when the nurse and the deputy probation officer arrived(101). Previously, this boy and four others, under the influence of glue, were sitting in a theater. Suddenly they grabbed a young girl sitting in front of them and tried to rape her. The girl screamed and they ran from the theater(101).

Several cases of addiction have been called to my attention(73,74,76, 89). A young boy was committed to a state institution after being judged addicted by a court judge. An 18-year-old glue sniffer, a junior college student, requested help from the juvenile authorities because of his desire to sniff glue. A 26-year-old male, with a history of sniffing glue for a period of 12 years, was addicted to toluene. A judge admitted him to a mental institution. He had a history of assaultive destructive outbursts following frequent episodes of glue sniffing, and revealed a brain syndrome associated with glue sniffing (Personal Communication).

Richard Satran, M.D. and Vernon N. Dodson, M.D. reported a case of toluene habituation(76). Strong indications that sniffing airplane glue and other solvents can cause chromosome damage are reported by a group of investigators in Toronto, Canada. Two extremely rare chromosome configurations — atriradial and aquadriradial — have been found in glue sniffers. However, the Canadian researchers emphasize that whether the chromosome damage will have any somatic or genetic effect is not known yet(32,43,54,66,78,98). Benzaldehyde, a substance in airplane glue, is a mutagen, according to Dr. Ernst Freeze of the National Institutes of Health Laboratory of Molecular Biology(43).

The juvenile will experience some of the following signs after sniffing glue: a buzzing sensation, dizziness, headaches, euphoria, somnolence at times, deplopia, dullness with poor concentration, nystagmus, forgetfulness, tremors (at times simulating a condition of alcoholic intoxication), spasmodic condition of muscles, especially the neck muscles and the muscles of the lower extremities, dilated pupils, decreased reflexes, numbness of extremities, sneezing, coughing, chest pain(1,2,3,7,8,13, 14,19,21,25,26,33,37,38,39,40,41,42,43,44,52,56,66,68).

Loss of weight is not uncommon. In one case, 30 lbs were lost by a youth who indulged in glue sniffing.

The physical examinations and laboratory tests conducted on glue sniffers admitted to Juvenile Hall revealed that glue sniffing causes brain, liver, kidney, bone marrow, and lung damage(1,2,3,14,39,40,59,69,70, 93,94,95,109,118–119,122,124). Our findings also reveal, among other things, that anemia has a particular manifestation among glue sniffers. In the *New England Journal of Medicine*, September 23, 1965, Dr. D. Powars describes two cases of aplastic-anemia and one death due to glue sniffing(27).

There is also a decrease in white blood cells and an increase in white cells. We find basophilic stippling and target cells which indicate a toxic condition. The urine analysis frequently reveals pus, albumin, casts, bacteria, and blood.

Enrico C. Vigliani, M.D. and Giulio Saita, M.D. of Milan, Italy, observed 47 patients with benzenehemopathy at the Clinica del Lavoro, Milan, between 1942 and 1963. Two showed anemia, 7 anemia with leukopenia, 5 anemia with thrombocytopenia, 26 pancytopenia, 6 leuke-mia, and 1 leukemoid reaction(117). The investigation states that in the province of Pavia many cases of chronic benzene poisoning arose from the use of glues containing benzene in the manufacturing of shoes(117).

The Institute of Occupational Health of the University of Pavia saw, during 1961–1964, 41 cases of benzene intoxication with hemopathy. Five of these cases came from factories where cases of aplastic-anemia also occurred. G. Hartwich, G. Schwanitz, and J. Becker of the Univer-sity of Erlangen-Nurnberg, Germany, described chromosome anomalies in a case of benzene leukemia(98).

A number of juveniles were subjected to electroencephalographic (EEG) examinations by Dr. Maurice L. Kamine, a medical neurologist. Examinations were given within 48 hours after admittance to Juvenile Hall, and occasional electroencephalographic changes were found.

Dr. M. Brozowsky and Dr. Emil G. Winkler, of Brooklyn and State University of New York Downstate Medical Center, found that among 10 sniffers, 6 had abnormal EEG findings. In 5 of these, the EEG changes were considered severe(96).

A number of deaths, directly or indirectly caused by glue sniffing, have been recorded in the United States(1,2,3,15,29,31,36,37,45,50a,55,59, 69,76,82,94,102,113,116,121). A high school student was found dead in Richmond County, California after sniffing glue. In Philadelphia, a youth was found dead after sniffing glue. In Washington, a student died after sniffing glue. In Oregon, one death is recorded. In Fremont, Kansas, a death is reported due to sniffing glue. In 1968 a Los Angeles boy, age 13, was found dead from sniffing airplane glue (29).

In January 1972 two members of a religious sect were found dead after inhaling a liquid substance as part of a church rite. The victims, age 22 and 26, had taken part in the Church of Armageddon's "rite of breathing," which involved the use of toluene placed in a plastic bag and held over their mouths (102). The anatomical findings for the 26-year-old revealed intense pulmonary edema with bloody fluid in the airway; a blood toluene level was 1.5 mg percent; microscopically the brain showed lytic changes in the basal ganglion cells and excess pigment in other nerve cells in the hypothalmus. The anatomical findings for the 22-year-old revealed marked cerebral edema with minute subarachnoid hemorrhages in the region of the right precentral gyrus, collapsed ventricles, and evidence of cerebral edema. The airway contained bloody fluid and the lungs were extremely congested and bloody (Personal Communication).

Suicide from the effects of glue sniffing was reported by the *Los Angeles Herald Examiner* when two California youths were found dead with towels saturated in model building glue near the bodies.

In Detroit, in 1967, two young sisters, 6- and 8-years old, were found strangled and raped. Police reported that 15 empty glue tubes, as well as a 6-pack of empty beer cans, were found near the bodies (121).

In Los Angeles in 1967, a 16-year-old sniper and suspected glue sniffer was killed after slaying one police officer and wounding another (113).

Four death cases due to glue sniffing are recorded in the State of California and I am presenting two autopsy reports.

Case: 41-year old man, 1963, Los Angeles County

Respiratory System: The right lung weighs 650 grams and the left 600 grams. Both lungs are markedly congested and voluminous. The pleural surfaces have a dark red mottled appearance. Sections of the right lung show marked congestion and areas of dark red hemogeneous appearance, indicating inter-alveolar hemorrhage. The blood of the pulmonary vein appears dark red and hemolyzed. The left lung is ligated at the bronchus and pulmonary vessels for gas chromatography studies. The larynx has a congested mucosa also. No area of obstruction is noted.

Liver and Biliary System: The liver weighs 2230 grams. The surface is dark brown and smooth. Multiple sections show a markedly congested lobular pattern. The gall bladder contains dark green mucoid fluid material.

Hemic and Lymphatic Systems: The spleen weighs 160 grams. The surface is dark red and smooth and its parenchyma is markedly congested.

Urinary System: The kidneys together weigh 350 grams. The capsules can be stripped without difficulty, revealing dark red, congested cortical surfaces. The corticomedullary demarcation is distinct. The mucosa of the pelves and ureters is not remarkable. The urinary bladder has an intact mucosa.

Case: A 13-year-old boy, 1968, Los Angeles County

Respiratory System: The lungs weigh 490 and 400 grams on the right and left, respectively. The pleural surfaces are smooth, and they appear somewhat generally congested. The left lung is tied off and remained intact for analysis for hydrocarbon substances. The right lung, when sectioned, shows moderate congestion. There is fluid within the tracheobronchial passages and the mucosal linings show slight inflammation. The hilar lymph nodes are not enlarged. The pulmonary vessels connect with the heart in a normal fashion and these are patent. The thymus is present and grossly normal weighing approximately 40 grams. The upper respiratory structures are removed and dissected. There is some reddening of the mucosa of the epiglottis, larynx, and upper trachea. Otherwise no lesions are found to involve this portion of the body.

Lungs: Marked hypermia of alveolar capillaries of the lungs and pink fluid, in some alveoli, focal hemorrhage into some alveoli.

The exact cause of the fatal mechanism due to sniffing is as yet unknown. A group of researchers found that exposing mice to fumes from toluene or airplane glue slows their hearts to asphyxia induced atrioventricular block. Although the relevance of these findings for man is untested, they suggest that arrhythmias may be the cause of human death after sniffing glue.

GENERAL CONCLUSIONS

In conclusion, may I say that thousands of adolescent and teen-age youngsters in many cities throughout the United States and other countries are deliberately inhaling vapors of a wide variety of volatile organic solvents in order to induce repeated states of inebriation. Although the practice itself is not new, its occurrence in epidemic proportions in many areas, and the passage of legislation prohibiting the act in many cities and states in the United States has brought the problem into nation-wide prominence.

Finally, I would like to say that the problem of the inhalation of solvents is primarily found among teen-age boys and girls. A variety of organic solvents are inhaled by juveniles for the intentional induction of intoxication. While different in some of their effects and in toxic potential, they all share a narcotic effect upon the central nervous system.

GASOLINE SNIFFING

Another fad today is the sniffing of gasoline. Gasoline, one of the most volatile substances, is a mixture mostly of C_4 to C_{12} saturated hydrocarbons with major components that have boiling points ranging from 60° to 200°C. Various additives may be present in commercial gasoline. The additive T.M.P. — trimethyl-phosphate — is a known mutagen. Dr. Epstein's group of Boston researchers reported that T.M.P. produces adverse genetic effects in mice (78).

Brief exposure to high concentrations of gasoline have caused fatal pulmonary edema, acute exudative tracheobronchitis, and passive congestion of the liver and spleen (48,50,51,61). Exposure to gasoline may damage the central nervous system, resulting in edema of the brain, petechial hemorrhages, and myelitic changes (48,50,51,61,67,68,84,94,105,109).

There are mild blood changes caused by gasoline sniffing. There is a reduction in red cells and in hemoglobin content, an increase in eosinophiles and leucocytes. In exposure to gasoline of high benzene content, the blood findings will also reveal leuopenia and thrombopenia.

Under the influence of gasoline sniffing the juvenile will experience some of the following: headaches, dizziness, drowsiness, nausea, vomiting, salivation, weakness, loss of appetite, blurred vision, buzzing sensation in the ears, excitement, combativeness, staggering gait, erotic feelings (transient erection), euphoria, grandiosity, visual and auditory and tactual hallucinations, altered shapes and colors, distorted spatial relations, sense of spinning, sense of moving, sense of floating, dyspnea, painful chest, cyanosia, delirium, coma, epileptoform seizures, and death (4,40,45,46, 47,48,49,50,50a,51,61,66,67,68,84,89,104,105,109,122).

Sylvan Bartlett and Fernando Tapia, M.D., describe a 15-year-old boy who "often felt that he was lying on a plush, reddish-purple velvet carpet that extended in every direction as far as he could see, and all above and around him was a dark blue sky with white clouds that passed over him" (89).

W. M. Easson describes an 11-year-old boy who, under the influence of gasoline sniffing, "talked constantly about the birds who talked with him, and said he saw monkeys and his friends swinging in the garden trees" (49).

N. W. Brown, M.D. describes a 15-year-old boy who claims to have seen Jesus and people in white robes. This same youngster, while under the influence of gasoline, also claimed communication with his dead sister. He occasionally felt that his size changed, so that sometimes he would be the size of a giant, and at other times he would be very small (133).

E. J. Tolon, M.D. and Frederich A. Lingl, M.D. describe a model psychosis produced by inhalation of gasoline fumes. A 15-year-old boy envisioned people who were half women and half cows and half horses and half people. He would dream that he was in Hell, lying in a fiery pit with flames rolling out. This youngster experienced amnesia after gasoline intoxication, culminating in an episode in which he broke furniture and a glass door and then attacked his mother's dog(123).

J. J. Larton, M.D. and Carl P. Molmqurt, M.D. describe a 15-year-old boy who inhaled gasoline fumes from 2 to 5 times a week over a 6-month period. This youngster experienced erotic gratification—transient erection. The above authors also describe a 13-year-old boy who was "drifting in space." He related to the nurses in a seductive manner, at times attempting to grab their breasts(124).

William R. Law, M.D. and Erland R. Nelson, M.D., Ph.D. describe a 41-year-old woman who chronically sniffed gasoline vapor. This sniffing resulted in leadencephalopathy. She hallucinated that she had placed a radar in her house to spy on her thoughts. She frequently had terrifying dreams(126).

Dawson Durden, Jr., M.D., M.C.U.S.A. and David W. Chipman, M.D., M.C.U.S.A. describe a 19-year-old marine who had been habituated to the practice of gasoline inhalation for 7 years, during which time he experienced euphoria, hilarity, and hallucinations. When he found no available gasoline, he inhaled the fumes from a can containing 60 percent carbon tetrachloride, which resulted in severe poisoning(127).

Four death cases caused by gasoline sniffing were reported in California. Below are two autopsy reports which reveal the similarities of the pathological conditions resulting from sniffing gasoline.

Case: R. F., 1966, Los Angeles County (This 23-year-old male was found dead in an automobile beside a can containing gasoline.)

Anatomical Summary
Respiratory System: (1) Acute Laryngotracheobronchitis; (2) pulmonary edema, minimal.

Microscopic Report
Microscopic Diagnosis: (1) Focal perivascular hemorrhage, cerebrum; (2) pulmonary edema, minimal; (3) intrapulmonary and hemorrhage, and congestion, marked; (4) acute epiglottis.

Case: R. G. C., 1968, Los Angeles

Anatomical Summary
External Injuries: Crusted abrasions, right temporal region; multiple ecchymoses, right lower extremity.

Respiratory System: Pulmonary edema, moderate; hypostatic pulmonary congestion, marked; hemorrhagic foam in the trachea.

Nervous System: Petechial hemorrhages in cerebral centrum, minimal.

Brain: The brain shows multiple sections scattered petechial hemorrhages, mainly of the cerebral centrum. In some sections, the dendritic architecture is somewhat blunted.

Heart: The heart shows normal size and amount of myocardial fibers and scattered evidence of hypoxia reflected in the nuclei. Another section is of similar appearance.

Lung: The lungs show severe congestion but no exudate. Another section is of similar appearance but shows moderate to regionally marked edema as well, without significant numbers of intra-alveolar macrophages.

Liver: The liver shows moderate congestion.

FREON SNIFFING

Apparently a new fad of collecting fluorinated-chlorinated hydrocarbons from aerosol glass chillers in ballons or bags and then inhaling the concentrated vapors has become popular. A number of such products have as chilling ingredients one of the Freons: Freon 11 (fluorotrichloromethane) or Freon 12 (dichlorodifluoromethane)(81).

The following pathological conditions may result from the inhaling of Freon: narcotizing effect, a feeling of an intense high, a pulsating sense throughout the body, the tendency to laugh, spasm of the larynx, freezing and frostbite when Freon is brought into contact with the skin, asphyxiation, and death. There is also possible decomposition of Freon into highly irritant and toxic gases such as hydrogen chloride, hydrogen fluoride, fluorine, chlorine, and even phosgene when the Freon is heated(97, 98, 129, 134, 135).

The inhaling of Freon was popular during 1967 at Reed College, Oregon. At that time, an Oregon Medical Investigator stated that stocks of the quick-freeze spray were bought up as quickly as they were put on the shelves in Portland, Oregon. Later this new fad spread among the students at Yale University in New Haven, Connecticut.

The law enforcement agencies in the city of Pasadena, California, were faced with the same problem. Lieutenant R. H. McGowan, Police Watch Commander, stated that the Juvenile Division had received information that teen-agers were inhaling aerosol fumes for a new thrill sensation. In 1968 the law enforcement agencies of Orange County, California, were faced with the serious problem of sniffing of Freon among juveniles.

On December 11, 1967, Peter J. Pitches, Sheriff of Los Angeles County, issued a press release regarding the danger of sniffing aerosol glass chillers.

A number of deaths have occurred throughout the United States, with 9 in the state of California reported as the result of inhalation of Freon (37,62,63,64,81,82,91,92,94,100).

Death is usually sudden and may occur in individuals who practice the inhalation of Freon only once as well as among those who have repeated these inhalations on different occasions.

Various mechanisms have been postulated as to the cause of death (63). The evidence suggested that the cause of death due to sniffing of aerosols is acute cardiac arrest. It could result from the sudden onset of ventricular fibrillation due to sensitization of the heart to ephinephrine by inhalation of high concentrations of aerosol contents. Experimental investigation revealed that the commonly-used aerosol propellants in high concentrations are capable of sensitizing the heart to ephinephrine, resulting in serious cardiac arrythmias (37,62,63,64,81,82,91,92,94,100).

Dr. Nancy Flowes and a group of researchers at the Medical College of Georgia exposed dogs to inhalation of several aerosols while monitoring electrocardiographic and blood gases data. The animals developed rhythm disturbances within seconds or minutes after inhalation had begun. The initial cardiac manifestations were profound sinus-slowing. Cardiac excitability, premature beats, and the like were only seen in the terminal state.

Researchers from the Department of Medicine, University of Illinois Hospital in Chicago, exposed aerosol propellants to adult mice of the ICR Strain. It revealed that fluoroalkaline gases were toxic to the hearts of 34 mice sensitizing them to asphyxia induced sinus-bradycardia atrioventricular block and T-W depression (62).

The cause of death is also probably due to ventricular fibrillation or to sudden alteration produced by a decrease in oxygen and an increase in carbon dioxide in the pulmonary alveoli, which induced a reflex effect and almost instantaneous cessation of respiration and heart beat.

There is therefore a possibility that, in humans, the cardiac toxicity aerosol propellants may be the cause of sudden death in youths who are inhaling propellants.

I am presenting verbatim cases of autopsy reports of two young men who lost their lives due to sniffing Freon.

The anatomical and microscopical findings for them are almost identical.

Autopsies were performed by the offices of the Chief Medical Examiner's Coroners of Los Angeles County, Orange County, and San Francisco County.

Case: J. S., 1968, Los Angeles

Anatomical Summary
Petechial hemorrhage left lateral sclera; hypermia of pleura—marked pulmonary edema—mild; hyposatic and alveolar hemorrhage; hemorrhage tracheal bronchitis, severe; hyperemia of superficial cerebral vessels; focal necrosis, left internal capsule.

Microscopic report
Lung: The lung shows comparatively small alveolar spaces containing variable amounts of edema and/or fresh hemorrhage. Some of this hemorrhage is nearly subpleural. No neutrophilic exudate is present.
Trachea: The trachea shows moderate dilation of the stroma but essentially intact respiratory epithelium. This section is from nearly the level of the carina and includes a paratracheal lymph node showing no abnormality. Another section taken more proximally shows complete loss of the respiratory epithelium and extreme edema, dilation and patchy hemorrhage of the stroma. Larger blood vessels in the even deeper areas are also engorged.
Spleen: The spleen shows mild congestion.
Kidney: The kidney shows moderate congestion.
Brain: The brain shows, in multiple sections, numerous petechial and larger hemorrhages, usually not associated with discrete blood vessels. There is a mild amount of subarachnoid dilation. No other characteristic change is found in these multiple sections of cerebrum, cerebellum, and brainstem.

Case: R. C., 1969, Los Angeles

Microscopic Report
Lungs: Passive congestion, moderate. The septal vessels are congested and the septal intersitium is edematous.
Liver: Moderate passive congestion.
Brain: Marked passive congestion.
Kidneys: Passive congestion, marked.
Spleen: Passive congestion.

It is evident from these autopsy reports that the inhalation of Freons for euphoric purposes is extremely dangerous and unpredictable as to its outcome. It appears that the young user is lulled into a false sense of security by having had, or knowing others who have had, previous "harmless" experiences.

LIGHTER FLUID SNIFFING

Deaths have also been caused by the inhalation of butane lighter fluids. This problem has been recognized only in recent years. The chief effect of the inhalation of lighter fluid fumes is euphoria, simulating intoxication by alcohol. There is a rapid induction of dizziness, confusion, muscular incoordination, and a pleasurable oblivion from reality. Other occasional symptoms are headaches, irritability, nausea, vomiting, anorexia, and irritation of the conjunctiva and mucus membranes of the nose, throat, and bronchial tree, with the end result of pneumonitis. Sustained use during any one episode can lead rapidly to unconsciousness(39,40,106, 109).

Chemically, lighter fluid varies from brand to brand, but essentially it contains a mixture of volatile and highly inflammable aliphatic hydrocarbons, primarily naphtha(38,39,40,106,109).

Under the influence of lighter fluid sniffing, youngsters may engage in both homosexual and heterosexual behavior. In 1964 the police of San Antonio, Texas were called to investigate an abandoned building where they apprehended 6 children who admitted to a year-long series of sniffing accompanied by sex parties(106).

Addiction to the sniffing of lighter fluid is a possibility. I have observed several juveniles at the Hall who revealed withdrawal symptons in the form of restlessness, anxiety, excitability, crying spells, and tremors of the hands. In 1967, a 15-year-old male of Oxnard, California died from acute pulmonary edema and anoxia due to inhalation of butane. The autopsy revealed the following findings in the respiratory system: both lungs were supcrepetant and heavy in character, lying free in the pleural spaces. The pleural surfaces were marked by scattered subpleural, petechial hemorrhages. Both lungs appeared to be considerably edematous and congested, as visualized and pulpated (Personal Communication).

CARBONA

For a time it was popular, among juveniles, to sniff Carbona. Carbona is a cleaning fluid containing Tri-Chlor-Ethylene and Petroleum-Hydrocarbons manufactured by Carbona Products Company.

The juvenile will experience some of the following after sniffing Carbona: forgetfulness, fatigue, insomnia, giddiness, intolerance to alcohol, diplopia, may exhibit polyneuritis, anginal pain, dermatitis, conjunctivitis, aversion to work, gastrointestinal disorders, mild trigeminal neuralgia, trigeminal/oculomotor/auditory or facial paresis, slight anemia/leukopenia, psychosis-paranoid, cerebellar symptoms, addiction, toxic encephaloses, which may change to chronic brain syndrome(39,40,60,75,83,84,85,86,99,109,110,130,131,132).

TRI–CHLOR–ETHYLENE $\underset{\underset{CCL_2}{\parallel}}{CHCL}$

Tri-chlor-ethylene possesses an anesthetic effect. It may cause: Transient impairment of liver function and pulmonary edema due to disintegration to phosgene and chlorine.

Tri-chlor-ethylene breaks down into hydrochloric acid and di-chlor-acetylene. Di-chlor-acetylene breaks down to phosgene and carbon monoxide or into (in the pressure of moisture) dichloacetylchloride and trichloracetylchloride (39,40,60,75,83,84,85,86,109,110).

I am presenting one case from the records of a university medical center in Los Angeles.

The patient is a 20-year-old Caucasian male who came to the Medical Hospital in 1967, with the complaints of malaise, myalgia, vomiting, diarrhea, and jaundice for the three days prior to admission. The patient related that his urine had been the color of tea and that his stools were dark. However, for the 24 hours before admission, the patient had not urinated.

There is a history of using dangerous drugs for the past six years. He also occasionally sniffed Carbona. Two days prior to admission patient sniffed Carbona for 6 hours continuously. He also sniffed AeroSpot Remover for 30 minutes. The patient's symptoms began that day.

Patient's condition required peritoneal dialysis and later hemodialysis (Personal Communication).

There are several death cases recorded due to sniffing Pam. Pam is an antisticking spray for pans. The main ingredients are Lecithin, and a-mono-amino-mon-phosphate. It is a colorless crystal compound soluble in alcohol. Lecithin is found in animal tissue, especially nerve tissue, semen, and in the yolk of eggs, also in smaller amounts in blood and bile. It is chemically the steary-loleyl-glycero-phosphate of choline.

In 1970, in Chula Vista, California, a 14-year-old girl lost her life due to sniffing Pam. The autopsy, performed by Dr. H. R. Irwin, revealed that the cause of death was edema and congestion, pulmonary, acute, due to anoxia, due to inhalation, lecithin (Personal Communication, 115).

Another death, that of a 13-year-old boy, was reported in Minneapolis, Minnesota in 1971. The autopsy was performed by Dr. John I. Coe and Dr. S. Gulmen in Hennepin County. The cause of death was aspiration, pulmonary hemorrhage and edema (Personal Communication).

REFERENCES

1. Sokol, J., M.D. and Robinson J. Glue sniffing. *Western Medicine*, June 1963, 4: 192.
2. Sokol, J., M.D. Glue sniffing. *Listen*, Jan.–Feb. 1964, Vol. 17, No. 1.
3. Sokol, J., M.D. Sniff of death. *F.B.I. Law Enforcement Bulletin*, Oct. 1965.
4. Krug, D. C., Sokol, J., and Nylander, L. Inhalation of commercial solvents: A form of deviance among adolescents in *Drug addiction of youth*. Edited by Ernest Harms. Pergamon Press, 1965.
5. Barker, G. H. and Adams, W. T. Glue sniffers in sociology and social research. *An International Journal*, April 1963, Vol. 47, No. 3.
6. Freer, A. B. About glue sniffing. *Children*, Sept.–Oct. 1963, Vol. 10, No. 3.
7. Glue sniffing. National Clearing House for Poison Control Centers, U.S. Dept. of Health, Education and Welfare, July–Aug. 1964.
8. Davis, M., R.N. Glue sniffers. *R.N.* Oct. 1965, Vol. 28, No. 10.
9. Merry, J. and Zachariadis, N. Addiction to glue sniffing. *Brit. Med. J.*, Dec. 1, 1962.
10. Burgess, W. Glue sniffing. A dangerous teen-age fad. *The P.T.A. Magazine*, Calif., March 1964.
11. Severin K. Dreams which turn to nightmares. *Listen*, July 1965, Vol. 18, No. 4.
12. Glaser, H. H. and Massengale, O. M. Glue sniffing in children. *JAMA.*, 1962, 181–300.
13. Jacobziner, H. Glue sniffing. *New York J. Med.*, Oct. 15, 1962.
14. Grabski, D. A. Case report of toluene sniffing producing cerebellar degeneration. *Amer. J. of Psych.*, 1961, 118–461.
15. Glue sniffing – Death of a baker. *Los Angeles Times*, May 10, 1963.
16. Hazards of glue sniffing to the young. *N.A.C.C.A. Newsletter*, Feb. 1964.
17. *Roanoke Times*, Va., Jan. 5, 1964.
18. Health Information Release. *California Medical Annual*. Glue sniffing, A dangerous form of juvenile misbehavior. Jan. 1965, 164.
19. Sterling, J. W. A comparative examination of two models of intoxication: An exploratory study of glue sniffing. *Criminology and Police Science*, 1964, 55.
20. *Evening Tribune*, San Diego, Calif., July 3, 1963.
21. Glue sniffing, *Brit. Med. J.*, Oct. 20, 1962.
22. *Los Angeles Herald Examiner*. If you sniff, don't drive. Nov. 5, 1967.
23. Drug abuse. California State Dept. of Education, 1967.
24. Smith, Kline, and French. Drug abuse escape to nowhere. 1967.
25. *San Jose Mercury*, Feb. 8, 9, 10, 1965.
26. Press, E. and Sterling, J. Glue sniffing. *Police*, March–April 1968.
27. Powars, D. Aplastic anemia secondary to glue sniffing. *New Eng. J. Med.*, Sept. 23, 1965.
28. Ellison, W. S. Portrait of a glue sniffer. *Criminal Delinquency*, Oct, 1965.
29. *Los Angeles Times*, Dec. 17, 1968.
30. Anspacher, C. Mental hospital pleads for help. *San Francisco Chronicle*, Aug. 10, 1968.
31. Goodman, G. Did glue sniffing kill B. Spencer? *Los Angeles Sentinel*, July 22, 1965.
32. Glue sniffing may alter chromosomes. *JAMA*, Feb. 24, 1969.
33. Massensale, O. N., Glaser, H. H., LeLievre, R. E., Dodds, J. B., and Kluck, M. E. Physical and psychologic factors in glue sniffing. *New Eng. J. Med.*, 1963, 269.
34. Drug dependence. American Medical Assoc., 1969.
35. Toxic effects of glue sniffing. In Question and Answers. *JAMA*, Dec. 23, 1968.
36. *Daily Oklahoma*, Jan. 17, 1969, 1.

37. *Los Angeles Times* Part II Editorial. Sniffing death trigger concern, April 21, 1969.
38. Task Force Report. Narcotics and drug abuse. The President's Commission of Law Enforcement and Administration of Justice, 1967.
39. Polson, C. J. and Tattersall, R. N. Glue sniffing. *Clinical Toxicology*, 1969.
40. Deichman, W. M. B. and Gerarne H. W. Symptomatological and therapy of toxicological emergencies, 1964.
41. Sokol, J., M.D. and Robinson, J. Glue sniffing. *Calif. Youth Authority Quarterly*, Fall 1964, Vol. 17, No. 3.
42. Sokol, J., M.D. Glue sniffing among juveniles. *Amer. J. Corr.*, Nov.–Dec. 1965.
43. Scientist sounds warning on wide field of drug products by Harry Nelson. *Los Angeles Times*, Nov. 1, 1969.
44. National Clearing House for Poison Control Center. *Bulletin*, March–April 1969, Sept.–Oct. 1969, Nov.–Dec. 1969.
45. Nitsehe, C. J. and Robinson, J. F. Case of gasoline addiction. *Amer. J. Ortho. Psych.*, 1959, Vol. 29.
46. Faucett, R. L. and Jensen, R. A. Addiction to inhalation of gasoline fumes in children. *Pediatrics*, 1952, Vol. 41.
47. Clinser, O. W., M.D. and Johnson, N. A., M.D. Purposeful inhalation of gasoline vapors. *Psych. Quarterly*, 1951, Vol. 25.
48. Co-Operative Kerosene Poisoning Study. *Pediatrics*, April 1962.
49. Easson, W. M., M.D. Gasoline addiction in children. *Pediatrics*, 1962, Vol. 29.
50. Edwards, R. V., M.D. Case reports of gasoline sniffing. *Amer. J. Psych.*, 1960, Vol. 117.
50a. Fluorocarbon Inhalation Deaths. National Clearinghouse for Poison Control Centers. *Bulletin*, July–Aug. 1969.
51. Read, A., M.D., D.C.P. Petrol Vapour Poisoning. *Brit. J. Med.*, Aug. 1958, Vol. 2.
52. Land, H. W. *What you can do about drugs and your child*. Pocket Books, New York, 1971.
53. Zinser, B. Quick death by sniffing aerosol gas. *Independent Press-Telegram*. Long Beach, Calif., Nov. 14, 1971.
54. Fornia, A., M.D., Pacifico, E., ScD., and Limonta, A., M.D. Chromosome studies in workers exposed to benzene or toluene or both. Milan, Italy, *Archs envir. Hlth*, March 1971, Vol. 22.
55. Sniffing death in aerosols. *Medical World News*, Jan. 8, 1971.
56. Einstein, S. *The use and misuse of drugs*. Wadsworth Publishing Co., Belmont, Calif., 1970.
57. Glue sniffing causes heart block in mice. *Science*, Nov. 1970.
58. Nelson, H. Aerosol sprays – Can steady use cause heart damage? *Los Angeles Times*, Nov. 14, 1971.
59. Winek, C. L., Collom, W. D., and Wecht, C. H. Fatal benzene exposure by glue-sniffing. *Lancet*, March 25, 1967.
60. Stewart, R. D., M.D. Human exposure to tetrachloroethylene vapor. *Archs envir. Hlth*, May 1961, Vol. 2.
61. Lt. Col. W. Dawson Durden, Jr. and Lt. Col. David W. Chipman. Gasoline sniffing complicated by acute carbon tetrachloride poisoning. *Archs Intern. Med.*, April 1967, Vol. 119.
62. Taylor, G. J., IV, and Harris, W. S., M.D. Cardiac toxicity of aerosol propellants. *JAMA*, Oct. 5, 1970, Vol. 214, No. 1.

63. Reinhardt, C. F., M.D. Cardiac arrhythmias and aerosol sniffing. *Archs envir. Hlth*, Feb. 1971, Vol. 22.
64. Arrhythmia held death cause in youths who sniff aerosols. *Med. Tribune*, April 28, 1971.
65. Phillips, T. J. and MacDonald, R. R. Comparative effect of pethidine, trichlorethylene, and entonox on fetal and neonatal acid base and PO_2. *Brit. Med. J.*, **3**: 558–560, Sept. 4, 1971.
66. Sokol, J., M.D., Sniffing is dangerous. *Listen*, Jan. 1972.
67. Deichman, Wm. B., M.D. and Gerarde, H. W., M.D., Ph.D. *Signs, symptoms, and treatment of certain acute intoxications*. Chas. C Thomas, 1958.
68. Deichman, Wm. B., M.D. and Gerarde, H. W., M.D., Ph.D. *Symptomatology and therapy of toxicological emergencies*. Academic Press, 1964.
69. Morley, R. Xylene poisoning: Report on one fatal case and two cases of recovery after prolonged unconsciousness. *Brit. Med. J.*, Aug. 22, 1970.
70. Brush factory employe kills 5, wounds 2. *Los Angeles Times*, Nov. 23, 1971.
71. Gellman, V. Glue-sniffing among Winnipeg school children. *Canad. Med. Ass. J.*, Feb. 24, 1968.
72. Anderson, P. and Kasada, B. R. Electroencephalogram in poisoning by lacquer thinner. *Acta Pharmacol. et Toxicol.*, 1953, 9: 125–130.
73. Silver, R. R. Long Island youths inhale glue in model kits for narcotic effect. *The New York Times*, Oct. 6, 1961. P. 31.
74. Wilson, R. H. Toluene poisoning. *JAMA*, 1943, **123**: 1106–1108.
75. Stewart, R. D., M.D. Acute tetrachloroethylene intoxication. *JAMA*, May 26, 1969, Vol. 208, No. 8.
76. Satran, R., M.D. and Dodson, V. N., M.D. Toluene habituation: Report of a case. *New Eng. J. Med.*, 1963, Vol. 268.
77. Corliss, L. M., M.D. A review of the evidence on glue-sniffing — A persistent problem. *The J. Sch. Hlth*, 1965, Vol. 35.
78. Birth defects and their environmental causes. *Medical World News*, Jan. 22, 1971.
79. Collon, W. D., M.D. and Winek, C. L., M.D. Detection of glue constituents in fatalities due to glue sniffing. *Clinical Toxicology*, March 1970, 3(1). Pp. 125–130.
80. Press, E., M.D. and Done, A. K., M.D. Solvent sniffing: Physiologic effects and community control measures for intoxication from the intentional inhalation of organic solvents. *Pediatrics*, March 1967, Vol. 39, No. 3.
81. Hallucinogens — Trips that kill. *Time*, Oct. 13, 1967.
82. Bass, M., DO, MPH. Sudden sniffing death. *JAMA*, June 22, 1970, Vol. 212, No. 12.
83. Stewart, R. D. Human exposure to tetrachloroethylene vapor. *Archs envir. Hlth*, May 1961.
84. Stewart, R. D. Diagnosis of solvent poisoning. *JAMA*, Sept., 27, 1965.
85. Kleinfeld, M. and Tabershaw, I. R. Trichloroethylene toxicity: Report of five fatal cases. *Archs Ind. Hyg.*, 1954.
86. Williams, J. W. The toxicity of trichloroethylene. *J. Occup. Med.*, 1959.
87. Dodds, J., Ph.D. and Santostefano, Ph.D. A comparison of the cognitive functioning of glue-sniffers and non-sniffers. *Pediatrics*, 1964, Vol. 64.
88. Sniffers get break — In chromosomes. *Medical World News*, March 21, 1969.
89. Bartlett, S. and Tapia, F., M.D. Glue and gasoline sniffing, the addiction of youth — Case Report. *Missouri Medicine*, April 1966.
90. Glue sniffing. *Pediatrics*, Oct. 1963.

91. Baselet, B. S. and Cravey, B. S. A fatal case involving Trichloromonofluoromethane and Dichlorodifluoromethane. *J. of Forens. Sci.*, July 1968, Vol. 13, No. 3.
92. Flowers, N. C., M.D. and Horan, L. G., M.D. Nonanoxic aerosol arrhythmias. *JAMA*, Jan. 3, 1972, Vol. 219, No. 1.
93. Sokol, J., M.D. Glue sniffing. *Listen*, Jan.–Feb. 1964, Vol. 17, No. 1.
94. Sokol, J., M.D. Glue sniffing. In *Drug Addiction in Youth* (E. Harms, Ed.). Pergamon Press, 1965.
95. O'Brien, E. T. and Yeoman, T. A. E. Hepato-renal damage from toluene in a glue sniffer. *Brit. Med. J.*, April 3, 1971.
96. Brozowsky, Y. M., M.D. and Winkler, E., M.D. Glue sniffing. *New York J. Med.*, Aug. 1, 1965.
97. Freon inhalation. *JAMA*, Aug. 1968, Vol. 205, p. 9.
98. Hartwich, G., Schwartz, G., and Becker, J. University of Erlangen-Germany. Chromosomes anomalies in a case of benzene leukemia. *German Medical Monthly*, Sept. 1969.
99. Heim, Von. F., Estler, C. J., Tamman, H. P. and Hähnel, U. University of Erlangen-Germany. Der Metabolitgehalt Der Leber Weise Mäuse by Akuter Trichloräthylen Vergiftung. *Med. Pharmacol. Exp.*, 1966. P. 15.
100. Dollery, C. T., M.B. Aerosol inhalers. *Consultant*, May 1972.
101. *Inhale . . . exhale . . . The new terror.* Film—A Stanley Brady Production. Los Angeles County Probation Dept., Calif.
102. Two sect members inhale fluid die. *Los Angeles Times*, Jan. 24, 1972.
103. Glasser, F. B., M.D. Inhalation psychosis and related states. *Arch. Gen. Psych.*, March 6, 1966.
104. Gold, N., M.B., D.P.M. Self intoxication by petrol vapor inhalation. *Med. J. of Australia*, Oct. 5, 1963.
105. Machle, W. Gasoline intoxication. *JAMA*, 1941.
106. Ackerly, W. C., M.D. and Dalupegibson, G. V. A., M.D. Lighter fluid sniffing. *Amer. J. Psych.*, 1963.
107. Boy 18 dies after sniffing propane gas. *Los Angeles Examiner*, Oct. 2, 1967.
108. Hazard of propane. *JAMA*, Sept. 4, 1967.
109. Thienes, H. and Halen, J. *Clinical Toxicology*, 1972.
110. Bartonicer, V. Metabolism and excretion of trichlorethylene after inhalation by human subjects. *Brit. J. Indus. Med.*, April 19, 1972.
111. Alcohol top of abused drugs among Hawaiians. *Med. Tribune*, June 30, 1971.
112. Smoking, drinking, and experimenting with other drugs among marijuana users and non-users. *Med. Tribune*, Oct. 6, 1971.
113. Boy officer slain. *Los Angeles Examiner*, May 9, 1967.
114. Girl reportedly sniffing fumes dies at party. *Los Angeles Times*, April 13, 1970.
115. Pam stops food from sticking. Pamphlet Distributed by Gibralter Industries, Inc. Chicago, Illinois 60611.
116. I helped him but he killed my son by John Bilby. *Los Angeles Herald Examiner*, May 5, 1968.
117. Vigliani, C., M.D. and Saita, G., M.D. Milan, Italy. Benzene and leukemia. *New Eng. J. Med.*, Oct. 22, 1964.
118. De Govin, R. N. Benzene exposure and aplastic anemia and leukemia 15 years later. *JAMA*, 1963.
119. Erythro-leukaemic myelosis in benzene poisoning. *Brit. J. of Ind. Med.*, 1950.

120. Boy dies after sniffing glue. *The Herald Statesman*, Jan. 14, 1963.

121. Stranger slays two sisters 6, 8. *Los Angeles Herald Examiner*, April 12, 1967.

122. Polson, C. J. and Tattersall, R. N. Halogenated hydrocarbons. *Clinical Toxicology*, 2nd edition, 1969.

123. Tolan, E. J. and Lingl, F. A. Model psychosis produced by inhalation of gasoline fumes. *Amer. J. Psych.*, Feb. 1964.

124. Lawton, J. J. and Malmquist, C. P. Gasoline addiction in children. *Psych. Quarterly*, 1961.

125. Gleason, M. N., Gosselin, R. E., and Hodge, H. C. Clinical Toxicology of Commercial Products.

126. Knox, J. W. and Nelson, J. R. Permanent encephalopathy from toluene inhalation. *New Eng. J. Med.*, Dec. 29, 1966.

127. Law, W. R. and Nelson, E. R. Gasoline sniffing by an adult. *JAMA*, June 10, 1968.

128. Durden, W. D. Jr. and Chipman, D. W. Gasoline sniffing complicated by acute carbon tetrachloride poisoning. *Arch. Intern. Med.*, April 1967.

129. Freon affects heart. *Listen News*, Oct. 1971.

130. Grandjeam, E., M.D. Trichloroethylene effects on animal behavior. *Archs envir. Hlth*, 1960, Vol. 1.

131. Spain, D. M., M.D. Trichloroethylene intoxication. *Archs envir. Hlth*, Sept. 1965, Vol. 11.

132. Longley, E. O., M.B., B.S. and Jones, R., B.S.C. Acute trichloro-ethylene narcosis. *Archs envir. Hlth*, Aug. 1963, Vol. 7.

133. Brown, N. W. Gasoline inhalation. *JMA*, Georgia, May 1968.

134. Freon sniffing risk told. *JAMA*, May 13, 1968.

135. Refrigerants manufacturers warn of dangers from sniffing. *Wilmington Press*, Delaware, 1968.

Glue Sniffing — A Communion*

EDWARD PREBLE and GABRIEL V. LAURY

Reports on the voluntary inhalation of volatile organic solvents started to appear around 1960. Before this time, there were reports in the literature of industrial medicine concerning the toxic effects of the solvents as a result of involuntary inhalation by workers in industry. The concern in these cases was exclusively for somatic damage. Recommendations were made as a result of these studies regarding the substitution of less toxic solvents, and for other measures such as better ventilation and air conditioning. There was little interest in the psychological effects of involuntary inhalation. Before 1960, there were also some anecdotal reports by individuals about getting dizzy and giddy on gasoline fumes, cleaning fluids, and carbon tetrachloride, and there were a few scientific reports from the early 1950s on the habit of gasoline sniffing. These reports, however, were rare and caused no general concern. Regular reports still appear in the literature regarding solvent poisoning in industry, almost always with an exclusive concern for physical damage.

Since 1960, the deliberate sniffing of volatile organic solvents by children and adolescents has become a significant phenomenon. The products used for this purpose include model airplane glue and plastic cements, paint thinner, shellac, carbon tetrachloride, cleaning fluids, lighter fluid, gasoline, and kerosene. By far the most popular products are the plastic

*Abstracted from "Plastic Cement: The Ten Cent Hallucinogen" by E. Preble and G. V. Laury in *The International Journal of the Addictions*, Fall 1967, Vol. 2, No. 2, pp. 271–281, by courtesy of Marcel Dekker, Inc.

cements used for assembling models. The major solvents used in these products are hydrocarbons (hexane), aromatic hydrocarbons (toluene), halogenated carbons (carbon tetrachloride), ketones (acetone), esters (ethyl acetate), alcohols (ethyl alcohol), and glycols (ethylene glycol). Where there is a choice of these products, the user selects those which have a relatively inoffensive odor, produce minimal irritation to the mucous membranes, and are relatively slow drying. In New York there is one brand that is always preferred.

There are several techniques for the inhalation of plastic cement vapors. In the most widely used one, a tube of cement is emptied into a small paper bag which has been wrinkled and massaged ahead of time so that in the process of breathing in and out of the bag there will be no distracting noise which will affect the concentration of the user. After the tube is emptied into the bag, the bag is placed over the mouth and nose, and the user breathes in and out rapidly, massaging the glue all the time to keep it from drying too fast. Plastic bags have also been used, but have been discontinued because of the cases of suffocation reported as a result of this technique. In some cases, the glue is emptied from the tube into a handkerchief and the user sniffs the vapors directly from that. Another technique is to empty out the original contents from a medicinal nose inhaler and insert the plastic cement into the empty inhaler. This technique is often used in school rooms and other public places where the user wants to avoid detection. In the home the glue is sometimes vaporized by means of placing it directly on an electric stove burner or in a frying pan on top of the stove. In a closed room the vapors quickly permeate the atmosphere.

The effects on behavior of inhaling these vapors are similar, in part, to those of alcohol intoxication. As with alcohol, these vapors act as depressants on the central nervous system. There is a feeling of inebriation, exhilaration, euphoria, and, in the extreme, stupor. But the avowed main incentive for sniffing glue is to experience hallucinations, a fact that has been reported in the literature, if at all, only in passing. It is, however, the primary and most significant feature of glue sniffing. The young people who sniff glue refer to these hallucinations as "dreams." They will commonly say: "let's go sniffing and have some dreams."

These hallucinations are primarily visual, frequently in bright colors. Sometimes there are auditory accompaniments. The themes are about equally divided between pleasant and unpleasant. As a rule, hallucinations occur only during the process of inhalation, but in some instances they persist for a period of up to 2 hours after inhalation. The onset of hallucinations is preceded by a "buzzing noise" in the ears (tinnitus) for about 5 minutes after inhalation of the vapors.

There is an important social element in the glue sniffing experience, in that the sniffers seek a communion with fellow sniffers through a sharing of the same "dream." Sniffing is usually done among two or more persons, with those who want to experience similar "dreams" (for example, pleasant or unpleasant) sitting together in a location apart from those who want to experience different "dreams." An enthusiastic account of an hallucination by one person will very often generate the same one in a sniffing partner, or partners. The precise location of the person or persons having a particular hallucination is important. If someone else wants to have the same hallucination he must come to the same location. In one case, two boys had a particularly enjoyable "dream" while sitting on some stairs. They told another boy about it and he wanted the same experience. He went to the same stairs but was unable to reproduce the "dream" until the other boys noticed that he was sitting on the wrong step. When he moved one step down he was able to experience the hallucination.

Sometimes the entire group will get together in a ritualistic position, such as in a circle with their feet or hands touching, and try to produce a common theme. This group experience can take the form of a "seance" in which deceased relatives or friends are manifested inside the sniffers' glue bags. This is usually regarded as a frightening experience; as one boy put it: "you could have heart failure."

Despite the considerable exhortative publicity about the alleged somatic damage to be expected from glue sniffing, most glue sniffers discount these dangers, believing that serious damage can result only after chronic and prolonged use of 1 or 2 years. In this belief they are in accord with most recent scientific evaluations of the phenomenon.

In the early studies of glue sniffing it was suspected that organic damage would result from the practice due to the high toxicity of the agents involved (National Clearinghouse for Poison Control Centers, 1962; Christiansson and Karlsson, 1957). More recent studies on the voluntary inhalation of plastic cement have not established that there is irreversible organic damage, although there are measurable transitory abnormalities (Barman, 1964; Brozovsky and Winkler, 1965; Gellman, 1968; Glaser and Massengale, 1962). The evidence at this time indicates that the toxicity of the cement vapors inhaled does not exceed body tolerance, and that there is an adequate period of time allowed for detoxification which prevents the development of permanent organic damage. One researcher, Dr. Thomas G. Ryley of Toronto's Wellesley Hospital, claims to have found evidence of some chromosome damage among the 14 glue sniffers he studied (*Medical World News*, 1969), but the small number of subjects does not permit a conclusive finding.

With regular sniffers, a tolerance to the plastic cement vapors develops which requires increasing amounts in order to experience the desired sensations. It is also "habit forming" in that the sniffer "feels bad" when he does not sniff on a regular basis.

There are immediate unpleasant physical effects – not always present – including nausea, vomiting, headaches, dizziness, tinnitus, and loss of energy. All of these effects are of short duration and are considered a fair price to pay for the hallucinations.

Probably the greatest physical dangers associated with glue sniffing lie in the uninhibited behavior which results from the depression of the central nervous system. The lack of judgment and awareness that goes with this condition, and the impairment of motor ability, can result in dangerous and reckless acts. Cases have been reported of youngsters falling off of roofs, being hit by vehicles, and suffering other, sometimes fatal, accidents after a glue sniffing experience. Uninhibited behavior can also present a danger to other persons. In 1967, a 14-year-old Westland, Michigan boy was reported to have raped and strangled two sisters, aged 6 and 8, after inhaling plastic cement (Mullings, 1966). Other reports of aggressive and assaultive behavior are common.

There are some obvious signs that indicate a person has been sniffing glue. The odor of plastic cement is strong and is detectable in the breath at close range. Small particles of glue often stick to the body (especially the face) and to clothing. The eyes become droopy and red and the sniffer may become somewhat incoherent. There is usually a noticeable loss of energy and a general lack of attention. More subtle signs include a partially red face, which results from the sniffer's effort to rub stuck glue from his face, and a change in his gait. In general, after a sniffing bout, the sniffer will look somewhat inebriated.

The present report is based on observations of and interviews with 3 groups of glue sniffers in New York City. Twenty subjects were studied in their community as voluntary research subjects in connection with a recreation program in a New York City slum neighborhood. Fourteen were Puerto Rican, 6 were Negro. Their ages ranged from 12 to 18 years, with an average age of 15. All were boys.

A second group of 20 was from a working, lower-middle class neighborhood in the city. All were white. Eleven were of Irish descent (second and third generation), 9 were of Italian descent (second and third generation). The ages ranged from 9 to 16, with an average age of 11. There were 12 boys and 8 girls. These subjects volunteered information on the basis of a long time acquaintance with one of the authors (anthropologist) who had worked in the neighborhood on other research projects.

The third group of 20 subjects were patients in a children's unit in a large mental institution in the New York metropolitan area. As a rule, these in-patients were admitted from referring hospitals, and, therefore, 2–5 weeks had elapsed since their last inhalation. Fifteen subjects were boys, 5 were girls. Their ages ranged from 8 to 15 years, with an average age of 12. They came predominately from the lower socioeconomic class of New York City's population. Twelve were Puerto Rican, 6 were Negro, 2 were non-Puerto Rican white. Their psychiatric diagnoses ran the gamut of mental illness.

Upon admission, a battery of tests was routinely performed: complete physical and mental examination, chest X-ray, hematological examination consisting of a complete blood-count, differential-count, hemoglobin and hematocrit determination, and serology. Urinalysis included physical examination (pH, specific gravity), chemical examination (albumen, sugar) and a microscopic examination (red and white cell count, detection of crystals and empthelial cells). The basic psychological tests included the Bender–Gestalt Test, Rorschach, House-Tree-Person, and WISC.

The physiological studies showed that all the subjects were within the normal limits for their ages. The psychological and psychiatric studies revealed a distribution of mental pathology that is found at large in the hospital population of the same age range. In all the studies there were no correlations associated with the history of plastic cement inhalation.

The authors believe that the most important feature of glue sniffing is the primary desire of glue sniffers to experience hallucinations in a social setting, and that a knowledge of the nature and function of these hallucinations is essential to an understanding of their motivations for this practice. Accordingly, reported below are verbatim accounts of hallucinations experienced by members of the three study groups.

First Group

My boy (friend) Indio said, "Lucky, come over here and I will show you a trick I invented with glue." Then we started sniffing glue in the hall and he said. "Open the window, open the window," and the window it started opening. I saw it open. I said, "What—this is true, this is true. If you sniff glue and tell the window to open, it opens." I kept sniffing and sniffing and the window opened, and I said, "Oh man, this is magic or something—I could rob me a lot of things like this. I could go to a fire escape and open a window like that and go in and rob the apartment."

We used to make electricity. We used to get a shock. One guy would stand over there and one guy here used to sniff glue and we used to touch our fingers and then we used to sniff glue and we used to scratch our feet and the guy used to get a shock. We could see the electricity going. We used to take pictures too. The guy would be standing there and it's dark. We used to sniff glue and then we would tell them to go out and when he goes out you see the smoke. Like smoke from his body and then it used to go away. When we used to take our bag out it would go away. We used to let him stand there and we'd think of Frankenstein and we would look at him and his face would be Frankenstein. Then we started staring at the wall and there was a picture of the devil there. The devil came out and went through Carlos and then we all started going and fighting with the devil and saying, "They ain't going to touch you. They ain't going to touch you."

It was about 1 o'clock in the morning and I was sniffing and I kept looking at the walls of the school and I was staring at the windows. All of a sudden the windows they disappeared. You know the school they have a lot of windows and all of a sudden they disappear. Then I got real scared. Something came out of the building towards me and I dropped my glue bag because I was really scared. I said, "Please, please give me a break. I swear, I swear I won't do it no more. I swear to God I won't sniff glue no more." Then I tried to run to the light and when I was going to jump to the light something held me, turned me back, and I said, "Please God, God give me a break." My highness went away. I got really scared and then I went to the light and I said. "I ain't going back there no more."

Then I closed my eyes and then I was going with a girl named Rosa on 139th. And I was thinking "Rosa I dig you a lot." And then I kept on thinking and thinking. Then some bells started ringing and I was dreaming that I was married to her. And I was walking down a big aisle with my bride. Then her father came out and said, "I don't want my daughter to get married. She is too young." And I said, "Don't break up my wedding now." And then he took a shotgun and then I said, "Okay, okay, I won't get married to her." And then I went and I was up on the roof and I said, "Oh man, now her father blew my cool and now I'll have to kill him or something. I'll have to do something to him because he blew my cool." And I was sniffing glue in the schoolyard and all of a sudden the cops came and they grabbed me and I thought that was her father grabbing me in my dreams and I tried to find a way out and I thought it was Rosa's father, and then I saw the cop was really there and not in my dream and I got really scared. I got really shook up and he took me to the precinct. He said, "What are you sniffing glue for?" And I told him. "I don't know, man." He said, "You know you should get sent away to a hospital or something. You know that is bad for you. You are going to mess up your lungs." And I said, "I don't think I got lungs." Then he searched me and he took off two bags of glue from me. And he took my glue bag. Then I said, "Can I go to the bathroom?" He let me go to the bathroom and when I got there I took off my sock and I started sniffing glue in the bathroom, because I had one bag he didn't find. Then I took my glue tube and put it in my sock again and sat down, and then about 3 o'clock in the morning my mother came and picked me up. Then I went home and I went to sleep.

There was around 20 of us in the yard sniffing glue. And all of us were stone high. We had around three things of glue in a bag. All of a sudden someone said, "Oh, there is a monkey." Everybody started running up to the roof. I stayed down there and I seen it too. I was fighting with him and he was a big man and he was with a hatchet. I tried to drop him to his legs and I tried to put him on the floor. Then all of a sudden he left. I went up on the roof and I saw all the guys up there and they said, "What happened to you, Tony?" I said, "Nothing."

We used to go down there and tell a story about a picture on T.V. that you haven't seen, or a monster picture, and you would see the picture of how it all happened. If you take the glue and sniff hard and don't take the bag off your nose and pay attention to what he was saying you used to go into the same dream. I saw one that made me run, man.

So I went there and I opened the door and I sat down on the mattress we had and I started sniffing. So I got high. So then I started talking to the mattress. I remember saying to the mattress, "Boy, oh boy, I can't sleep on you no more." The mattress just seemed to me like it was moving back and forth. And like if somebody else sat on the mattress it was all right but if I was on it myself the mattress would puff up. It was a nice mattress, you know. Now if I was to tell this to somebody, you know, they'd tell me I was funny in the head. So I just kept it to myself most of the time.

One day me and Mousey were sniffing in the backyard and we thought it was caving in. And then I said, "Watch out he is coming closer. Watch out, watch out." Then this guy goes, "boo!" And we dropped the bag and we started running. A lot of things can happen while you are sniffing glue. You imagine that a puppy dog is just a puppet and you can bring him to life like that and you can make him rough and make him bite you. You can do everything you want with glue.

Second Group

They had like buttons in the wall. And say you press this button and talk to a lady and she'll open a little door through the wall. You make like a wish to her and like you say: "I wish I had some money." Then you get money. Then I went and got more glue.

Once I saw a crack in the wall and I concentrated on this crack and the wall opened up and I saw diamonds, and then I saw a monster.

For instance I can see you with two heads or with a big foot. You could do things without realizing it. You could be crossing a highway and you feel like you're on the sidewalk and all of a sudden you jump and you're dead. Or you could go on the roof and dive off the roof.

I was looking at this rock and it turned different colors. I could see names on it. Then I saw a war on it, like with the Nazis.

I went right into this dream and thought I was blind and crippled. Then I saw the sky closing over me and I saw it was snowing. I wanted to go out and make a snowball, but it was summer.

I thought I was watching T.V., and all the things were moving backwards in slow motion. Then I was listening to a radio and I could see people acting the song out.

I was looking into the bag and a machine came out of the bag and went on to my wrist and made it bleed. I pushed buttons on the machine and blood came out of me at different places.

I saw a little man in the bag, and went after it. Then he was above me, and said that sniffing glue was bad for me, but I didn't pay any attention to him. Then a bee stung me — it really did — and I threw the bag away.

We had this seance sitting in a circle with a candle in the middle, and I saw in the bag some of my dead relatives and pets that I had.

Third Group

I sniffed glue only once, about 8 months ago. I was 15. Three boys came and they had bought 5 tubes of glue. I had prepared the paper bags. I rapidly got very high. It made me dream colored dreams with dark colors. I was able to sniff the bag for about 20 minutes. The dreams were pleasant. I was with friends laughing and I was laughing too. I heard them laugh and we were all laughing together. Meanwhile, I felt dizzy while I was sniffing. I've never had any hallucinations otherwise in my life, not even when I'm drinking, although I have been high under the influence of drinking.

I dream; it's like television. I see nice things, nice colors – orange, yellow, black. Orange are the clowns. I don't know what they say. When we sniff we don't talk at all about what we see. Only later on or some other day do we talk about it. My friends see animals; it's a real show. At times I see nice girls and toys and big cars, but I don't always see the same. It changes. If I take glue now I would see different things than last time.

Sometimes when you sniff glue it makes you act stupid and other times you laugh a lot. Glue doesn't make you feel sleepy and does not make me forget things. When you are high on glue you can dream about whatever you want. I used to dream about my boyfriend and I also saw and heard the spirits with the ugly faces. They told me that I would lose my boyfriend and go away and both these things were true. I recall one time I was with my girlfriend and there was this boy, John, and myself. We were sniffing and we saw the same ghosts. All 3 of us saw them, although the boy was sober. I've never seen ghosts before I started sniffing, but once I started I even saw them twice while I was at home and sober. Once, high on glue, I felt like killing my ex-boyfriend and girlfriend. The voices then had told me to do so.

Another time, when I was sniffing glue, I had visions of Christ and of Bishops and of Mary and Joseph. Several times I had seen them before. At other times I have seen these ghosts while on glue and they told me to go and kill my parents.

I saw other boys sniffing. I took a sniff and liked it. I was like in a dream thinking of being a millionaire. Things were going very fast and there was no sense of time. At other times it was like a bad dream and things suddenly looked bigger. I was walking on top of a car and I was getting electrocuted.

At first I liked it. I would feel high. You dream what you want. It is like when you drink but you do not stay high for long.

I always sniff one tube at a time, never more. I stopped because I felt bad and I thought I would die from sniffing. When sniffing I would see the walls moving and on the walls I could make out these space movies. Sometimes my friend and I would see the same movie on the wall.

I had sniffed glue, and I was going home. A duck was chasing me down the block; I started running; I was scared. People were looking at me. It was a straw duck with a long neck and a big face. I got so scared I promised myself to give up sniffing.

When I sniff glue I start hearing voices; they are voices of spirits — men and women. Sometimes it's like a stupid dream. I see the spirits; they are always the same ones. There are good ones and bad ones. Once they told me to kill my girlfriend with scissors. These spirits have weird faces. Some have only one arm; some have one leg; and some are in color.

I was lying on my bed leaning forward about 10 inches from the glue I had squeezed on the floor. I felt nauseated; I felt like throwing up. I saw ducks like in a circus; some were yellow, some orange, some purple. They were all different colors.

DISCUSSION

The voluntary inhalation of vapors for the purpose of altering psychological states has a long history. At Delphi, in the ancient Greek world, the Pythia sat on a tripod above a cleft in the rocks and inhaled cold vapors emanating from inside the earth, which induced in her an ecstatic alteration of mind. In this altered state she uttered mystical observations in the presence of the Delphi Prophet, who translated them into oracular pronouncements.

In the ancient Judaic world, the vapors from burnt spices and aromatic gums were considered part of a pleasurable act of worship. In Proverbs, (XXVII, 9), it is said that "ointment and perfume rejoice the heart." Perfumes were widely used in Egyptian worship. Stone altars have been unearthed in Babylon and Palestine which had been used for burning incense made of aromatic wood and spices. In the Christian era, "noble guests were honored by being sprinkled with perfume or incense" (St. Luke, VII, 46).

Maimonides, the great Jewish philosopher and physician of the Middle

Ages, regarded incense as a means to animate the spirits of the Priests. In the Renaissance, the French writer Montaigne wrote: "The physicians should make more use of odors; I have often found that they can change me and also act upon my spirits. Incenses and perfumes awaken our senses and put us in the proper frame of mind for contemplation." (Essais, I, LV).

In the nineteenth century, the inhalation of nitrous oxide (laughing gas) became a fashionable indulgence. The effects of laughing gas were described as delightful, intoxicating, and productive of beautiful visions. A person under its influence staggered and talked nonsense. The practice was considered a genteel way of getting intoxicated at fashionable parties. In the same century the inhalation of ether vapor was also popular. The writers Charles Baudelaire and Guy deMaupassant found delight and inspiration in inhaling ether. DeMaupassant inhaled it initially to relieve his migraine headaches, and, in his novel, *Sur L'eau*, described the sensation of intoxication from ether. In the medical literature of this period physicians were alerted to the reddish coloration of the epiderm of the nose and of the upper lip as a clinical sign of ether inhalation. Chloroform inhalation was also used during this period as an agent of exhilaration and intoxication.

Vapor inhalation, then, has for a long time been a source of pleasure and gratification and a means of psychological and emotional adaptation. In the present case of the voluntary inhalation of volatile organic solvents by children and adolescents, there are dangerous side-effects, if not in permanent somatic damage, in the uninhibited, reckless behavior and loss of judgment which result from a depressed central nervous system. For this reason, it is a dangerous activity, both for glue sniffers and for society, and some speculation about the causes is needed.

The 60 children and adolescents who were the subjects of this report did not exhibit an unusual degree of psychopathology. In general, they were active, behavior problem children who had histories of truancy, fighting, and other acting-out behavior. The usual explanations of delinquent type behavior are as applicable to these glue sniffers as they are to similar non-sniffing types: broken home, weak father image, overprotective mother, need for sensory gratification, peer support, demand for attention, escape from unpleasant realities, self-destructive inclinations, superego lacunae, and so on.

One obvious question is why the practice of plastic cement inhalation or glue sniffing did not become an important phenomenon until 1960. The products used for this purpose had been available for a long time, and they could be purchased inexpensively and legally. Also, prior to 1960, there were many children and adolescents with a tendency toward deviant and escapist behavior.

A general answer to this question is that the preoccupation with getting "high" is part of a widespread interest in chemically induced altered states of mind among all members and classes of our society. This interest started after World War II, grew slowly and surreptitiously through the early 1950s, began to accelerate and move into the open in the late 1950s, and became blatant in the 1960s.

This progression of interest in drugs applies to both the "body" drugs (to use the hipster terminology), such as the opiates and hypnotics, and to the "head" drugs, such as marijuana, peyote, mescaline, LSD, and the amphetamines. Today in New York City anyone can observe groups of heroin addicts in any slum neighborhood waiting on a corner or in a bar for the heroin dealer to come into the block; and anyone can observe hundreds of young, middle- and upper-class "teenyboppers" from the suburbs mobbing the "head shops" in the West and East Village in search of the appurtenances and trinkets associated with the use of "head" drugs.

More specifically, however, the glue sniffing experience is special in that a central feature is the social communion through shared hallucinations. It facilitates for the participants a psychological and emotional intimacy with others which they may not be able to achieve in a society where television viewing and other forms of "parallel play" increasingly dominate leisure time activities. Interpreted this way, it is a positive adaptive effort, but with sometimes unfortunate consequences.

REFERENCES

Allen, S. M. Glue sniffing. *Intern. J. Addict.*, Jan. 1966, 1(1): 147–149.

Barker, G. H. and Adams, W. T. Glue sniffers. *Sociology and social Research*, April 1963, 47 (3): 298–310.

Barman, M., *et al.* Acute and chronic effects of glue sniffing. *Calif. Med.*, 1964, 100: 19–22.

Brewer, W. R., *et al.* Hazards of intentional inhalation of plastic cement fumes. *Ariz. Med.*, 1960, 17: 747.

Brozovsky, M. and Winkler, E. G. Glue sniffing in children and adolescents. *New York J. Med.*, 1965, 65: 1984–1989.

Christiansson, G. and Karlsson, B. Sniffing: Method of intoxication among children. *Svenska Lakartidningen*, 1957, 54: 33–47.

Dodds, J. and Santostefano, S. A comparison of the cognitive functioning of glue sniffers and non sniffers. *Pediatrics*, April 1964, 64 (4): 565–570.

Gellman, V. Glue sniffing among Winnipeg school children. *Can. Med. Assoc. J.*, Feb. 24, 1968, **98**: 411–413.

Glaser, H. H. and Massengale, O. N. Glue sniffing in children. *JAMA*, July 28, 1962, **181** (4): 300–303.

Gleason, M. N., Gosselier, R. E., and Hodge, H. C. *Clinical toxicology of commercial products.* Baltimore: Williams and Wilkins, 1957.

Jacobziner, H. and Raybin, H. Glue sniffing. *New York J. Med.*, Oct. 15, 1962, **62**(20): 3294–3296.

Jacobziner, H. and Raybin, H. Lead poisoning and glue sniffing intoxications. *New York J. Med.*, Oct. 1, 1963, **63**: 2846.

La Bene, W. *Psychology*, 1968, **5** (4), 14–16.

Laury, G. V. Glue inhalation, *Medicine and Hygiene*, July 30, 1966, **24** (742): 728–729.

Massengale, O. N., *et al.* Physical and psychologic factors in glue sniffing. *New Eng. J. Med.*, 1963, **269**: 1340–1344.

Medical World News, March 21, 1969.

Merry, J. and Zachariadis, N. Addiction to glue sniffing. *Brit. Med. J.*, Dec. 1962, 5317: 1448.

Mullings, E. B., Flying high on airplane glue. *Michigan's Health*, Sept.–Oct. 1966, **54**: 3.

National Clearinghouse for Poison Control Centers. Glue Sniffing I (1962) and Glue Sniffing II (1964). Washington, D.C.: U.S. Department of Health, Education and Welfare, Public Health Service.

New England Journal of Medicine. Glue sniffing. *New Eng. J. Med.*, Nov. 8, 1962, **267** (19): 993–994.

Pierson, H. W. Glue sniffing, A hazardous hobby. *J. Sch. Hlth*, May 1964, **34**: 252.

Press, E. Glue sniffing. *Pediatrics*, 1963, **63**: 516–518.

Sokol, J. and Robinson, I. L. Glue sniffing. *Western Med.*, 1963, **4**: 192ff.

Sterling, J. W. A comparative examination of two modes of intoxication: An exploratory study of glue sniffing. *J. Criminal Law, Criminology and Police Science*, March 1964, **55** (1): 94–99.

Winick, C. Teenage glue sniffers reported in many areas. *Social Health News*, Nov. 1962, **37** (9): 1–2.

Winick, C. and Goldstein, J. *The glue sniffing problem.* New York: American Social Health Association, 1965.

Physical and Mental Pathology Due to Drug Addiction

STUART L. NIGHTINGALE

The physical and mental pathology due to drug addiction is a large and complex subject. When viewing the issues surrounding drug addiction in youth, there are many compelling reasons to focus specifically on the problem of heroin addiction. Although heroin addiction is currently responsible for a significant amount of morbidity and mortality in all age groups, it is particularly so in the young. Direct and indirect complications and sequelae of heroin use are now the leading causes of death in adolescents and young adults in New York City (Helpern, 1970). Overdose deaths among the young are increasing throughout this country. The non-fatal medical effects are felt particularly keenly among adolescents, traditionally viewed as the healthiest sub-group in our population.

The actual health status of the active heroin addict is difficult to assess. Our current information is drawn largely from "snapshots" obtained by various investigators who have reported series of acute medical problems or fatalities. The observations differ according to the population examined. Many variables operate within this framework: age, race, sex, socio-economic class, area of residence, type of drug or drugs used, source of drugs, and particular "life-style" are but a few.

While repeated physical and laboratory examinations on some addicts with access to pure drugs (e.g., those in the medical and paramedical professions) have established that stable administration of narcotics can be compatible with good health and adequate social functioning, this group represents only a small percentage of all active addicts. So-called street heroin addicts comprise the majority of the individuals who are incarcerated, hospitalized, or who apply for treatment in large metropolitan areas. Dole *et al.* (1966) describe the status of the typical heroin addict in the following way: "Although he has some periods of normal alertness and well-being which he calls 'straight,' the typical addict spends a major part of his day in two other conditions — 'high' and 'sick'... When 'high' — or euphoric — he is sedated, tranquilized, absorbed in himself, and lost to responsibilities. When 'sick' — or abstinent — he is desperate in his need for narcotic drug, with symptoms of general malaise, nausea, lacrimation and perspiration, tremors and cramps. Because of the short period of action of heroin, he oscillates between the limits of 'high' and 'sick' with insufficient time in the normal condition of 'straight' to hold a steady job. Addiction leaves little time for a normal life." These addicts generally have had multiple arrests and convictions. Often, they have spent long periods of time incarcerated. These functionally disabled "hard-core" addicts are typically at the lowest rung of society. They are usually people who function at the poverty level, even though large sums of money may daily pass through their hands. Since all money goes for drugs, malnutrition, poor oral hygiene, and dental caries are almost uniformly present. Hepatitis, venereal disease, and tuberculosis are much more prevalent than in the general population. Preventive medical care, even if available, is not utilized, while medical services in general are avoided in all but emergency situations.

An understanding of the health hazards of heroin addiction is essential for all those who would attempt to help the drug addict; physicians, other health professionals, social workers and community workers need to be aware of the acute and chronic effects of narcotic addiction. With the greater availability of narcotic treatment facilities and increasing accessibility of medical care in the inner-city, knowledge of the physiologic and behavioral realities and consequences of addiction becomes paramount. To be concerned only with the medical complications and sequelae of heroin addiction is no longer sufficient. The full functional and social disability related to narcotic addiction must be appreciated in order to render comprehensive medical care and facilitate rehabilitation. This brief survey will delineate some of the physiologic effects of narcotic drugs and the relationship of these effects to the problems of the street heroin addict.

ACUTE AND CHRONIC EFFECTS OF NARCOTIC ADMINISTRATION

Heroin, or diacetylmorphine, is rapidly distributed throughout the body following administration. Mainly within the liver, heroin is soon deacetylated to 3- or 6-monoacetylmorphine and then to morphine (Way *et al.*, 1960). The drug then enters the brain largely as 6-monoacetylmorphine, and to a lesser extent, morphine (Murphree, 1971). These two compounds appear to be responsible for the pharmacologic effects of heroin. Heroin is excreted in the urine mostly as free and conjugated morphine (Jaffe, 1970). Analgesic and sedative doses of morphine depress all phases of respiration. Moreover, the respiratory depression can be detected even with doses too small to produce sleep or disturb consciousness. This effect increases progressively as the dose is increased and culminates in hypoxia, carbon dioxide retention, acidosis, and finally death in respiratory arrest. Morphine and related narcotics also increase vagal tone. The combination of hypoxia and increased vagal tone has been postulated to cause the transient cardiac arrhythmias observed during hospital treatment of heroin overdose (Labe, 1969).

Tolerance, the increased resistance to the usual effects of a drug, has been reported to have developed after only one dose of a narcotic. Significant tolerance, however, develops generally only with continuous drug use and, even then, does not develop equally to all actions of narcotics. Tolerance develops primarily to the respiratory depressant, analgesic, sedative, and euphorigenic effects of narcotics. Physical dependence on a drug exists when a specific (stereotyped) abstinence syndrome develops upon withdrawal of the drug in question. This dependence usually is produced by continued administration of a drug over a certain minimal length of time. About 40 to 80 mg of morphine must be taken daily for at least a month for detectable signs of abstinence to occur (Isbell, 1971). The symptoms and signs of the opiate abstinence syndrome have been recognized and studied for many years. Jaffe (1970) points out that the character and severity of the withdrawal syndrome that appears on abrupt discontinuation of a narcotic depends upon the particular drug, route of administration, total daily dose used, interval between doses, duration of use, and health and personality of the addict. Symptoms and signs, aside from drug craving, include yawning, lacrimation, rhinorrhea, perspiration, dilated pupils and "goose-flesh." More severe symptoms include tremor, insomnia, anorexia, weakness, nausea, vomiting, abdominal cramps and bone pain. Signs of central nervous system irritability are prominent in and, indeed, typify the opiate abstinence syndrome. Martin *et al.*, (1967) have divided the opiate abstinence syndrome into two phases based upon physical and laboratory examination. The *early phase* consists of the classical symptoms and signs described above as well as increases in blood pressure, heart rate, temperature, respiratory rate, and increased sensitivity of the respiratory center to carbon dioxide. This phase persists in a diminishing form for several months after the cessation of drug use. There follows a second, *late phase* which consists of a decrease in blood pressure, heart rate, and temperature as well as pupillary constriction and increased sensitivity of the respiratory center to carbon dioxide. This second phase appears several months after withdrawal and persists for at least 4 months. The magnitude of the changes associated with this phase of the abstinence syndrome is small and is within the so-called normal range. Whether or not these changes are really pathologic or whether they are related to behavioral abnormalities is unknown at present (Martin *et al.*, 1967). Other changes described in the post-addiction period include EEG abnormalities, feelings of weakness, insomnia, anorexia, irritability, and muscular aches and pains. Changes in catecholamine metabolism following addiction and withdrawal from morphine have been observed for up to 6 months (Sloan and Eisenman, 1968).

THE MORBIDITY AND MORTALITY OF THE STREET HEROIN ADDICT

Assessment of the health of the street heroin addict is most difficult. A variety of factors combine to keep the addict from "surfacing" at traditional medical facilities. Though adequate data are unavailable, it may be assumed that active heroin addicts are subject to at least the same medical problems afflicting individuals of similar demographic characteristics, as well as certain unique addiction-related problems. The same symptoms or illnesses which would lead a non-addict to medical attention, however, would be far less likely to induce the addict to seek medical assistance. This not surprising fact is based on reports in the medical literature as well as on personal observation and flows from certain legal, social, and medical facts of life operational in inner-city areas. Aside from the fact that preoccupation with drugs and drug-seeking behavior are central in the addict's life, he is often reluctant to seek medical care because of expense, impatience with waiting in hospital emergency rooms, and fear of being labeled as an addict, and, in some cases, arrest while at the hospital. Common physician attitudes toward drug addicts, ranging from lack of interest to contempt, are well known to addicts and generally reinforce their distaste for traditional medical assistance. Obviously, the attitude and approach of individual physicians is variable, as is the individual addict's perception of symptoms and appreciation of need for medical care. Whether or not a particular hospital treats addicts with opioids, the therapy of choice for withdrawal, probably influences patterns of addict emergency room usage. The presence or absence of hospital-based long-term treatment programs may also partially determine emergency room usage by addicts at any particular hospital.

The above factors should be taken into account when evaluating the meaning of data from series reported by various institutions. Such data, moreover, may only be applicable to addicts of the type treated at these facilities. Other reporting agencies (e.g., Medical Examiner) while cutting across demographic lines, include data based on only one type of outcome. To apply these figures to the spectrum of street heroin addicts or post-addicts in treatment is often unwarranted. Nevertheless, various investigators have made unique contributions to our knowledge of the morbidity and mortality of the heroin addict by carefully presenting demographic data, circumstances of medical treatment, and criteria for inclusion in treatment or institutionalization. The following observations are culled from a variety of sources and may be applicable to the street heroin addict within the context of his contacts with that type of facility or agency.

THE DRUG, THE NEEDLE, AND THE HABIT

The Drug

The great majority of street-bought narcotics are "unknowns" in respect to drug(s) present, quantity, and quality. While in some instances a pharmaceutically pure substance may be obtained in unopened vials (e.g., morphine sulfate, Dilaudid, etc.), the majority of narcotics either injected or snorted is only defined in street terms. Studies of confiscated street samples of purported heroin in glassine envelopes (bags) or gelatine capsules (caps) have shown wide variations in the actual percentage of heroin present. One survey reported a range from 0 to 36 percent in most samples (Fulton, 1966). The hazard of a purely narcotic drug overdosage is always present, regardless of the state of tolerance of an individual addict. Street heroin is traditionally "cut" with milk-sugar (lactose) and quinine. When administered in this manner, quinine has been demonstrated to produce visual loss (Brust and Richter, 1971) and has been implicated in the production of certain hematologic and other phenomena associated with heroin use and overdose. Other ingredients have been found on toxicologic examination of bags of heroin. These have ranged from the innocuous to the lethal. Substances such as talc and baking soda are not uncommon "fillers." Talc granules, in fact, along with the fibers of cotton, through which the heroin is strained prior to injection, have been associated with pulmonary scarring (granuloma formation) found at post-mortem examination (Helpern and Rho, 1966). Strychnine and other poisons have been suspected in street samples of heroin, but none were found in Fulton's large series.

Certain skin findings are hallmarks of intravenous drug abuse (Sapira, 1968). Sclerosed veins (tracks) are almost pathognomonic. These represent hyperpigmented and hypertrophic scarring of the veins secondary to "mainlining." Microscopic examinations of involved veins reveal evidence of infection and inflammation, the latter probably a consequence of the toxicity of quinine and cocaine, as well as bacterial contamination. Certain drugs rapidly lead to sclerosis of the veins into which they are instilled. This has been seen with paregoric, an opium tincture intended for oral use, due to ingredients such as benzoic acid, camphor, and anise which have limited solubilities and are irritants (Lerner and Oerther, 1966). The concomitant use of triphenamine hydrochloride or barbiturates can enhance the process of sclerosis. Chronic superficial ulcers of the skin have been reported following the intravenous use of barbiturates; ulcerating subcutaneous nodules following subcutaneous heroin injection alone have also been observed (Minkin and Cohen, 1967). When the drug has been taken subcutaneously (skin-popping), circular, depressed scars (quinine-burns) are often seen at old injection sites. This technique is usually employed when all available veins have been rendered unusable through scarring, but (particularly in females) this is also done to conceal drug use. Nasal inhalation of heroin alone or, more commonly, with quinine (and sometimes with cocaine) may lead to necrosis of the nasal mucosa and perforation of the nasal septum with long-term use (Messinger, 1962). Intercurrent epistaxis and chronic sinusitis have been observed when this route of administration is employed.

Infection

Regardless of drug purity, including freedom from pharmacologically toxic ingredients, the bag of heroin is by no means free of major hazard. The bag of heroin reaches the addict only after it has been diluted (cut) repeatedly under unsterile conditions. It is well recognized that bacteria, fungi, and pyrogens are often present in the bag. However, even if the drug is not contaminated by toxicologic or microbiologic standards, the preparation and administration of the drug can lead to other minor or major complications.

Bewley *et al.* (1968) reported the practices of 50 addict-patients. Their findings in Great Britain are generally consistent with those observed in this country. Needles and syringes are usually wrapped in tissue in both countries, but in the United States they are hidden, rather than carried on the person. While disposable equipment may be utilized, it is almost never used only once. Needles are generally discarded only when blocked or blunt and medicine-droppers or syringes only when stuck, broken, or lost. Attempts at cleaning narcotic paraphernalia (works) consist mostly in flushing syringes or medicine-droppers with cold water or, less commonly, hot tap water. The process of preparing heroin for injection usually involves dissolving it in tap water and boiling (cooking). Dissolving heroin in water which is drawn from lavatory bowls has been described in Great Britain and America. Many addicts feel the needles with their fingers or lips for barbs before use and some blow through a blocked needle. The skin is rarely cleansed before a "fix." Blood is commonly licked off the skin following the injection. Bewley even reports incidents of injections through the clothing when "in haste." Gross abscess formation commonly occurs with intravenous use and cellulitis or thrombophlebitis often supervenes. It is not rare for all three to be present concomitantly (Sapira, 1968). While abscesses may go unnoticed by the addict, he may seek medical attention and be hospitalized for septicemia, bacterial endocarditis, septic pulmonary infarction, empyema, brain abscess, or meningitis—all with or without clinically recognizable or actual superficial skin infection. Cases of gas gangrene have also been reported.

A high incidence of tetanus has been found in black females in Harlem. This has been related to their preference for "skin-popping" (Cherubin *et al.*, 1968). The septic complications of parenteral heroin use have been well reviewed by several authors (Cherubin, 1967; Hussey and Katz, 1950; and Louria *et al.*, 1967). Because most addicts use drugs in a communal setting where one set of "works" is shared within the group, conditions such as hepatitis and malaria have been reported in outbreaks and epidemics among addicts (Helpern, 1934; Levine and Payne, 1960; Rosenblatt and Marsh, 1971).

Hepatitis, so common among addicts that it has been used as a means of detecting addicts in a defined population (Alarcón and Rathod, 1968) as well as of identifying an individual who is at high risk of being an addict, has been a subject of great interest in the controversy surrounding the hazards of narcotics use. Indeed, the role of "the needle vs. the drug" in hepatitis in the addict has received a great deal of attention from hepatologists as well as physicians with a primary interest in treating addicts.

Much data support the theory that the hepatitis is on an infectious basis, i.e., transmitted by the needle, and not a toxic effect of the drug (Gorodetzky *et al.*, 1968; Sutnick *et al.*, 1971). Extensive laboratory studies have revealed a high incidence of liver function abnormalities which are not clinically apparent. Surveys of addicts usually uncover a history of prior jaundice diagnosed as viral hepatitis in up to one-third of the total. Various estimates place the ratio of anicteric, or clinically inapparent hepatitis, to clinical hepatitis with jaundice at 2–8 : 1. Hepatitis, then, is probably present at some point in any addict's drug using career. Recent serologic advances have given us much data on the prevalence of the hepatitis-related antigen in the addict population. With the development of more sensitive techniques, more information on hepatitis in the addict will be available. At present, however, this technique has proved useful in screening blood donors. This is especially relevant, because addict blood donors have been found to be a definite source of transfusion induced hepatitis (Cohen and Dougherty, 1968).

Intoxication

The respiratory depressant effects of heroin when administered acutely and chronically, in a stable manner, have been described previously. The street addict, however, takes heroin irregularly; dosage and schedule depend on funds available as well as on impulse. Moreover, actual heroin per bag, the street dosage-unit, varies widely as stated previously. Thus, the degree of tolerance and state of physical dependence of the street addict is quite variable and is as much an unknown at any given time as is the amount of the drug itself. This combination of circumstances sets the stage for untoward reactions ranging from prolonged intoxication to death.

Heroin intoxication, the euphoric state characterized by "nodding" and periods of somnolence with associated hypoventilation, may lead to the observed prevalence of pulmonary atelectasis (Gelfand *et al.*, 1967). The latter situation as well as stupor, narcotic induced vomiting, depression of the epiglottal and cough reflexes, and decreased activity of the respiratory epithelial cilia, probably contribute to the increased incidence of bacterial pneumonia in this population. Since alcohol shares the ability to depress the epiglottal reflex, it is not surprising that both narcotics and alcohol facilitate aspiration. A great many narcotics addicts drink heavily while taking drugs. Similarly, the use of barbiturates at the time of heroin use is not uncommon. Indeed, barbiturate addiction and chronic alcoholism are not rare among street heroin addicts. The prevalence of mixed addictions, however, appears to vary by locality and to be related to certain demographic characteristics. Although the recreational use of alcohol and barbiturates far exceeds the compulsive use of these agents by the narcotics addict, this does make him more susceptible to the acute complications of heroin use. Alcohol and barbiturates are frequently found in the blood of patients who recover from "heroin overdose" reactions in the hospital as well as in those who succumb. The most common cause of death among heroin addicts, the acute reaction or over-dose, in many instances is probably compounded, when not actually produced by other central nervous system depressant drugs.

Although the frequency cannot be adequately determined, there are probably a number of homicides committed by the selling or giving of pure heroin to unsuspecting individuals with little tolerance. More obvious, but probably far less in number, are homicides committed through the substi-tution of known poisons for heroin in the bag before it reaches the user. Suicide has also been committed by addicts by knowingly administering a quantity of heroin far in excess of their normal habit. How many of the so-called accidental overdoses with heroin fall into this category is open to question.

Overdose

While narcotics addicts have a high mortality rate due to acute reactions and illnesses associated with drug use, non-suicidal overdose is the major cause of death in heroin addicts in both Great Britain and the United States. Between 1950 and 1961 in New York City, 48 percent of all addict deaths were due to "acute reaction to dosage or overdosage" (Helpern and Rho, 1966). In 1970, the number of deaths among addicts in this population equalled 75 percent of the total deaths for the 11-year period 1950–1961. Moreover, of this large number, 80 percent rather than 48 percent were due to overdose. Since 1967, heroin overdose has been the leading cause of death in the 15–35 year age group in that city (Helpern, 1970). There are various theories concerning the pathogenesis of the overdose phenomenon. Indeed, Helpern and Rho (1966) do not use the term overdose alone. They prefer the designation "acute re-action," implying that death may result from a form of hypersensitivity reaction to the drug itself. The frequently observed suddenness of death and the unexplained almost uniform finding of pulmonary edema at death (and often, clinically, in those who survive) suggest an acute, massive, allergic-type of response. Regardless of the exact mechanism, death from narcotic poisoning is characterized by respiratory arrest which may be compounded by other factors. Large doses of pharmaceutically pure narcotics (e.g., methadone in the United States and heroin in Great Britain) have produced the classic syndrome of pulmonary edema, respiratory arrest, and death as it is seen in the street heroin addict. Moreover, cases of death where dosage is unknown (the majority of cases) have been found in increasing incidence where tolerance has been lost or is small. Gardner (1970) reported that 55 percent of 47 cases dying of accidental overdosage died shortly after detoxification. These addicts had been either recently released from an institution (hospital, prison, or detention center), or had undergone outpatient narcotic withdrawal. Similarly, cases of overdose death are not uncommonly seen in drug experimenters or detoxified addicts with only recent resumption of use. Furthermore, although not always clinically recognized, many so-called heroin overdoses represent combined drug intoxications, as stated previously. While larger than usual quantities of heroin might have been taken, alcohol and/or barbiturates were frequently consumed prior to the episode, as evidenced by appropriate blood and urine tests as well as histories of hospitalized addicts recovering from these "heroin overdoses."

Memory deficits and encephalopathy have been reported as sequelae to the heroin overdose (Protass, 1971). The latter apparently represents a delayed effect of the hypoxic episode and is secondary to respiratory depression at the time of overdose. Encephalopathy has been reported to occur with other agents causing anoxia (e.g., carbon monoxide) and in those cases are associated with definite pathologic changes in the brain. Strassmann et al. (1969) have related similar pathologic findings in the brains of addicts to subfatal episodes of anoxia during "acute reactions" which may or may not have brought the addict to medical attention. Karliner et al. (1969) have demonstrated changes in pulmonary function up to 3 months following episodes of pulmonary edema associated with heroin overdoses.

Withdrawal

As outlined previously, the severity of the opiate abstinence syndrome is related to many factors which contribute to the degree of physical dependence. Regardless of the actual state of physical dependence, however, the tendency among long-time addicts is to feel highly dependent and, consequently, to fear the abstinence syndrome. Many addicts claim to use narcotics only to feel normal, that is, to alleviate withdrawal symptoms. It has been hypothesized that narcotic drug hunger itself has a biochemical basis (Dole and Nyswander, 1967). Whether fear of withdrawal, subjective complaints, drug hunger, or other factors are primary in the observed drug-seeking behavior of the street heroin addict, the subjective experiences of addicts undergoing withdrawal are of great significance for both the physician and the patient.

Recent reports have focused on the subjective experiences produced by the withdrawal of opiates (Haertzen and Meketon, 1968; Haertzen et al., 1970). Some of the common symptoms found in both weak and strong opiate withdrawal include tension, worry, dysphoria, insomnia, poor cognitive and social efficiency, loss of sense of humor, and a feeling of subjective need for the drug of choice. The oft-described goose-flesh, hot and cold spells, sweating, watering eyes, difficulty in movement, cramps, and yawning are more common during strong opiate withdrawal (Haertzen et al., 1970). Jaffe (1970) has singled out manifestations of the opiate abstinence syndrome that represent goal-oriented behavior and may be classified as "purposive symptoms." These include complaints, pleas, demands, and generally manipulative behavior. This behavior is directed at getting more drug and is highly dependent on the observer and on the environment.

Psychotic manifestations were reported to have developed in 2.4 percent of a series of 500 patients undergoing narcotic withdrawal (Pfeffer, 1947). Chessick (1960) subsequently commented on the lack of psychotic deterioration seen in addicts. Psychosis or suicide as a sequel of drug addiction in general or of repeated addiction and withdrawal cycles was not found in many patients who had undergone detoxification even 10–20 times.

Death has been mentioned as a potential complication of the opiate abstinence syndrome. Glaser and Ball (1970) reviewed the 55 deaths reported to be associated with narcotic withdrawal in the medical literature. They found no instances where the withdrawal syndrome itself could be implicated as a direct cause of death. Furthermore, they reviewed the 25 deaths which occurred during the withdrawal period at the Lexington Hospital over 31 years (a total of almost 30,000 patients detoxified) and found no cases that appeared directly related to withdrawal. In fact, most deaths in both series appeared to be associated with complications of the medical treatment or organic disease which may or may not have been exacerbated by withdrawal. It should be noted, also, that some deaths which have occurred during narcotic withdrawal have occurred because complaints of severe pain were neglected by physicians who felt the latter were either attempts to obtain more narcotics or were merely manifestations of the withdrawal syndrome itself. In these cases, death has been caused by such conditions as perforated duodenal ulcer with peritonitis. Of particular significance is the reported incidence of suicide, a total of 5 of the 80 deaths in the combined series of Glaser and Ball. Suicidal tendencies may be more pronounced during the withdrawal period, especially if the latter is extended to cover the 4–6 months after termination of physical dependence, the time for the return to normal of the physiological variables mentioned previously. Glaser and Ball found that suicide accounted for 12 percent of the deaths during the withdrawal period, but for only 3.6 percent of all deaths occurring at other periods of hospitalization at Lexington.

Subjective Effects and Behavioral Toxicity

The subjective effects and behavioral toxicity produced by drugs are complex and problematic. Lasagna et al. (1955) point out that the subjective effects of drugs are dependent on the drug dosage, the route of administration, the nature of the subject, and the situation in which the drug is taken. Moreover, the production of a given mental state, even in the same situation, may be experienced as pleasant by some and unpleasant by others.

Post-addicts tend to experience euphoria from morphine or heroin, while non-addicts generally do not find the effects pleasant (Lasagna et al., 1955). Observers have noted that non-addicts are indifferent to or actually dislike opiates. The medical patient who receives morphine for analgesia does not find narcotics euphorient. Kolb (1925) has suggested that only the emotionally unstable individual actually experiences euphoria from morphine; the psychologically sicker he is, the greater is his euphoria. Many addicts have reported sensations similar to sexual orgasm following the intravenous administration of heroin. Chessick (1960) has labeled this the "pharmacogenic orgasm." Tolerance does not seem to develop to these orgastic effects. This, perhaps, reinforces the views of those investigators who emphasize the ritualistic preparation and administration of narcotics in producing subjective effects.

The effects of narcotics on psychologic functioning have been reviewed by Laskowitz (1964). Mental impairment with single doses of heroin and morphine has been well documented. A recent study with stabilized methadone maintained patients has revealed reaction-times equal to or shorter than those of non-addict controls (Gordon, 1970).

Suicide

Chambers and Ball (1970) consider various factors which might be related to suicidal behavior in addicts. They base their views on data obtained on patients who committed suicide at the Lexington Hospital. While their observations may pertain only to hospitalized addicts, at least some appear to have relevance for the street heroin addict, not institutionalized, but subjected to the attitudes and pressures of society. Of particular interest is the fact that suicide was not associated with whether the patient was in the Lexington Hospital on a compulsory or voluntary basis. Probable causes or related factors were: (a) the psychological and physiological discomfort of drug withdrawal, (b) physical illness not related to addiction, (c) difficulties of institutional adjustment, (d) the inability to accept the severity of legal punishment for crimes related to addiction, and (e) the inability to cope with the personal problems addiction brings to the addict and his family. They identify depression resulting from the filing of criminal charges, lengths of sentences, fear of other patients, and depression resulting from chronic and irreversible physical illness as being factors. There appeared to be little relationship to the actual process of detoxification since some of the patients were not even physically dependent on drugs at the time of their admission.

There is evidence that the incidence of suicide in addicts is far greater than the Lexington in-patient data suggest. A follow-up study on patients discharged from that hospital disclosed a suicide rate of 263 per 10,000 (O'Donnell, 1969). Mason (1967) reported a suicide rate of 85 per 10,000 among adolescent opiate addicts during the first year after hospitalization. Suicide occurs not uncommonly in penal institutions in known narcotics addicts who are undergoing or fear withdrawal, or have been detoxified. What other circumstances obtain in these cases are unknown and presumably varied.

Narcotics in Pregnancy and the Newborn

While few animal studies have been done to investigate the teratogenicity of narcotics, some have revealed dose-related teratogenic effects (Geber and Schramm, 1970). These generally involved single doses in early gestation, as opposed to chronic, stable administration of narcotics prior to and following conception. It is difficult to extrapolate these results to humans. Mechanisms that might be involved in producing congenital abnormalities include a decrease in uteroplacental blood flow leading to fetal hypoxia, a known effective teratogenic condition. Also, increased catecholamine production by the narcotics could lead to interference with normal protein, RNA, and DNA synthesis (Geber and Schramm, 1970).

The pregnant heroin addict is notorious for her failure to obtain proper prenatal care. Studies have revealed a high incidence of maternal complications. While prematurity by weight is commonly seen, this is difficult to assess because of uncertainty surrounding the date of conception. Nevertheless, factors other than drugs may contribute to conditions such as prematurity. These include maternal malnutrition, chronic illness, cigarette smoking and, perhaps, merely living in poverty conditions of the inner-city.

Blatman (1971) has reviewed the early experience with high-dose methadone maintained pregnant women. While prematurity by weight was found in some, the babies had good Apgar scores, had no congenital malformations, and showed no evidence of laboratory abnormalities. Follow-up of 19 of these babies, now up to 4 years, has revealed normal physical and mental development.

CONCLUSIONS

The street heroin addict's life-style carries with it many risks and exposes him to medical problems which are either directly or indirectly related to drugs.

The physical and mental pathology associated with narcotic abuse must be viewed in the context of the individual user and his current negative position in society.

While present knowledge of the mental and physical health of the street heroin addict is inadequate, we know even less about the pre-addict. This lack of information must be remedied before we can really delineate the physical and mental pathology currently observed with narcotic drug abuse and addiction.

REFERENCES

Alarcón, R. and Rathod, N. H. Prevalence and early detection of heroin abuse. *Brit. Med. J.*, 1968, 2: 549–553.

Bewley, T. H., Ben-Arie, O., and Marks, V. Morbidity and mortality from heroin dependence. III. Relation of hepatitis to self-injection techniques. *Brit. Med. J.*, 1968, 1: 730–732.

Blatman, S. Neonatal and followup. *Proceedings, Third National Conference on Methadone Treatment*, Nov. 14–16, 1970, N.I.M.H., Public Health Service Publication No. 2172, 82–85, 1971.

Brust, J. C. M. and Richter, R. W. Quinine amblyopia related to heroin addiction. *Ann. intern. Med.*, 1971, 74: 84–86.

Chambers, C. D. and Ball, J. C. Suicide among hospitalized opiate addicts. In John C. Ball and Carl D. Chambers (Eds.), *The epidemiology of opiate addiction in the United States*. Springfield, Ill.: Charles C Thomas, 1970. Pp. 288–300.

Cherubin, C. E. The medical sequelae of narcotic addiction. *Ann. intern. Med.*, 1967, **67**: 23–33.

Cherubin, C. E., Palusci, E., and Fortunato, M. The epidemiology of "skin popping" in New York City. *The Int. J. Addict.* 1968, 3(1): 107–112.

Chessick, R. D. The "pharmacogenic orgasm" in the drug addict. *Arch. Gen. Psych*, 1960, 3: 545–556.

Cohen, S. N. and Dougherty, W. J. Transfusion hepatitis arising from addict blood donors. *JAMA*, 1968, **203**: 427–429.

Dole, V. P. and Nyswander, M. E. Heroin addiction—A metabolic disease. *Arch. intern. Med.*, 1967, **120**: 19–24.

Dole, V. P., Nyswander, M. E., and Kreek, M. J. Narcotic blockade. *Arch. intern. Med.*, 1966, **118**: 304–309.

Fulton, C. C. An analytical study of confiscated samples of narcotic drugs. *Int. Microfilm J. Legal Med.*, Fall 1966, 1(1).

Gardner, R. Deaths in United Kingdom opioid users 1965–69. *Lancet*, 1970, **II**: 650–653.

Geber, W. F. and Schramm, L. C. Teratogenic potential of various narcotic and non-narcotic analgesic agents. *Proceedings of the Committee on Problems of Drug Dependence, National Academy of Sciences*, N.R.C., 1970, 6571–6577.

Gelfand, M. L., Hammer, H., and Hevizy, T. Asymptomatic pulmonary atelectasis in drug addicts. *Diseases of the Chest*. 1967, **52**: 782–787.

Glaser, F. B. and Ball, J. C. Death due to withdrawal from narcotics. In John C. Ball and Carl D. Chambers (Eds.), *The epidemiology of opiate addiction in the United States*. Springfield, Ill.: Charles C Thomas, 1970. Pp. 263–287.

Gordon, N. B. Reaction-times of methadone treated ex-heroin addicts. *Psychopharmacologia*, 1970, **16**: 337–344.

Gorodetzky, C. W., Sapira, J. D., Jasinski, D. R., and Martin, W. R. Liver disease in narcotic addicts. I. The role of the drug. *Clin. Pharm. and Ther.* 1968, 9: 720–724.

Haertzen, C. A. and Meketon, M. J. Opiate withdrawal as measured by the Addiction Research Center Inventory (ARCI). *Dis. Nerv. Syst.*, 1968, **29**: 450–455.

Haertzen, C. A., Meketon, M. J., and Hooks, N. T. Jr. Subjective experiences produced by the withdrawal of opiates. *Brit. J. Addict.* 1970, **65**: 245–255.

Helpern, M. Epidemic of fatal estivo-autumnal malaria. *Amer. J. Surg.* 1934, **26**: 111–123.

Helpern, M. Statistics for 1970, Office of the Chief Medical Examiner. New York City.

Helpern, M. and Rho, Y. M. Deaths from narcotism in New York City. *New York J. Med.*, 1966, **66**: 2391–2408.

Hussey, H. and Katz, S. Infections resulting from narcotic addiction. *Amer. J. Med.* 1950, **9**: 186–193.

Isbell, H. Drug dependence, addiction and intoxication. In P. B. Beeson and W. McDermott (Eds.), *Textbook of Medicine*, Cecil-Loeb, 13th edition, 1971.

Jaffe, J. H. Drug addiction and drug abuse. In L. A. Goodman and A. Gilman (Eds.), *The pharmacological basis of therapeutics*. New York: Macmillan, 4th edition, 1970.

Karliner, J. S., Steinberg, A. D., and Williams, M. H. Jr. Lung function after pulmonary edema associated with heroin overdose. *Arch. intern. Med.*, 1969, **124**: 350–353.

Kolb, L. Pleasure and deterioration from narcotic addiction. *Mental Hygiene*, 1925, **9**: 699–724.

Labe, M. Paroxysmal atrial fibrillation in heroin intoxication. *Ann. intern. Med.*, 1969, **72**: 951–959.

Lasagna, L., von Felsinger, J. M., and Beecher, H. K. Drug induced mood changes in man. I. Observations on healthy subjects, chronically ill patients, and postaddicts. *JAMA*, 1955, **157**: 1006–1020.

Laskowitz, D. Psychological characteristics of the adolescent addict. In E. Harms (Ed.), *Drug addiction in youth*. Pergamon Press, 1964.

Lerner, A. M. and Oerther, F. J. Characteristics and sequelae of paregoric abuse. *Ann. intern. Med.*, 1966, **65**: 1019–1030.

Levine, R. A. and Payne, M. A. Homologous serum hepatitis in youthful heroin users. *Ann. intern. Med.*, 1960, **53**: 164–178.

Louria, D. B., Hensle, T., and Rose, J. R. The major medical complications of heroin addiction. *Ann. intern. Med.*, 1967, **67**: 1–22.

Martin, W. R., Jasinski, D. R., Sapira, J. D., Flanary, H. G., Van Horn, G. D., Thompson, A. K., Logan, C. R., and Kelly, O. A. Drug dependence of morphine type: Physiological parameters, early abstinence, protracted abstinence. *Proceedings of the Committee on Problems of Drug Dependence, National Academy of Sciences*, N.R.C., 1967, 4929–4941.

Mason, P. Mortality among young narcotic addicts. *J. Mt. Sinai Hospital*, 1967, **34**: 4–10.

Messinger, E. Narcotic septal perforations due to drug addiction. *JAMA*, 1962, **179**: 964–965.

Minkin, W. and Cohen, H. J. Dermatologic complications of heroin addiction. Report of a new complication. *New Eng. J. Med.*, 1967, **277**: 473–475.

Murphree, H. B. Narcotic analgesics. I. Opium alkaloids. In J. R. DiPalma (Ed.), *Drill's pharmacology in medicine*. New York: McGraw-Hill, 4th edition, 1971.

O'Donnell, J. A. *Narcotic addicts in Kentucky*. U.S. Government Printing Office, 1969.

Pfeffer, A. Z. Psychosis during withdrawal of morphine. *Arch. Neurol. Psychiat.*, 1947, **58**: 221–226.

Protass, L. Delayed postanoxic encephalopathy after heroin use. *Ann. intern. Med.*, 1971, **74**: 738–739.

Rosenblatt, J. E. and Marsh, V. H. Induced malaria in narcotic addicts. *Lancet*, 1971, **II**: 189–190.

Sapira, J. D. The narcotic addict as a medical patient. *Am. J. Med.*, 1968, **45**: 555–588.

Sloan, J. W. and Eisenman, A. J. Long persisting changes in catecholamine metabolism following addiction to and withdrawal from morphine. *Assoc. Res. Nerv. Ment. Dis.*, 1968, **46**: 96–105.

Strassmann, G., Sturner, W., and Helpern, M. *Beitraege zur Gerichtlichen Medizin.*, 1969, **25**: 236–242.

Sutnick, A. I., Cerda, J. J., Toskes, P. P., London, W. T., and Blumberg, B. B. Australia antigen and viral hepatitis in drug abusers. *Arch. intern. Med.*, 1971, **127**: 939–941.

Way, E. L., Kemp, J. W., Young, J. M., and Grassetti, D. R. The pharmacologic effects of heroin in relationship to its rate of biotransformation. *J. Pharmac. exp. Ther.*, 1960, **129**: 144–154.

Psychopathology in the Juvenile Drug Addict*

ERNEST HARMS

Certain researchers claim that all desire for addictive drugs, especially among the young, ought to be considered psychopathological. In view of today's general punitive attitude toward addiction, one might say we attribute too little to its psychopathological aspects. However, any opinion that would blame all craving for wilful deviation of the conscious mind by some form of chemical intake on the pathology of the mind undoubtedly goes to the other extreme. We see that even rather young children scare one another, or dizzy themselves by spinning their bodies dozens of times just for the thrill of it. The search for adventure or thrills is common to juveniles. We have a great deal of evidence which suggests that much drug abuse in the young started with a desire for a "kick" (addict's slang for thrill). A first or second try may lead even the very young to become "hugged."

This, of course, is only one consideration in our attempt to reach an objective overview. Also, it should be recognized that there is a rather wide area in which there must be agreement that neurotic tendencies prove to be the starting point for minor and major juvenile addiction. It seems questionable whether the secret nightly marijuana smoking sessions of boys, and especially girls, in prep-school and college dormitories ought to be labeled psychopathological. I have often heard it said among the non-addicted that "if we did not do this we did something

*Because of the special structure given to this volume, the Psychopathological and Psychotherapeutic sections have been separated and appear in different places in the book.

else crazy." Such juvenile extravagances also should not casually be labeled neurotic excesses. However, we are justified in pointing here to the "pill-taking neurosis" which has been correctly pointed to as a major causal factor of drug taking tendencies in the young. We must also consider the small moat between sane desire for excitement and hysterical spells which definitely fall within the psychopathological field.

Adolescence has been called the first life period of depression. The almost natural tendencies of the puberty period, from its pre- to its post-stage, are loaded with emotional upsets. It is difficult to be confronted with challenges which have depressive experiences as their constant shadows. It is a small and easy step to one of the many anti-depressives, to be had either over the drug store counter or from a parent's medicine chest. On this level, drug addiction or dependency is all too human and it is not just to deal with it punitively. Later on we shall discuss the means by which it may be possible to avoid railroading teen-agers onto the road to drug abuse.

Sniffing or "snorting" of a variety of substances such as airplane glue, gasoline, Carbona, and even actual anesthetics is the earliest form of drug abuse. I have heard many 7, 8, and 9-year olds give the same reply when asked "why" — "It is fun." Fun to get dizzy or feel faint or ill? Answer: "I guess so." We see here the actual primitive enigma of all drug taking from its religious beginnings to contemporary severe addiction in its nuclear form. Only a small step over the borders of human consciousness leads from playfulness and daring adventure to the area of beginning addiction neurosis which may end in severe psychopathology.

I like to tell of an experience of my own since it may contribute to an understanding of the impulse behind juvenile addiction. When I began my German education, at the equivalent stage of the first year of high school here, the class was rather upset. In the lower grades it had been accepted practice for the custodian to place a piece of chalk and a whipping stick on the teacher's desk each morning. However, when this whipping stick appeared in the high school class, the students protested. Although no teacher would have dared to use such a cane on any of us, our pride was challenged by the presence of this tool of punishment. Frequently, the cane disappeared; but again and again it was replaced. After a few weeks, a whispering campaign started. Someone had the idea of smoking the cane. A secret hiding place was arranged and in an almost ritualistic manner the cane was cut up and smoked. The stuff tasted awful, and sometimes caused nausea and vomiting. There were — insofar as I can remember — no psychological effects. The "cult" lasted only a few weeks.

Apparently the repeated disappearance of the cane convinced the custodian not to replace it anymore. There doubtless had been behind our behavior a revenge impulse which was so strong that it overcame the ill-effects of the fumes. I have never established what chemical the cane contained.

If we remind ourselves how many youngsters start to smoke cigarettes because of the wish to feel grown-up, the idea of revenge in the cane-smoking episode appears to have the same psychological background as such other impulses as daring, competition, showing up, revolt, even punishment, which lead to abuse impulses. We cannot call these impulses directly psychopathic, but they do result from a neurotic and socio-neurotic trend which, unfortunately, is all too common among our adolescents.

Earliest addiction tendencies appear mostly in the pre-adolescent years, around the age of 10. It is the period when hero worship, competition, and "doing big" are major forces. Fortunately, it is not often that criminals are the ideals. But the model of the Indian chief and his peace pipe seems to have taken hold and this may lead from tobacco to "pot" smoking, especially where high school children are pushers in the schools.

With the advent of adolescence, psychological features change. The acknowledgment of the self as a deciding agent becomes increasingly strong, and with this comes rejection of parental and other authority. The thrust toward self-determination and protest against doing what one does not wish to do, or against suppression and prohibition, become major drives behind which may hide many negative struggles and feelings. Protest and revenge loom and grow into a definite abuse pattern for which the pot euphoria is almost an ideal release. A realistic scoutmaster once told me that he was astonished that more kids did not turn to marijuana because it is a real compensation for the negativism and anger which we are not able to stem or sublimate in many. To a large degree, group pot smoking comes about in this way. These are angry "kids" who want to air their negative feelings, and this togetherness, with one or two puffs of pot, is what they want and get.

The post-adolescent struggles with ego extension, social adjustment problems, acknowledgment, choice of profession, and with love. Depression and defeatism are the Scylla and Charybdis of the later high school years. When serious problems and actual neuroses get in the way of sound advancement and development, the euphoria of pot no longer does the trick. Then first comes the search for an anti-depressant, and finally the trip is on to heroin. This is a realistic picture of the genetic development of adolescent addiction impulses. It must be viewed objectively by society and with a desire to attempt a psychological and social change, rather than punitively. Help must be strong enough to induce alteration in the developmental impulses and to instill the strength to move in a positive psychic direction.

In the life periods which follow there are numerous, mostly negative, impulses which seek compensation and relief in addictive materials. We now have statistical evidence that a very high percentage of addicts are "ignited" during their post-adolescent and young adult period of life. These are periods of preparation for the greatest life challenges, and our desperate desire to fight addictive impulses should have its major point of assault at this time. How can we actually—if we are honest—have any success in freeing anyone from drug dependency if we are not able or not willing to eliminate the causes which have driven him to this dependency? All too frequently, we hear the unjust, superficial opinion that youth must be moved away from a particular drug to something else. Where is the positive response to the unfortunate conditioning which has created the tendency to addiction in the first place? The most immediate task must be to unravel and lay bare the causes of the neuroses which have created the problem. Not until we have done this can we expect to find the "means and medicine" to help victims out of their dilemma.

Some say that teen-age addiction generally is not as deep-seated as it may become in later life. This is doubtlessly true. In my dealing with adolescent psychopathology, I have been convinced that growth power, so long as it is active, can be viewed as a source of health in the fight against the strength of the ill. But before this growth power can resume true activity, we must root out the sources of pathological impulses and clear the ground for the new growth.

Much has been written about the negative, sick-making, destructive impact of drugs; we are badly in need of a clear picture of the basic afflictions that result from drug addiction.

It has been observed, for instance, that the physical impact appears much more quickly in the earlier years than later on. Knowing the sensitivity of the juvenile constitution, one can easily understand this. On the other hand, whatever damage has occurred disappears more readily in the younger years than later. More serious damage, however, will be carried over from youth into adulthood.

Just as the impact of the drugs varies, so does their psychopathic effect differ. In addiction slang, there are "ups" and "downs," the designation of pharmaceuticals according to their depressive or anti-depressive effects.

The most clear difference known is that between marijuana and heroin. There are a number of toxological writings which describe this more or less phenomenologically. However, as we mentioned above, since we do not have a proper theoretical and basic point of view, most of these records are of little concrete value.

One of the essentials to bear in mind regarding the pathology which results from drug abuse is the difference in the effect of each stage in addictive drug use. There are psychopathic experiences during the intake. Then there are those during the period of "full effect" or "influence," and, finally, there are those of the withdrawal stage and of the after-effects.

There are quite a number of extraordinary pre-addiction experiences. There are adolescent, and also older girls who are "mortally afraid" of drugs. They do not want to know or read anything about that "stuff." They give up friends who smoke pot. But one day . . . . This phenomenon can be explained psychoanalytically. However, this explanation does not give us the full background for the task we have set for ourselves.

There are actually many youngsters who, before they smoke pot, take the heroin needle or a small bit of LSD and undergo a severe phobic episode. They are afraid, on the one hand, of the deviation of consciousness which, on the other hand, they want. Many would not be alone or smoke alone during a heroin, marijuana, or LSD trip. Some feel unable to give themselves the needle, but have a friend give them the injection. They feel nauseous, faint; often they vomit. Many hallucinate and want someone nearby during the entire "trip." The essential point is that these negative experiences do not prevent addiction. The dependency is stronger than these initial negative effects. These negative effects are "taken in the bargain" as "going with the trip." This is the explanation given to me by a highly intelligent student who was "hopelessly hugged by heroin."

For the most part, the actual addiction episode is not experienced with clear consciousness. Judgment is too much impaired in most addicts to allow them to feel that the entire experience is, to a large degree, a pathological one. Any change in consciousness which cannot shortly be reversed to bring back full consciousness and self-control must be designated as pathological. The comparison remains, of course, with drunkenness and anesthesia, and whether they ought to be designated as pathological. In any case, these also must be considered abnormal states. Similarly, states of religious excitement in primitives and even of the more sophisticated religions observed in this country must be labeled abnormal although designated as higher states of mind by the practicing group.

There is an entire set of pathological phenomena which has been observed and described by various authors: logorrhea, laughing and crying spells, incoherent speech, hallucinations, inability to recognize known objects and persons, states akin to sleep walking, and episodes of violence. The memory of euphoria as well as oblivion is for the most part rather dim. However, the memory that they "want to have it again" remains. In my opinion, the major dependency or desire for the addiction experience seems to occur to a large degree in the *unconscious*. Intellectual students, who are frequently quite keen observers of the addiction experience, and therefore the best source for the reporter on youth addiction, speak of the essential factor of dependency as an "unconscious reaction against being too overpowered by disagreeable outside experiences." It means "going out" for a while, "behind the curtain."

The most serious and disagreeable of addiction episodes are in the withdrawal and after-effect periods. Even rather young abusers are very aware of the severe experiences which follow the receding of an addiction episode. Nine and 10-year-old boys who have formed the habit of snorting solvents accept the headaches, dizziness, and "not feeling good afterwards," confessing that they want to do it again. Marijuana, amphetamine, and barbiturate after-effects, as different as they are in their content and different for each individual, give off a general neurotic letdown in their mildest forms. However, they can accelerate to severe psychopathic states. In continuous addiction the individual will soon feel that he cannot function at all, a state similar to the psychopathic personality.

All heroin addiction, especially in the teen-ager, leads to psychopathic and even psychotic impairment. "Starting with heroin has no end." This feeling is frequently found in post-adolescents. "I am not myself anymore," and he thinks heroin alone can give him back himself, but the more heroin he tries the more he weakens his sense of self. There is also heroin tolerance, which has a worse result. The addict with this tolerance no longer knows whether he is physically or mentally ill. He finally does seek help, often wandering from one treatment center to another without getting the help he really wants and needs. "I need help for MYSELF." And this means *psychological help* which he rarely gets. An addicted medical student once told me that anyone "who is hugged on heroin really needs a new self." This is not generally realized, especially by those who think that chemical replacement therapy can exorcise the grip of heroin addiction. *Intensive psychological reconstruction of the basic function of personality is what is needed.*

We cannot offer, in this short presentation, either a detailed survey of the effect of a large number of earlier or presently used addictive substances, nor can we give a detailed description of the entire psychological structure, which might be expected in an instruction to professionals. What we have tried to offer here are some important and partially new thoughts for the general reader which can also be applied to the fundamentals of detailed pathological and toxological studies. For this reason, we have tried to present certain major types and symptoms which long experience has taught are important and helpful in administering relief. In our still rather limited field, we face universal problems about which man is trying to reach an understanding. It is a principle that the functioning of the many internal states rests on the functioning of a basic few. If we succeed in understanding these few, we have the common denominator of the many. However, we should avoid being dogmatic. Principles can only be fruitful if they are applied as primers for extending further insight.

We have presented the main pathological trends in the two major types of pathology, one of which is called euphoric and the other *depressive*, descending to the actual state of *oblivion*.

A third major area of drug addiction – the hallucinatory or hallucinating state – still remains to be discussed. Those who are informed know that this is the most troublesome and complicated of all addictions. Its primary form goes back in personal history and is known to be widely associated with religious or religious-like procedures. We do not need to discuss the use of drug-like substances, such as peyote, by primitives or aborigines since they have actually not reached into our civilization. We are covering practically all that need concern us in discussing the problems of hallucinating experiences under the signum LSD with substances having, chemically, the same effect as lysergic acid.

The first thing to be aware of is that LSD is one of the most potent, deadly drugs available anywhere. It was produced a few decades ago by the Sandoz Pharmaceutical Company, but was strictly forbidden entry to this country. According to some researchers, LSD has possibilities for a dual impact. Highly respected specialists have claimed benefits from small doses of LSD in serious pathological cases. Although writings advocating the use of LSD have a rather dubious character, Richard Blum's substantial book, *Utopiates**, demands to be taken seriously. However, all the acknowledged applications of LSD have been made under the strictest medical and scientific controls. Most of these experimental applications were terminated years ago and hardly any research seems presently underway to support the claims of the possibilities of benefit from LSD.

*Atherton Press, New York, 1964.

In mentioning the possibility of advantage from LSD, we have expressed our willingness to acknowledge positive factors even where judgment pointing to negative results seems to be overwhelming. There have been claims that only 5 percent of the LSD applied has been of a positive character, while the rest falls within the area of serious danger. It is a fact to be faced that the chemical formula of LSD is widely known and its production is a rather simple pharmaceutical procedure with which practically every chemistry student is familiar. Accordingly, LSD, or rather LSD derivatives have been produced in unlimited quantities, and relatively small amounts are available everywhere on the illegal market. Because of its easy manufacture, there can be no guarantee of the chemical contents of LSD used, nor of its strength and toxic effect. Some estimates attest that more than half of all fatalities from drug abuse are attributable to LSD mixtures. Serious mental and physical damage has been reported in cases of repeated LSD use. This extends from impairment of thinking and derangement of emotional experience to actual psychotic patterns, and cases of dementia, because of the inability to "come out" of an LSD state. Cataleptic states have resulted and even leukemia has been reported. It must be assumed that an individual who has taken a relatively small dose of LSD three or four times has afflicted himself physically with some kind of chronic impairment. Even in cases reported by Dr. Blum, one is justified in assuming that somehow somewhere damage can be expected. After a certain period this may become apparent. There is no doubt that any intake of LSD has psychopathic impact, be it nervousness, sleeplessness, or worse.

The tales regarding the possibility of extending consciousness or "getting insight" into the beyond may have a fascination, but, viewed realistically, the experiences border on a disintegration of sound reality. Indeed, throughout the history of mankind, going back to primitive man, we find a partially religious urge to obtain experience from or in what is called the theistic sphere. Vision, clairvoyance, premonition, atavism are spheres of extrasensory perception which often are tied to the gods or other metaphysical realities named. In many primitive societies, various substances derived mostly from plants have been known to put individuals into ecstatic or visionary states. There are myths about travel into the underworld, from which, however, usually one in three returns — one dies, and one becomes insane. One can easily apply the essence of the myth without getting into unrealistic phantasies about present hallucinism and the dangers involved. As a young man once told me: "LSD puts you on the road to insanity." There are a number of drugs which are basically of this type. In addition to such substances as certain types of eastern morphine, there are absinthe, mescaline, peyote. Undoubtedly, these addictive substances present the greatest danger to the human mind. There is no more serious task than keeping our teen-age youth from this danger.

In order to get a short overview about the variety of impacts of drug abuse on psychic and mental life, we should make ourselves aware of the psychological regions which abuse of drugs may attack. There is hardly any part of our psychic and mental organization which cannot be impaired by the administration of one or another drug.

Repeated deviations of sense perception appear from practically all corners. Numbness occurs generally or in parts of the body; there is impairment of taste, hearing, and seeing. In contradiction, there are reports of high grades of hypersensitivity to the degree experienced in hebephrenia. Speech disturbances as well as logorrhea appear.

The most common disturbances are those in the thinking process. As the most sensitive of the human faculties, thinking is easily influenced by overstimulation as well as by a lowering of the conscious state. We learn how easily an excited consciousness "runs away" to uncontrolled activity of thought or unrealistic thought phantasmagoria to the point of becoming hallucinatory. We have countless reports of the inability to control thought. Such experiences create severe states of fear, since humans tend to feel safest in the thought strata of self-experience. "Headlessness," as it is frequently described, brings out the fear of losing oneself. On the other hand, in some addictions having one's thoughts and thinking "knocked out" is felt to be the desired state: numbness, no-ness, and forgetting. Lack or loss of memory is frequently an "after-trip" or a withdrawal symptom. Some are glad that there is no memory to bother them. Some become frantic because they cannot or cannot easily remember what they know they know but are unable to reach.

The broadest and most frequent, and also most severely experienced, psychopathologies concern the emotional arena of inner life. Bliss and excitement, one swing of emotional expression frequently aligned with euphoric addiction experiences, become a psychopathological experience when they overreach the individual's strength of control. A psychoanalytical writer has spoken of an Icarus experience, comparing with the Greek myth the states into which addicts are precipitated from an emotional overreaching. Such incidents are almost always followed by severe depression which is especially hard to deal with therapeutically because the euphoric line of experience is phobically affected, being almost totally blocked by the previous experience, and will be useless therapeutically in lifting the individual out of this kind of depression.

Depressions are the most extensive problem in drug abuse. In many cases, depression haunts the individual prior to the addiction. In many cases, this is the direct motivation for the actual abuse. Several times I have heard from sensitive addicts: "Dependency means more a feeling of depression than of a desire." "Being severely depressed again and again leads into the mud." "Depression also warms up the tolerance." "If one could do away with feeling depressed, much of the need for the 'stuff' would not arise."

Almost everywhere, depression is the major component of the aftertrip or withdrawal experience. They may be light and bearable depressions or they may be severe, approaching the abyss of a catastrophe. I have heard it said that "if you recognize your depression as it comes, usually you are able to cope with it." A certain pattern of depression is accepted, like the "blues" after drinking. Many claim they need company to stand the depression. "As long as I feel it will get better, it is all right." It is most important in dealing with addiction depression to have some knowledge of the psychological type to which the individual belongs. Introverts and manic types sink deeper into depressions and are harder to lift out. More serious states occur when emotional depressions combine with rational pitfalls. It is through rationality, especially in adolescents, that depressions can be solved.

The impairment of will and activation impulses is especially dominant in the younger group of adolescents and in the later phase of post-adolescence when the struggles of life and vocation adjustment are the core of existence. The comment, "I don't want to do anything" from a youth lying on his bed or sitting in a corner, is a characteristic one of the addict. The basic experience of discouragement is one of the hardest with which to deal because it is apt to ignite more easily the desire for repetition. This type is frequently led to a total involvement of his not quite fully developed ego. This condition in many cases leads to the need for institutionalization. In most of these cases a neurological involvement, resulting from chronic aggravation, has developed, and we can only attempt to help such individuals through longer institutionalization.

Most of our present dealings with drug abuse, especially with youth, have little or no consideration of the specific psychopathological conditions which are the real center, the nucleus of the addiction. We always deal with a specific addiction in a young addict, be it a glue sniffer, a marijuana smoker, a heroin mainliner, or an LSD eater. All punitive and social manipulations are fringe or shell dealings with the actual addiction and do not touch the inner source of the abuse, which can only be dealt with, and possibly eliminated, by proper individual psychotherapy.

REFERENCES

Anslinger, H. J. Psychiatric aspect of marijuana. *JAMA*, 1950, **34**.
Ausubel, O. P. Psychopathology and therapy of drug addiction. *Psychiat: Quarterly Suppl.*, 1948, **22**.
Bromberg, W. Marijuana, A psychiatric study. *JAMA*, 1939, **113**.
Brown, T. T. *The enigma of drug addiction*. Thomas, 1961.
Cain, A. H. *Young people and drugs*. Day, 1969.
Comprehensive Psychiatry. A Special Issue. 1963, **4**.
Curtis, H. C. Psychosis following the use of marijuana. *Kansas Med. J.*, 1939, **40**.
Darrow, C. W. Psychological effect of drugs. *Psychol. Bull.*, 1929, **26**.
Haertzen, C. A. Changes of personality from opiates. *J. Nerv. & Mental Diseases*, 1969, **148**.
Imada, Y. Attitudes of females in treatment of drug addiction. *J. Mental Health*, 1965, **14**.
Isbel, H. Symposium on Medical Therapie. *Clinics of North America*, 1950, **34**.
Kolb, L. Pleasure and deterioration in narcotic addiction. *Amer. J. Psychiatry*, 1925, **94**.
Kolb, L. and Himmelsbach, C. K. Clin. study of drug addiction. *Mental Hygiene*, 1925, **9**.
Kolb, L. Theory and treatment of drug addiction. *J. Med. Assoc. District of Columbia*, 1939.
Kolb, L. *Drug addiction as a medical problem*. Thomas, 1962.
Lord, J. R. *Marijuana and personality*. Heath, 1971.
Mauer, D. W. and Vogel, V. H. *Narcotics and narcotic addiction*. Thomas, 1954.
Meerloo, A. M. On drug addiction and its effects. *Acta Psychiatrica*, 1935, **10**.
Shooter, A. Psychology of drug addiction. *Rorschach Newletter*, 1935, **10**.
Thorpe, J. J. and Smith, B. Phases of group development. *J. Group Psychotherapy*, 1953, **3**.
Torda, C. An effective procedure for heroin addicts. *Perception and Motor Skills*, 1968, **26**.
Walton, D. Drug addiction. *J. Mental Science*, 1960, **106**.
Zucker, A. H. Group psychotherapy and the nature of drug addiction. *Intern. J. Group Psychotherp.*, 1961, **II**.

The Social Patterns of the Teen-age Drug Abuser

NATHAN LANDER

There is a clearly defined social process by which individuals in our study became involved with drugs and ultimately addicted. Exposure to stimulants occurred early in their lives and continued for as long as they resided in the area of their addiction.

Roughly one-third to one-half of the boys by age of 10 engaged in glue sniffing. It normally occurs in a group setting, frequently on rooftops away from prying eyes. The practice is inexpensive — simply the cost of airplane glue.

However, recently some merchants have become reluctant to sell glue to youngsters because of the publicity surrounding their use for "kicks."

Glue sniffing frequently results in a violent headache and at times renders its user unconscious. Its main importance lies in its being the bottom rung on the scale of "highs" — in part, its negative effects prompt users to seek elsewhere for bigger and better "highs."

At this stage, 10–11 years old, there is also use of pills, particularly barbiturates and marijuana. These are usually used separately from glue. Easily available in the neighborhood, pills and "pot" are seen as a step up the ladder — they give a different "head."

In junior high school (starting around the age of 12), the drug process assumes a more formal and involved pattern. Drug use, for most, becomes intimately tied to sexual and educational patterns. That is, the "hookey party" becomes the core around which drug activity centers. Several times a week groups of boys and girls chip in for drugs and wine, and

131

spend the 9–3 school day at the home of someone whose parents are working, or in a vacant apartment. At 3 o'clock, the hour at which school lets out, they leave the "gig" (party) and go home as if they were returning from a normal day at school. The fact that truancy is endemic to the neighborhood accounts for the lackluster diligence of truant officers. It seems that it is indeed a rare instance when someone playing hookey is disciplined by the school authorities.

At the hookey party, equal numbers of boys and girls congregate for the pleasures of sex and highs of drugs. By this time, glue sniffing is considered a little boy's activity. Marijuana becomes the prime means of attaining a high. Used within varying combinations are all kinds of pills. Sometimes amphetamines are used with marijuana to increase the high. At other times, particularly when there is less money available, pot is used in conjunction with barbiturates, resulting in the user being "knocked out."

Due to its cheapness, wine instead of whiskey is the alcoholic staple. In addition to alleviating thirst from pot smoking, it is effective as a booster to the "head" one gets from drugs.

Only those prepared to engage in sexual and drug activity are allowed to attend a hookey party. Since its whole purpose is to facilitate the attaining of "highs," there is little patience with anyone who attends, but refrains from engaging in the requisite rituals.Sexual partners are exchanged in the course of the party, the byplay eased by the euphoria resulting from drugs. Many claim that the combination of sex and marijuana results in a heightened experience. It is clear also, however, that pot and other stimulants have the effect of breaking down inhibitions in dealing with the other sex. Thus, one boy stated that if he has sex with a girl who is "straight," he feels flustered after finishing. He said he did not even want to look at the girl; but under the influence of marijuana the "good" feeling continued uninhibited after consummation.

Generally speaking, heroin use is sporadic and minimal at hookey parties. For several years, most rest content in nourishing the "highs" connected with marijuana, pills, and wine. Heroin use is the exception. Once it becomes important to someone, he leaves the "hookey party" scene and "graduates" to more extreme activities.

Significant is the pressure exerted by older adolescents on the 12–14-year olds who attend the hookey parties. Homosexuals and older men introduce some to stronger drugs and also furnish them with money to experiment with drugs on a wider scale if they wish.

By the time they are 14 or 15, most of those who frequent the hookey parties have been at least exposed to heroin and many have, to some degree, tried it. For about 75 percent of the boys and half of the girls who do so, the result is disastrous, for it is the beginning of a long road of suffering. For the others, the experiment is only that, and they eschew heroin completely, continuing in their accustomed round of hookey parties or dropping them altogether, and at 16–17 finishing school and going out to work.

The heroin users follow no one pattern. They may be introduced to heroin at one of the hookey parties, elsewhere, or by one of the older users. First experiences are extremely varied – some speak of emptiness and others record vomiting.

But in both cases, the user is so affected that he returns for more (although bad first reactions can delay the time of a second use for long periods – some only try again after a year's wait). In all cases, however, there is talk of how much "better" the heroin "high" is – it clearly functions on the psychological level as the big leagues do to the minors. We are talking here, of course, of those who continued on heroin. Some use it once or a few times, are scared by its effects, and discontinue use.

In most cases, the 14–15-year olds who use heroin do so on the sly. They often still participate in the conventional hookey parties, but their heavy drug taking is done either in other neighborhoods or secretly in a group of fellow users. They continue the group experience of the hookey party in their heroin use. At first the mood is fairly easy – they are often given drugs by other users and if they need money they can use lunch money to finance their experience. They are young and healthy and do not yet feel any of the physical dependence of drug use. However, it is not long before their use of heroin tends to dominate their lives. Then school work, such as it is, is affected and after several months of regular use, there inevitably comes a time when they feel craving for a fix which is not immediately available. They must then "hustle" to overcome the discomfort. They might "bum" the needed fix or "bum" the money for it, or they might have to steal from their parents. In any case, they have for the first time been truly exposed to the demands of their habit.

The pattern of use varies greatly. Some almost immediately become daily users while others use only on weekends. Thus, "becoming an addict" is no simple process. Neither, therefore, is the speed with which a user is exposed to the implications of his adopted style of life. It should not, either, be assumed that all heroin users, from a high use area, are intimately aware of the effects of heroin use. There is a clear distinction between intellectual knowledge and immediate experience of such effects.

Further, there are some who with apparent sincerity claim that they were unaware of the effects of heroin when they started using it. One subject claims that he started using junk because he thought users were hip and tough. Thus, he did not even attempt to hide his use, for he wanted to be identified as a heroin user.

On starting to use heroin, when the first ill-effects manifest themselves, it is usually too late to "simply" stop using it. It is invariably easier to get another fix and postpone the hard decision for some vague future. This is to assume that the user sees himself as in some sense addicted — which is definitely not the case. It usually takes a long time before a user is ready to admit he is addicted. For the honeymoon period when money and drugs are easily available there is no question at all of being an addict. The user functions just as he always did, but as drugs become more dominant, his life is changed — he drops out of school, is unable or unwilling to maintain a job, becomes gradually more alienated from his family and friends. Drugs come to monopolize his every moment — it is somewhere at the level of commitment to the drug culture that the fact of being an addict is brought home to him as a user. It is also at this point that the community tends to designate a member as an addict.

By this time, of course, the hookey party is a remembrance from the past. As the demands of heroin use become more compelling, the user gradually becomes isolated. At first he used heroin and functioned normally. He still attended the parties while using junk in a group with fellow initiates. As money becomes necessary for the habit, the user usually teams up with one or two friends for money-making purposes. Stealing too becomes a way of life — from friend, foe, and stranger. Normally teams are short-lived — distrust is endemic among addicts.

The addict usually ends up functioning alone, scampering and dodging as best he can to guarantee the next fix. A few manage to continue on an even keel in the community; they have very understanding families or jobs that permit them to maintain their habit while doing their work. However, most operate on a shoestring or less. The "junkies" are those whose appearance becomes shabby and who live in basements; others still live at home and get regular family meals, but spend all their waking hours hustling to pursue their habit. Sex soon becomes secondary to the addict and by his early thirties is often non-existent.

When questioned, nearly all youngsters express contempt or pity for addicts regardless of their own later fate. Those who start using heroin as indicated are ashamed of their actions and almost always will deny that they are or will become addicts. They will either deny they are using heroin or say they are seeking a better high — in the latter case either "ignoring" the danger of addiction or confidently asserting they will know when to stop.

For a long time the user will attempt to hide his use from the neighborhood and, in particular, his family. Often parents are completely ignorant of drugs (they may have come from Puerto Rico where drugs were not a big problem or from the rural south where there is little drug use), so the user can fairly easily escape detection. Often he goes out of the immediate area to buy and use drugs, staying away until the drug effects wear off.

As the "straight" life — school, a job, etc. — recedes into the background, the defenses are dropped and the user, busy financing his next fix, has little respect for the opinion of others. His life is on the line, which is not conducive to alternate role playing. However, the possibility of quitting drugs is never completely absent. Numerous attempts are made to "kick" the habit, to varying degrees of success. At some point the "shame" exhibited in the initial stages of use arises again and self-contempt drives some to transcend this hell, but this is never a simple process. Backsliding is the dominant fact.

Basic Aspects of the Drug Addict's Conflict With Law and Society

RODERIC V. O. BOGGS and JAMES V. DELONG

INTRODUCTION

During the 1960s a series of social ills were discovered and publicized by America's politicians and addressed with varying degrees of success by its institutions. Racial discrimination, urban decay, poverty, hunger, and crime have each in their turn been dramatized in crisis terms and then been permitted to fade as issues, though not as conditions. Today a new issue — heroin addiction — appears likely to follow the familiar pattern.

Heroin addiction today is largely and increasingly a problem of the young, particularly young urban male minority group members. The addicts on New York City's Narcotics Register in 1969, for example, were 47 percent black and 27 percent Puerto Rican(1). The patients in the Washington, D.C. Narcotics Treatment Agency are 95 percent black(2), and in the Model Cities area of that city the addiction rate for men between 20 and 24 may be as high as 36 percent(3). Nineteen percent of persons being treated in NIMH programs are under 21(4). A study of a sample of New York male addicts found that the peak age of incidence was 16 and that 64 percent were under 21 when they started on heroin(5). In 1936, 15 percent of the patients admitted to Lexington were under 20; in 1970, 53 percent were under 19(6).

In short, what once might have been dismissed as the isolated deviance of individuals has become a life-style of a significant portion of the urban young in many of our larger cities(7).

136

BACKGROUND OF THE PROBLEM

In the early part of the century the United States had an opiate problem. Estimates vary widely and wildly, but somewhere between 200,000 and 1,000,000 people were addicted to opiates in some form(8). The demographic characteristics of the addict population were different from those of contemporary addicts in that they were primarily rural, middle or lower-middle class, female, and white. The age of onset was usually in middle age(9). In 1900, fewer than 10 percent of all addicts were black; today, the figure is at least 50 percent and probably higher(10).

The problem was not one that suddenly burst upon the nation in the early 1900s. It had been present at least since the Civil War, and had been a subject of individual and medical concern for over 40 years. State laws purporting to deal with it had been passed as early as 1885(11). In 1914, the Harrison Act, the first major Federal attempt at control, was passed.

It is sometimes stated that the Harrison Act was meant simply to bring the traffic into the open, not to outlaw the use of the opiates. In a sense this is correct, because the Act says nothing about addiction *per se*, and one of the sponsors had mentioned the "out in the open" point(12). But the Act was clearly intended to eliminate the non-medical use of opiates and place control of the drug in the hands of physicians. The Opium Exclusion Act of 1909 had already prohibited the importation of opium except for medicinal purposes, though it was ineffective, and the Harrison Act was meant to perfect the medicalization of opiate use. Unregistered persons (i.e., the general public) could obtain drugs only upon the prescription of a physician, and such a prescription could be given by a doctor only for a legitimate purpose(13).

It is not clear what Congress intended to do about existing addicts. There were as many theories about addiction and its cure then as there are now, and they were equally unproven(14). It may well be that the lawmakers thought that the termination of supply would simply force people out of addiction and that would be the end of it, or they may have expected the medical profession to give drugs to existing addicts — or they may not have thought about it at all. In any event, over the next 15 years, a battle was fought between the Federal law enforcers and some elements of the medical profession. The doctors believed it legitimate to maintain addicts on opiates. The law enforcers believed that "It is well established that the ordinary case of addiction yields to proper treatment, and that addicts will remain permanently cured when drug taking is stopped and they are otherwise physically restored to health and strengthened in will power." In this view, prescriptions for maintenance purposes were not legitimate medical practice (15).

The law enforcers won unequivocally. Several Supreme Court decisions between 1916 and 1926 first upheld the view that maintenance was not medical treatment and then, at best, waffled on the issue (16). The question never again reached the Supreme Court, and the Narcotics Bureau was left free to impose its own interpretation of the law. The Narcotics Division of The Treasury Department mounted a serious campaign against recalcitrant physicians between 1914 and 1940 and for all practical purposes drove them from the field (17).

This series of events set the pattern of United States' narcotic policy that has continued to the present day. The basic tool is to outlaw distribution or possession of the drugs (18). This was not simply Federal policy, with the states left free to go their own way. In 1938, Congress enacted a model state law patterned closely on Federal law for the District of Columbia, and other jurisdictions were encouraged to adopt it (19). Opiate maintenance was to be forbidden, but, since no one knows any other treatment that is effective on a large scale, no effective treatment would be provided. Efforts were made by opening the Public Health Service hospitals at Lexington and Fort Worth in 1935 and 1938, and by starting civil commitment programs in some states in the early 1960s, but none of these worked well (20).

During the 1930s, and possibly even earlier, a new type of addict began to appear. He was poorer than the prior addicts, and more concentrated among minority group and urban males. From the mid-1930s to the present, this group has increased steadily, both absolutely and as a proportion of total addicts (21).

Dr. Troy Duster has pointed out that as the addict population became more a product of the minority and poverty culture the laws directed against it became steadily harsher. The first mandatory minimum penalty statutes were introduced in 1951, for example, and they were raised in 1956 (22). After that, possession of heroin was punishable under Federal law by a minimum of 5 years in prison. No such sanction was ever invoked against the rural housewife of 1920.

THE 1960s

In 1960, the addicted population of the United States appeared relatively stable. It was clear that there had been a wave of addiction in the late 1940s and early 1950s, but this had subsided. Many attributed this decline to the harsher penalties introduced in the early 1950s. Control of other drugs was still not an important issue. Marijuana, the "killer weed" and the "first step on the road to addiction," had been outlawed in 1937 and its use had been subjected to almost the same penalties as that of heroin during the 1950s. Cocaine was also classified as a narcotic. There were no other drugs of concern.

This stability, and the assumption that it would continue, were illusory. The addicted population expanded dramatically in the 1960s, particularly after 1966. There is no easy answer to why this happened, but the best brief explanation is that the assumptions about addiction that appeared to explain the stability were too simplistic, and that—contrary to general belief—the incidence of addiction was very sensitive to the social unrest that was to occur during the decade.

The assumption of the law enforcement system was that addicts could be deterred from heroin use by harsh penalties. Yet it is difficult, at best, to keep people from doing something they want to do. Drug addiction is an extreme case of this because heroin is notorious for its gripping power. Whether the causes of addiction are psychological, physical, or both, it is a hard condition to change. The law enforcement system was assuming that it possessed a power that it did not have (23).

A second premise was that addiction was an aberrational product of individual psychopathology. Implicit in this was an assumption that the population at risk was small and that addiction would never be more than a nagging problem. This view also turned out to be much too simple. While most addicts did show symptoms of psychopathology it was by no means certain that this pathology was related to the desire for heroin *per se* rather than to a more general propensity to deviance—a willingness to engage in an action that was abhorrent to society. The possibility that, under certain conditions, people who were not pathological would be drawn in was ignored. A few years later it was to be shown that the average addict from any area of low social pathology and social disorganization was more pathological individually than the average addict from an urban slum, with its high social pathology (24). Experts also began to note the recreational aspects of drug use and the subcultural reinforcements. By 1970 it could be stated:

> ... most opiate addicts are part of a drug subculture, and they begin to use drugs at the time they enter this group; consequently, arguments which are based on individual pathology seem inadequate as explanations of a group process.... If mental illness were the principal cause of drug addiction, this condition would have to precede the event and be closely associated with it; there is no evidence that this is so (25).

Finally, there was a general assumption in the society that using drugs of any kind was an aberrational activity. But between 1955 and 1970 a drug revolution occurred. Some of the landmarks were:

> Between 1958 and 1967 the number of new prescriptions of psychoactive drugs rose by 65 percent (all other prescriptions rose 35 percent). By 1967 approximately 50 percent of American adults had used a psychoactive drug at some time in their lives, and 17 percent of all prescriptions written were for such drugs. The trend has kept gaining since (26).
>
> Marijuana exploded into the educated, young, middle class. By the end of the decade it was perfectly clear that most marijuana users were not inherently deviant, not mentally ill, not criminal, and not hurting themselves. There was no way to fit them into the classic drug scheme.
>
> Beginning in the 1950s the use of tranquilizers caused a major breakthrough in the treatment of mental illness.
>
> The methadone experiments of the Dole-Nyswander project in New York found that the most effective method of rehabilitating heroin addicts was to use a narcotic maintenance system.

The variety of factors which combined to encourage increasing drug use throughout society during the 1960s inevitably had some effect on the young minority group members of our cities. Perhaps most important to the rapid spread of heroin in particular, however, was the growing social disorientation and breakdown of our urban centers. One need look no further than the Kerner Commission report on the massive urban riots of the mid-1960s to see the dimensions of this institutional collapse (27).

Increasing alienation, frustration, and desperation dominate the lives of many minority residents of our metropolitan centers. The debilitating effects of racial discrimination in housing, education, employment coupled with the failures of the present welfare system and the frustrated hopes raised by legal and judicial victories of the early civil rights movement combined to produce an urban crisis of massive proportion. Under these circumstances, the availability of heroin assured its use by an increasingly large number of people, and rising addiction, in turn, accelerated the cycle of urban decline.

The Judicial Response

In many areas of the law, such as civil rights, legislative inaction has prompted judicial initiative. This has not been true for heroin use, where the failure of legislation to eliminate the drug traffic or provide adequate treatment for addicts has not yet evoked a coherent response from the courts. In some ways this is surprising, because in *Robinson v. California* (28), decided in 1962, the Supreme Court raised hopes that the judiciary might reform the criminal law as applied to addiction. California, like several other states, applied criminal penalties to the condition of being a heroin addict. The thrust of the decision was that the status of addiction could not be made criminal because of the Eighth Amendment's prohibition of cruel and unusual punishment. The uncertainties of *Robinson*, which have troubled lower courts and continue to trouble them to this day, concern the application of the case to the acts of an addict, such as possessing drugs or needles, as distinct from the mere status of being addicted. What little litigation immediately followed *Robinson* on this issue saw courts reluctant to extend the Supreme Court ruling. Given the prevailing attitude of our society on the issue of heroin addiction throughout most of the 1960s and the absence of a well-founded commitment to treatment, the unsympathetic response to the *Robinson* case is not hard to understand. As long as crime, addiction, and race were so closely linked, there were strong pressures to maintain the existing penalty structure of the criminal law. The immediate attempts to capitalize upon the implications of the *Robinson* case sought either to expand upon the notion of cruel and unusual punishment as applied to actions beyond mere status or to seek application of the mental illness or insanity concept to addiction. Courts in the early and mid-1960s demonstrated a clear reluctance to move in this direction. In a number of cases *Robinson* was restricted to its facts — the statute in that case punished the status of addiction — and in other instances courts held that heroin addiction in and of itself could not raise the issue of insanity as an affirmative defense (29). The clear implication of these cases was to inhibit the movement toward a judicially-mandated program of treatment for those dependent upon heroin.

Within the last few years, a new, more enlightened approach to these issues has begun to emerge from Federal court decisions in the District of Columbia. Ironically, this new judicial activism can be traced not so much to the *Robinson* case or to the developing concepts of mental illness, but rather to historic notions of criminal responsibility rooted in the common law.

The renewed progress toward a new judicial attitude began with the 1966 decision of the U.S. Court of Appeals, D.C., in the landmark case of *Easter v. District of Columbia* (30). This case, which concerned a destitute alcoholic prosecuted under a law punishing public drunkenness, established the basic principle that "An essential element of criminal responsibility is the ability to avoid conduct specified in the definition of the crime. Action within the definition is not enough. To be guilty of a crime a person must engage responsibility in the action" (31). Under this guiding principle of diminished criminal responsibility, the court held the District of Columbia's public drunkenness statute inapplicable to a chronic alcoholic.

The full significance of this case was not readily apparent, since not only did *Easter* deal with alcoholism rather than heroin addiction, but also because the 1968 Supreme Court ruling in the case of *Powell v. Texas* (32) contained a complicated division of opinions about the parameters of diminished criminal responsibility. Specifically, while the court declined to apply the defense of diminished criminal responsibility to a case of public drunkenness by an alcoholic in the absence of convincing evidence of the defendant's need to drink *in public*, a five-judge majority did accept the *Easter* principle that the disease of alcoholism could create an overwhelming compulsion which would place consumption of alcohol by a chronic drinker beyond the reach of the criminal law. He had lost the ability to control his behavior with respect to the alcohol use, and whether this loss was based on physiological or psychological factors was irrelevant.

For Mr. Justice White, whose opinion was decisive in sustaining Powell's conviction, the critical point was the public nature of the conduct. While affirming the conviction on this narrow ground, the Justice indicated that the concept of duress as applied to an alcoholic could find logical application in the case of a heroin addict as well.

> If it cannot be a crime to have an irresistible compulsion to use narcotics, *Robinson v. California* . . . . I do not see how it can constitutionally be a crime to yield to such a compulsion. Punishing an addict for using drugs convicts for addiction under a different name. Distinguishing between the two crimes is like forbidding criminal conviction for being sick with the flu but permitting punishment for running a fever or having a convulsion. Unless *Robinson* is to be abandoned, the use of narcotics by an addict must be beyond the reach of the criminal law. Similarly, the chronic alcoholic with the irresistible urge to consume alcohol should not be punishable for drinking or being drunk (33).

The implications of the arguments accepted in *Powell* have since been applied to a succession of recent cases. The first of these, *U.S. v. Watson* (34), resulted in a technical decision holding unconstitutional a provision of the Narcotic Addict Rehabilitation Act of 1966 which makes treatment in lieu of incarceration unavailable to an addict with two prior felony convictions. Implicit in the *Watson* ruling was the invitation to explore in future cases the concept of compulsive addiction as an affirmative defense to a charge of possession of drugs for personal use by an addict.

The first full test of the Watson dicta has now reached the U.S. Court of Appeals for the District of Columbia in the case of *U.S. v. Moore*(35), which was heard *en banc* in September 1971. This case presents squarely the issue of diminished criminal responsibility due to heroin dependence as an appropriate defense to a charge of heroin possession. There are no other issues upon which the case can be decided.

Legislative and Administrative Response

The legislative response during the 1960s was equally piecemeal and confused. The Federal government pursued its hard line against drugs and against treatment based on narcotic maintenance. When the hallucinogens became an issue, they were subjected to the same type of control, though the penalties were not as stringent and a new organization – the Bureau of Drug Abuse Control – was established in the Department of Health, Education and Welfare. The job was not given to the Bureau of Narcotics in the Treasury Department.

Changes of emphasis did occur. California and New York began civil commitment programs for addicts designed to allow their removal from the criminal justice process into treatment. The Narcotic Addict Rehabilitation Act of 1966 did the same thing for the Federal government. In general, civil commitment has proven ineffective as a form of rehabilitation(36), and NARA in particular has been grossly underused(37), but the passage of these statutes did at least indicate a willingness to regard addicts as something other than degenerate criminals.

In 1968, a significant action was taken when the Bureau of Narcotics and the Bureau of Drug Abuse Control were combined into the Bureau of Narcotics and Dangerous Drugs, located in the Department of Justice. The motives for this were complex. Partly, a strong feeling had developed that FBN had become, or perhaps had always been, hopelessly rigid and that something, *anything*, had to be done to shake it up. In part, large-scale corruption among FBN agents had been discovered and the need for the more stringent control of Government's main law enforcement agency was felt(38). Most observers believe this has been a productive move and that the new BNDD is far more sympathetic to treatment than its predecessor.

While BNDD still opposes heroin maintenance, it has acquiesced in the development of methadone maintenance on the grounds that it is an experimental drug and that research is allowable(39). As of late 1971, there were approximately 25,000 patients in methadone "research" programs, and there is some chance that within the near future the Food and Drug Administration will approve institutionalized methadone maintenance as a proven rather than an experimental treatment method(40).

In 1970, the first major law reform measure in 56 years was passed, the Comprehensive Drug Abuse Prevention and Control Act of 1970(41). The primary purpose of the legislation was to rationalize the penalty structure for different drugs and bring it more into accord with the public sense of felt morality. For example, the penalty for marijuana had been high and that for LSD low, a reversal of the actual danger involved in the two drugs. The law also brought illegal use of legal psychoactive drugs under more stringent control and set up a more effective administrative mechanism for controlling drugs generally.

Insofar as the bill concerns heroin, it did not work any fundamental changes. The first title emphasizes rehabilitation and education, thus continuing the trend begun with the NARA Act in 1966, but this was not in the original bill and was not by any means the major purpose of the legislation.

The law did do one very important thing—it eliminated the mandatory minimum sentence. It also established a more rigorous penalty structure for those engaged in the business of importing and distributing narcotics, and it contains several specific provisions for extra penalties on persons engaged in continuing criminal enterprises or falling in the category of "dangerous special drug offender." These provisions raise constitutional problems and their ultimate fate is uncertain.

THE ROAD AHEAD

No one knows the cause of initial or continued addiction, beyond the elementary point that psychological, sociological, and physiological factors all interact. No one knows if all addicts share some as yet undiscovered psychological trait, or if heroin causes some long-term metabolic change in the body. It is unclear if other factors are involved and it is unlikely that any sudden breakthrough will tell us. No matter what theory one believes, however, we know by experience that the criminal process is not an effective way of handling addicts. The threat of jail for drug use or for commission of crimes to support a habit simply does not weigh against the need for the drug; nor is prison an effective mechanism of rehabilitation. The fundamental difficulty with most of the institutional responses to the addiction problem has been that they keep addiction within the framework of the criminal process, thus ensuring their irrelevance.

As this difficulty has become recognized, there have been increasingly frequent suggestions that known addicts should be diverted from the criminal process. Diversion programs, some of which apply solely to drug charges, and others to a range of offenses when the defendant is an addict, are in operation or under consideration by the Federal government (under NARA) and in Boston, New York, Philadelphia, Chicago, and Washington. The models vary, but usually successful completion of a treatment program results in either dismissal of the charges or suspension of criminal sentence (42).

These programs involve two problems. First, it is difficult for an addict to become permanently free of opiate use. In the words of Dr. John Kramer:

> The roadblocks to the abstinence programs are based in a well-known but little understood fact; that is, that once an individual has been seriously addicted for a relatively prolonged period of time to opiates, the desire to reproduce that opiate effect is so persistent and powerful that very few people have successfully given up their drug (43).

To the extent that such programs assume that treatment will be successful, there will be disappointments.

Second, the drift of the law may be toward decriminalization of addiction and addiction-related conduct. If this occurs, diversion will become possible only through the threat of unconstitutional or illegal prosecution.

What is needed is a far more flexible system that avoids the rigidities and hard categories of the criminal law, allowing for such differences as those between the veteran addict and the youthful beginner. In the *Moore* case the defense proposed a system of minimal civil restraint based on outpatient care, optional methadone maintenance, and available supportive services. The degree of control exercised over an addict would be dependent wholly upon his or her ability to refrain from criminal activity and illegal drug use (44).

Beyond this suggested policy lie two areas of important future litigation. One is the concept that an individual should have freedom to control his body through the use of drugs or in any other manner not endangering the lives and safety of others. Under any system of civil restraint, however minimal, this issue of bodily freedom will be raised (45).

A second will be the existence and scope of a constitutional right to treatment. Most often raised in the context of treatment for the mentally ill, this theory injects judicial review of acceptable minimum standards of treatment into any situation where a government sanctions commitment for non-criminal conduct (46). Just as this developing area of the law places a burden upon the administration of mental institutions, so it could be applied to the standards of treatment provided for drug dependent individuals whose liberty has been restricted.

Finally, it is not enough to talk solely of past mistakes or the present need for law reform. It is clear that the prevention and eradication of addiction entail far more than the establishment of treatment centers, however numerous, or the repeal of criminal laws, however onerous. For those who have studied the condition of our cities and relations between the races the agenda for action is obvious — housing, education, individual security, welfare and prison reform, equal employment opportunity — all of these have been repeatedly catalogued.

Until these issues are meaningfully addressed, it is doubtful that heroin addiction will be eliminated as a major problem. In the interim, it can only be hoped that recognition of the extent of the heroin crisis in this country, with its fantastic crime costs and increasing threat to the children of the middle class, will speed the national response required to reform these basic conditions of urban life.

REFERENCES

1. Gearing, F. Methadone maintenance treatment program: Progress report of evaluation through March 31, 1970 (mimeo., 1970), p. 11.
2. Dupont, R. Statement in *Narcotics research, rehabilitation, and treatment*, Hearings Before the Select Committee on Crime, House of Representatives, 92nd Congress, 1st Session, April 27, 1971 (1971), p. 173. [Hereinafter cited as *Crime Committee Hearings*.]
3. District of Columbia Government, Report of the Professional Advisory Committee on Heroin Addiction in the District of Columbia (May 1971), p. 5.
4. Brown, B. Statement, *Crime Committee Hearings*, p. 466.
5. Ball, J. and Chambers, C. Overview of the problem, in Ball and Chambers, *The epidemiology of opiate addiction in the United States* (1970), pp. 5, 18–19.
6. Jones, H. Statement, *Crime Committee Hearings*, p. 560.
7. A Commissioner of New York's Narcotic Addiction Control Commission recently stated:

    Our division of research has made the projection that, out of every 1,000 non-white ghetto males, 500 will experiment with drugs, 470 will smoke marihuana, 300 will try amphetamines, 280 will try barbiturates, 190 will try narcotics, 60 will try all four, and 100 will become addicts. We similarly project that 70 percent of these addicts will become known to the police, 60 percent will receive some form of formal treatment, and 40 percent will remain addicts for at least 10 years.

    Ibid., p. 586.
8. For a review of the different estimates, see Lindesmith A., *The addict and the law* (Vintage ed. 1967), pp. 99–134 [hereinafter cited as Lindesmith]; Terry, C. and Pellens M., *The opium problem* (1928), pp. 1–52. (An abbreviated version of the Terry and Pellens chapter is reprinted in Ball and Chambers, *op. cit.* note 5, pp. 36–67.)

9. Lindesmith, pp. 105–106, 124; Duster, T., *The legislation of morality* (1970), pp. 6–13 [hereinafter cited as *Duster*].
10. Lindesmith, p. 132.
11. Simrell, E. History of legal and medical roles in narcotic abuse in the U.S., in Ball and Chambers, *op. cit.* note 5, pp. 22, 23.
12. Terry and Pellens, *op. cit.* note 8, pp. 751–752.
13. Duster, pp. 14–15; Lindesmith, pp. 4–5.
14. These theories are reviewed in Terry and Pellens, *op. cit.* note 8, pp. 94–166.
15. *Ibid.*, pp. 756, 758.
16. *Webb v. United States*, 249 U.S. 96 (1919); *Jin Fuey Moy v. United States*, 254 U.S. 189 (1920); *United States v. Behrman*, 258 U.S. 280 (1922); *Linder v. United States*, 268 U.S. 5 (1925); *Boyd v. United States*, 271 U.S. 104 (1926).

   For a review of subsequent lower court cases, and the confusion of the state of the law, see Note, 78 *Yale, L.J.*, 1175, 1202–03 (1969).

17. King, R. *The drug hang-up* (1972).
18. Despite all the criticism that has been made of this policy, it is far from clear that the Harrison Act as interpreted and enforced by the FBN was unsuccessful as far as it related to the 1914 addict population. While no one knows what happened to people who were already addicted, that population did not replace itself over time. This could be judged a success. It might have happened anyway, even without the Harrison Act, but no one will ever know. As Lindesmith says, "One can make a case for any trend one chooses by judiciously selecting the estimates." (p. 100).
19. Simrell, *op. cit.* note 11, p. 28.
20. See, e.g., Cole, J. "Report of the treatment of drug addiction," and Aronowitz, D. "Civil committment of narcotic addicts and sentencing for narcotic drug offenses," in President's Commission on Law Enforcement and the Administration of Justice, *Task Force Report: Narcotics and Drug Abuse* (1967), pp. 135–58; Kramer, J., Statement, Crime Committee Hearings, pp. 662–69.
21. Ball, J. Two patterns of opiate addiction, in Ball and Chambers, *op. cit.* note 5, pp. 81–94.
22. Duster, pp. 20–21.
23. Law enforcement can be effective in other ways, of course. The top level suppliers are not addicts and are capable of responding to deterrence. And it may be effective to remove the first few addicts who appear in a new area to keep them from addicting others. The point made in text applies only to the practice of arresting addicts or street pushers who deal to support a habit without regard to their place in the total scheme.
24. Chein, I., Gerard, D., Lee, R., and Rosenfeld, E. *The road to H.* New York: Basic Books (1964).
25. Ball and Chambers, *op. cit.* note 5, pp. 19–20.
26. Balter, M. and Levine, J. The nature and extent of psychotropic drug use in the United States, Statement presented to the Subcommittee on Monopoly of the Select Committee on Small Business; U.S. Senate, July 16, 1969; Brown, *op. cit.* note 4, p. 457.
27. Report of the National Advisory Commission on Civil Disorders (March 1, 1968).
28. 370 U.S. 660 (1962).
29. See, e.g., *Heard v. United States*, 121 U.S. App. D.C. 37, 348 F. 2d, 43 (1964).
30. 124 U.S. App. D.C. 33, 361 F. 2nd 50 (1966) (*en banc*).
31. 361 F. 2nd at 52.
32. 392 U.S. 514 (1968).

33. *Ibid.*, pp. 548–549.
34. 439 F. 2d. 442 (1970).
35. ____ U.S. App. D.C., ____, ____ F. 2d ____, (heard *en banc* September 10, 1971).
36. See sources cited in note 20.
37. See Comptroller General of the United States, *Report to the Congress: Limited Use of Federal Programs To Commit Narcotic Addicts for Treatment and Rehabilitation* (Rept. No. B-164031(2): September 20, 1971).
38. In the words of Attorney-General John Mitchell:

> There was considerable lack of integrity on the part of many agents of predecessor organizations [of BNDD] . . . Some of them have been indicted. Others have had administrative procedures instituted against them, and a lot of them have left. I believe that is being overcome.

Mitchell, Statement, House of Representatives, Committee on Appropriations, *Hearings: Department of Justice*, 91st Congress, 2nd Session, (1970), Part 1, p. 220.
39. Ingersoll, J. Statement, *Crime Committee Hearings*, pp. 346–48.
40. Edwards, C. Statement, *Crime Committee Hearings*, pp. 393–422.
41. P.L. 91–513, 84 Stat. 1236 (1970).
42. See Bellassai, J. and Segal P. Addict diversion: An alternative for the criminal justice system, 60 *Georgetown L. J.* (in press).
43. Kramer, Statement, *Crime Committee Hearings*, p. 649.
44. Brief for Appellant, *United States v. Raymond Moore*, ____ U.S. App. D.C. ____, ____ F. 2d ____, (1971), pp. 110, 112.
45. See Lister, C. The right to control the use of one's body in Dorsen, N. (ed.), *The rights of Americans* (1970), pp. 348–364.
46. See generally A symposium: The right to treatment, 57 *Georgetown L. J.* 673 (1969); "Symposium," 36 *U. of Chicago L. R.* 742 (1969).

Sex-crazed Dope Fiends! —
Myth or Reality?

GEORGE R. GAY and CHARLES W. SHEPPARD

There isn't any question about marijuana being a sexual stimulant. It has been used throughout the ages for that . . . its use in colleges today has sexual connotations. A classical example of amatory activities is contained in the article "Hashish Poisoning in England" from the *London Police Journal* of 1934. In this remarkable case, a young man and his girl friend planted marijuana seeds in their backyard and when the stalks matured they crushed the flowering tops and smoked *one* cigarette . . . and then engaged in *such erotic* activities that the neighbors called the police and they were taken to jail . . .

> Harry J. Anslinger, former
> Commissioner of U.S. Bureau of Narcotics(1).

Until quite recently, with some notable historic exceptions (2) this rather slanted opinion has prevailed considering marijuana as an aphrodisiac, (or direct sexual stimulant) and as a "killer-weed" which "destroys will-power and makes a jellyfish of the user . . . He cannot say no . . . (it) eliminates the line between right and wrong, and substitutes one's own warped desires or the base suggestion of others as the standard of right" (3).

It is the purpose of this study to evaluate the validity of this long held and emotionally charged point of view regarding the relationship of marijuana (and other commonly used drugs) to human sexual function. Further, the authors hope to shed some light into some darkened corners of the current young drug using subculture of the Haight-Ashbury neighborhood of San Francisco.

In order to understand the drug user as an individual, it is essential to closely examine not only the pharmacological action of each drug, but also the total spectrum of subtle interactions between existing cultural sociological, ecological, psychological, and sexual aspects of his personality (4, 5).

We, at the Haight-Ashbury Free Medical Clinic, are in a particularly advantageous position to explore in depth and at first hand intercurrent patterns of drug use and abuse, and their sexual ramifications. Long established, located in a recognized area of high drug use density, an ongoing rapport exists between patients and clinic staff (many of whom reside in the area and belong to the same peer group). The population we serve is made up largely of disaffiliated and disillusioned young people who invariably have a wide pattern of drug experience (6, 7).

METHODS

In an attempt to evaluate the effects of various drugs on sex practices, a series of intensive confidential interviews were conducted. Free subjective expression was encouraged, and tape recording was employed. Individuals were interviewed singly, as cohabiting couples (both heterosexual and homosexual), and commune-living groups (where often partner-sharing and group sex was practiced).

This report is based on 50 such interviews, which included 25 males and 25 females. (Three individuals refused to participate, and are not included.) The age range was 18–30 years; the mean age was 24. Those

Table 1 Drug experience.

Group	No.	Alcohol	Grass	Barbs	I.V. Speed	Cocaine	Psychedelics	Heroin
Heroin Clinic Males	15	15	15	15	15	15	14	15
Heroin Clinic Females	15	15	15	15	15	15	15	15
Medical Clinic Males	10	10	10	3	3	5	9	2
Medical Clinic Females	10	10	10	3	3	4	10	0

interviewed were chosen randomly from patients seen at our Heroin and Drug Detoxification Clinic (30 patients: 15 male, 15 female) and our General Medical Clinic (20 patients: 10 male, 10 female).

RESULTS

Drug use as reported here was defined as more than merely "experimental"; i.e., marijuana on more than 30 occasions, more than 10 psychedelic "trips," intravenous amphetamine use on more than 10 occasions, barbiturate and alcohol use "daily" for extended periods of time, and cocaine use over 30 times. In no case was the use reported felt to be questionable to any significant degree (i.e., experiences reported were not at significant variance with the norm for this population).

We found the respondents to be generally uninhibited and articulate regarding their drug use and sex practices. Many were "turned on" by the interest of the interviewers and were quite voluble.

Validity of the responses was evaluated by the built-in male-female and partner-partner cross-checks. The results were generally agreed upon and so also validated by other members of the clinic population. (No major idiosyncrasies were noted from our general clinic population who are interviewed and counseled daily.)

As expected, and noted, the patients of the Heroin and Drug Detoxification Clinic had more widespread and prolonged involvement with all classifications of drugs. The patients of the Medical Clinic provided a ready-made non-addict control population existing in the same subculture.

ALCOHOL

Historical reference is replete with examples of the use of alcohol as an aphrodisiac. The utilization of the "demon rum" in the process of seduction is not without its pitfalls, however, as expressed by the gatekeeper in *Macbeth*: (II, iii).

Drink, sir...is a great provoker...of lechery...it provokes and it unprovokes; it provokes the desire, but it takes away the performance: therefore, much drink may be said to be an equivocator with lechery: it makes him and it mars him; it takes him on and it takes him off: it persuades him and disheartens him: makes him stand to and not stand to: in conclusion, equivocates him in a sleep, and giving him the lie, leaves him.

The sex act itself was seldom reported to be enhanced by alcohol. Only 4 of 50 patients felt that alcohol enhanced their physical sexual performance or increased their pleasure. ("It makes sloppy sex"); rather the effect is one of disinhibition. This may indeed contribute to increased sexual activity as well as other normally repressed behavior. While these effects are seen at low dosages, with increasing dosage the predominant effect may be loss of potency (much more noticeable in the male because of loss of erection)(8).

Alcohol, due to its current status as the "legal" drug of relaxation in Western Society, is repeatedly turned to as that drug used to facilitate social and interpersonal reactions, including sexual relations. Many of our female heroin patients support their habit by frequenting bars and offering themselves in prostitution to males (tourists, businessmen relaxing after the day's work, etc.) who seek such atmosphere and company(9).

Alcohol is regarded as the drug of the dominant culture (or "Establishment") by our population ("Juice is a 'redneck' drink . . . 'rednecks' and 'straights'"); nonetheless, perhaps paradoxically, it is utilized almost universally by our population, although usually in the form of wine rather than the "hard liquor" of the "Establishment"! Also, when "poor dope" is on hand, alcohol is always available, and *cheap*.

Alcohol (mainly wine) is repeatedly seen in the same social settings as marijuana, and the disinhibitory effects of both drugs are repeatedly mentioned in "breaking down sexual barriers" (reported in heterosexual, homosexual, and group sexual encounters).

One patient (with a history of overindulgence of several drugs) called alcohol "a second-rate substitute for sex." On further questioning it was discovered that he repeatedly "fell-out" when drinking; viz. he was unable to "titrate" a level of intoxication satisfactory for sexual enjoyment; rather he progressed to a level of true anesthesia.

MARIJUANA

The very mention of marijuana for years caused the average American to envision such erotic scenes as that described in this paper's opening paragraph(10).

Due to its very illegality, "grass" has become (as well as a symbol of open rebellion) the social drug of the counter-culture. Every respondent questioned professed a preference for "grass" over alcohol as a drug of social interaction(7).

"Grass" was reported by 40 of our 50 respondents as the one drug which most enhanced their sexual pleasure. ("It's the one drug better than natural")(16). This enhancement appears to be due in part to a disinhibitory effect similar to moderate doses of alcohol; but, in addition it provided increased sensory awareness and time distortion. Further, although the individual level of intoxication is titrated in an analogous manner to alcohol (by the number of inhalations or "tokes"), the genital — and general — anesthesia reported with alcohol is not seen with "grass."

Color, sound, and texture, as well as other modalities appear to be enhanced. Feelings of general body warmth, brotherhood, empathy, and oneness with others are reported to contribute to more pleasurable sexual relationships.

Regarding "grass" and sex, the following are representative statements:

"An orgasm lasts forever."

"A 'little number' is a part of my sexual ritual. It makes it prolonged and I appreciate it more."

"My sensations are heightened — such as the savor of lips, nipples, skin texture, and the sunlight reflecting off pubic hair."

"I'm more awed by being with another person's body."

"It's like being tickled all over. I'm really loose."

One female reported that "I'm up-tight until I smoke grass; then I can more easily conjure up (sexual fantasies) and come."

The physiologic sexual responses noted would definitely appear of disinhibitory, sedative, and mild psychedelic nature. The disinhibitory effect as well appears to produce euphoria and relief of anxiety (12, 13, 14).

Mild anxiety or "paranoia" was noted by some "pot-heads," usually associated with fear of arrest. This "paranoia" may have some basis in fact.

BARBITURATES

Barbiturates, as do alcohol and marijuana in moderate dosage, produce a cerebral disinhibition and may cause behavioral excitation and stimulation. In higher dosage, a true sedative-hypnotic effect is seen, and loss of sexual ability, as with excessive alcohol, is seen. Emotional control is quite labile. Reaction time is slowed; physical coordination is directly impaired. Movements are cumbersome, awkward (15, 16, 17).

True "barb-freaks" are not highly regarded in the drug using subculture, either as lovers, or otherwise.

The disinhibitory effect of "barbs" was only occasionally noted as contributory to a satisfactory (i.e., pleasurable) sex act (two patients). "Barbs" are reportedly sometimes taken by couples or groups "to relax" (i.e., relieve anxiety), but their sexual appetite and ability are invariably diminished.

"It takes longer . . . and sometimes he falls asleep on top of me, but that's really cool." (The warmth and physical companionship related to loss of inhibition and anxiety appear to be the factors of enjoyment to this girl).

AMPHETAMINES

Thirty of 36 respondents interviewed (who had been "speed freaks") stated that the "sexual drive" was greatly augmented with amphetamines, especially when taken intravenously.

With intravenous injection, an overwhelming, total body orgasmic "flash" or "rush" is repeatedly described(18). This response is the motivating factor for use in many cases, with shared sexual activity a secondary factor. In either case, a desire for sexual activity is almost always reported, as is augmented aggressiveness in the sex act.

"Speed freak chicks turn into aggressive, excited, active nymphos."

High dose intravenous amphetamines, more than any other drug, appear to dispense with usual sexual barriers, and group sex, bisexuality, and trios commonly develop.

"Speed makes strange bedfellows."

"The only time I was ever in threesomes was when I was shooting speed. Afterward it seemed weird."

"Sometimes I'll spend the whole day (in intercourse), and rub her and me raw."

"My old man is like a pile-driver; he'll go all day, but maybe come once or not at all."

Ten of 18 males interviewed who had used intravenous amphetamines reported the simultaneous occurrence of erection upon injection of the drug.

Three of 18 females reported "orgasm" upon injection.

Frequently, a couple would prepare for intercourse, or actually be underway, then "shoot-up" to enhance the sex-drug intensification.

Although erection in the male is prolonged, as is pelvic thrusting in the female, and although sexual activity is prolonged (for sometimes hours) orgasm may be difficult or impossible (reported in 5 of 18 males, 3 of 18 females). On the other hand, multiple orgasm was reported in several cases (10 of 18 males, 5 of 18 females). One vigorous young man reported that he would achieve orgasm "seven or eight times . . . every time" (19).

Two of 18 males reported inability to achieve erection after intravenous "speed."

Several patterns appear consistently here: The euphoria ("I'm larger than life . . . Clark Kent becomes Superman!") and sudden new confidence, associated with great aggressiveness and increased sex drive tend to immediately dispel any learned sexual shyness, and a whole gamut of repressed sexual activity may take place (with startling ferocity). (viz. A true aphrodisiac, or direct sexual stimulating effect may be seen.) Further, this sexual excitement seems to produce a fantasy state easily satisfied by casual sexual contacts (20).

A pleasure-pain correlation is also noted, as prolonged sexual activity may lead to muscle spasm, and literally "raw" genitalia. A direct effect of amphetamines is drying of secretions (including vaginal) that increases the pain of intercourse.

Most sexual activity is reported at the start of a "run"; after several days, as an exhaustion phase appears, potency and drive are definitely diminished. In addition, paranoia increases toward the end of a run.

The days of the "Speed Scene" are past in the Haight. None of the former "speed freaks" interviewed were currently involved, nor did they express any desire to return to "speed." Some spoke with almost fond recollection of past sexual feats, but shuddered at the "brutal come down" of speed, with teeth grinding, hepatitis, insomnia, weight loss, depression, and inevitable paranoia that they had experienced (21). (One girl had reported that she knew her "body smelled bad," and was continually suspicious of why any male would seek intercourse with her.)

It is of interest that intravenous amphetamines are sometimes used in our population by females who are unhappily pregnant and who wish to abort.

THE "NEEDLE FREAK"

Mention should be made of the sexual implications of needle puncture and needle sharing, beyond a feeling of "brotherhood or closeness."

Howard and Borges (22) questioned 36 intravenous drug users in the Haight-Ashbury. Sixty-four percent reported that there were sexual overtones related to needle use either for themselves or for others. Six individuals (17 percent) described the "rush" as "orgasmic" and 7 (19 percent) drew the analogy between the penetration of a needle and penetration of a penis. The needle is described as a phallic symbol, and "boosting" (letting blood in and out of the needle) "is like masturbating."

They quote: "There's no need to go into Freudian symbolism. Guys dig chicks hitting them and vice versa . . . It's a sexual thing to me to have a chick hit me . . . having a person stick something in you is very sexual. Girls particularly like to be injected by boys."

We have particularly noted the reported phenomenon of "pure needle flash" in our population; one "needle freak" regularly injects saline solution—for him, at least, the medium is the message.

COCAINE

As "Rolling Stone" has noted: "coke-time" is no longer the Eddie Fisher T.V. Show (23). Used much as the amphetamines, cocaine is described as giving an intravenous "splash."

"Intravenous C is electricity through the brain, activating cocaine pleasure centers" (24). "The full exhilaration of cocaine can only be realized by an intravenous injection. The pleasurable effects do not last more than five or ten minutes . . . rapid elimination . . ." (25).

Because of its expense on the illicit market (as much as $10.00 for "a snort"), cocaine is usually doled out "like champagne." A full 15 percent of patients seen in our Heroin and Drug Detoxification Clinic have used cocaine 30 or more times; it was usually "snorted," and usually saved for sexual situations.

Ten of 20 male respondents who had used cocaine intravenously reported spontaneous erection upon injection of the drug. Two males with a long history of cocaine use reported extremely painful episodes of priapism, lasting for 24 hours or longer. One vigorous young male reported episodes of multiple orgasm after sniffing "coke," then engaging in intercourse. This type of reaction to cocaine may account for its street name of "girl." It is also known as "the pimp's drug" because it costs so much.

Continuing use of cocaine, as with amphetamines, leads to a pleasure-pain threshold, after which nervousness, exhaustion, and paranoia prevail.

Cocaine is sometimes rubbed on the penis, effectively locally anesthetizing it, thereby affording the male "an ego trip" in his ability to provide prolonged intercourse without orgasm. We have treated several females (who had been the partners of males who have engaged in this practice) for inflamed "raw" mucosa of the vaginal vault.

AMYL NITRITE

Previously heavily used only in "gay" cults, amyl nitrite is now increasingly used in heterosexual settings. "Snappers" or "poppers" have been used by virtually all of our respondents for stimulation during the sex act, either at insertion or directly before climax. It is described as a "head *and* body trip", with a warmth rushing to the pelvis and genitalia and the mind "zooming off" for 3–4 minutes.

Terms used are "exotic addition to the (sex) act"; "I blew my mind at the intensity and sheer abandonment"; "I felt like a car with brand new superchargers and barrels added."

Also noted was: "It gave me a headache!"

The "high" is described as similar to sniffing cocaine, but "shorter and of greater intensity." "Poppers" are reported to be used frequently to "break down barriers," especially in group-sex situations.

THE PSYCHEDELICS: LSD, MESCALINE, PSILOCYBIN, STP, MDA

"As to LSD . . . the principal side effect of taking it is pregnancy . . . we should call LSD "Let's Start Degeneracy." Harry J. Anslinger(1).

Although few confuse sex with degeneracy, most authorities feel that LSD *per se* does *not* have an aphrodisiac effect(13,26).

Fourty-four of 48 of our respondents echoed this feeling. Four of 48, however, expressed that their sex desire was indeed increased with "acid."

The range of response reported while on a "trip" was from decreased desire and impotence to greatly increased sexual desire. Certainly a lessening of inhibitions, an increase in emotionality, heightened and altered awareness of many senses, and an increased feeling of love for one's fellow man, oneness with the universe, and thereby greatly heightened interpersonal affection may occur(27). This, in turn, may give way to an exquisite sexual experience(28).

A few representative quotations follow:

"A compatible partner is essential because of the tremendous sexual energies released."

"To make love on acid is to make perfect love and gain protoplasmic unity."

One girl stated that "acid" allowed her to "fantasize that I've found the perfect lover, and I would 'dig' the cat for days after the trip."

"I can't get it together enough on 'acid' (to sexually perform)."

"When I come (on acid) my whole soul and body seem to fuse (with my partner)."

A pleasant sexual experience with LSD, more than with all other drugs (and in direct contradistinction to the stimulation of amphetamine, cocaine, and their surrogates) appears to be directly related to the empathy which exists between partners, and to an appropriate "setting" in which the drug is taken.

Mescaline and Psilocybin are reported as "more a body trip, less a mind-blower" than is LSD; i.e., the sensory bombardment is less extreme— although physical coordination is again impaired, as is the ability to perform sexually. A not uncommonly noted experience with use of LSD is the person "tripping" may reach such a state of ecstasy as to consider sex inconsequential, either for the whole of the trip or during its peak. Sexual activity while on LSD usually takes place after the "peak," "on the way down."

"STP" is reported as "heavier" and much longer lasting than the other psychedelics. *None* of our respondents reported a satisfactory sexual experience while "on STP."

There *does* appear to be one psychedelic drug that has a sexually stimulating effect. This is MDA (alpha-methyl-3,4-methylene-dioxy-phenethylamine), an amphetamine-related hallucinogen. MDA is called the "love drug," and was so reported by the press when a quantity was found at the site of the Sharon Tate killings.

Fifteen of 20 of our respondents reported using MDA in conjunction with sex, and noted exotic fantasies as well as a compelling "speed like sex drive." Prolonged intercourse and multiple orgasm were described in 3 instances. One patient (male) reported impotence ("an acid like" incoordination), and one male respondent reported embracing and attempting to have intercourse with a tree (which he interpreted as being "mother earth").

HEROIN

William Burroughs has stated: "Junk shortcircuits sex"(30), and . . . "junk suspends the whole cycle of tension, discharge, and rest. The orgasm has no function in the junkie"(31).

Libido in the heroin user, however, appears to fluctuate markedly, depending on his immediate physical state. Certainly when "on the nod," Burroughs statements hold true. In this case heroin becomes a true sexual substitute.

The initial "rush" derived from intravenously injected heroin is described as "warm, drifting sensation," qualitatively different from the "flash" or "splash" of amphetamines or cocaine (32, 33).

The heroin addict's sexual relationships dissolve into a non-physical partnership dedicated to the daily procurement of "dope" (9).

If "kicking," or "coming off" heroin, however, sexual interest appears fairly rapidly, and some addicts state that sex is "best when the junk wears off, just before getting sick." Addicts who are incarcerated and forced to kick "cold turkey" report repeated masturbation in jail "to keep their minds off" a combination of physical and emotional discomfort.

Although "strung out" couples do not pursue intercourse to orgasm, a "warm" close physical relationship may take its place. Non-demanding touching and caressing are not uncommonly reported. Oro-genital fondling—never to climax—is also reported with some regularity, which is often seen in male homosexual heroin-using "hustlers" who turn many "tricks," but rarely achieve orgasm. (This relationship is analogous to that sometimes seen with barbiturate or other sedative-hypnotic drug users.)

It is not uncommon to observe erection, which quickly fades, in the male addict on injection of intravenous heroin.

Certainly little sexual activity is expected of heroin addicts. With the euphoric "total body orgasm" of injected heroin, the addict rationalizes his decreased libido (and/or potency) by stating that he does not miss the "genital orgasm." Our respondents reported that "when strung out" they had intercourse on an average of once a month. This figure concurs with the data gathered in our Heroin Clinic on a population of over 1600 addicts.

Any sexual failure can, after all, be blamed on the heroin. "I'm too stoned to ball tonight."

DISCUSSION

In an extensive in-depth series of interviews with patients seen at the Haight-Ashbury Free Medical Clinic in regard to the relationship of drugs to sex, an extremely wide range of response was noted.

The subjective, extremely personal nature of the responses must be reemphasized. Further, it must be stressed that each sexual response

Table 2 General subjective "sex-drug" responses. (Based on 50 respondents at the HAFMC.)

Drug	Increases sex activity			Decreases sex activity	
	Decreases Inhibition	Enhances Pleasure	Aphrodisiac	Decreases Desire	Decreases Potency
Alcohol	+/+	—	—	+/ in high doses	+/+ in high doses
Marijuana	+/+	+/+	—	—	—
Barbiturates other Sedative-Hypnotics	+/+	—	—	+/ in high doses	+/+ in high doses
Amphetamines	+/+	+/—	+/+	—	—
Cocaine	+/+	+/—	+/+	—	—
Amyl Nitrite	+/+	+/—	+/—	—	—
Psychedelics LSD, Mescaline, Psilocybin	+/—	+/—	—	+/—	+/
MDA	+/—	+/—	+/+	—	—
Heroin	—	—	—	+/+	+/+

reported was as highly dependent on the particular physical setting involved and each individual's particular psychological "set" as on the drug itself. Unique individual personal characteristics, past drug experiences, "attitude" toward the drug, motivations and expectations (both sexual and pharmacologic) collectively interact to produce psychological "set," and can color a sex-drug act anywhere on the spectrum from impotence or a "complete bummer" to profound orgiastic ecstasy.

As one of our more hedonistic respondents noted:

"I dig sex on uppers, downers ... drugs that take me sideways ... and those that turn me inside-out ... even a placebo would probably sex me up if I thought it would alter me in *some* way!"

As has been suggested for alcohol and marijuana, and what undoubtedly holds true for *all* drugs ... they bring out the fundamental traits of the personality. While the true pharmacologic pattern of each drug indeed produces a certain patina or overlay to the personality of the user, nonetheless, what was there to begin with must be first considered.

With these thoughts in mind, let us turn to such generalizations and conclusions as we may.

First, we may consider those drugs which may stimulate sexual activity by either releasing inhibitions (alcohol, barbiturates, and other sedative hypnotics in small doses), or by directly stimulating sexual desire—or "drive" (amphetamines, cocaine). Marijuana appears to fit both groups, by decreasing inhibitions while at the same time enhancing enjoyment. The psychedelic drugs are difficult to pigeon-hole, at times creating greatly increased enjoyment (and in the case of MDA apparently capable of strongly stimulating sexual desire).

Second, we note those drugs that may decrease sexual activity. Two mechanisms are apparent here: that of diminishment of desire, and that (particularly in the male) of decreasing potency. This group includes heroin and other euphoria-producing narcotic analgesics, and high doses of barbiturates or alcohol. To some degree, the psychedelic drugs fit into this category in that their use may create physical incoordination and inability to bring the concentration necessary to the consummation of the sex act. There is no doubt that a few micrograms too many may send the psyche soaring, but ground the soma.

CONCLUSION

"Sex-crazed dope fields" . . . "warped desires" . . . "killer-weed." These emotionally charged and outmoded phrases are "high camp" to the New Generation—the new young society reared in an age of electronically huckstered pharmacologic panaceas. Better living through "chemistry". . . penicillin, "Romilar," gentle blue "Compoz" and birth control pills are representative of the "wonder drugs" to which these young people have ready daily access.

And, lacking the puritanical guilt of their parents, the new society finds "Free Love," or at least casual sexual contact equally readily available (4). If many are not yet prepared to accept the responsibilities of shared sexuality, then surely a pharmacologic escape for this problem must exist, as well. And, for many of this generation, sex without guilt can appear bland and spiceless; it just does not live up to the teasing expectations that their parents knew (34). The programmed logic in their minds, then, is to turn to drugs—of many kinds—as a source of additional excitement and stimulation . . . or as an escape.

As we have noted, drugs may serve to release repressed behavior (thus allowing acting out of sexual fantasies); or drugs may serve as a "replacement" for sex, and we repeatedly have seen the use of the "phallic symbolism" of needle puncture, the vividly described orgasmic rush, and the use of the varied paraphernalia of drug use as a subordinate to the need for a conventional sex partner.

In the subculture studied here, we may see a fascinating array of apparatus at the bedside: hash pipes, "poppers," "coke-spoons," or "outfits" of "speed" ready for injection.

For most of our population, however, the added sexual "spice" of the drugs described is of transitory importance, and an almost invariable return to "sex on the natch" ("natural") is described.

The important point, however, is the vast drug sophistication of the new generation. "Scare" phrases, such as those quoted earlier, serve only to alienate and faintly amuse this population.

Finally, it is hoped that this report, felt to be extremely candid and valid for the subculture studied, may lend some insights into their drug-sex practices and mores.

REFERENCES

1. Anslinger, H. J., quoted in "Playboy" Panel Interview, "The Drug Revolution," 1969.
2. Mayor's Committee on Marijuana, *The marijuana problem in the City of New York.* Cattell, Lancaster, Pa., 1944.
3. Smith, R. C. In *The new social drug,* D. E. Smith, (Ed.), Englewood Cliffs, N.J., Prentice-Hall, 1970. P. 106.
4. Simmons, J. L. and Winograd, B. *It's happening.* Santa Barbara, Calif.: Marc-Laird, 1966. Pp. 105–119.
5. *Interim Report of the Commission of Inquiry into the Non-Medical Use of Drugs.* Crown Copyrights, Ottawa, Canada, 1970, P.41.
6. Sheppard, C. W., Gay, G. R., and Smith, D. E. The changing patterns of heroin addiction in the Haight-Ashbury subculture. *J. of Psychedelic Drugs,* 1971, 3 (2): 22–30.
7. Shick, J. F. E., Smith, D. E., and Meyers, F. H. Patterns of drug use in the Haight-Ashbury neighborhood: *Clin. Toxicology,* 1970, 3 (1): 19–56.
8. *Interim Report of the Commission of Inquiry into the Non-Medical Use of Drugs.* Crown Copyrights, Ottawa, Canada, 1970. P. 41.
9. Wellisch, D. K., Gay, G. R., and McEntee, R. The Easy Rider Syndrome: A pattern of heterosexual and homosexual relationships in a heroin addict population. *J. Fam. Proc.,* 1970, 9 (4): 425–430.
10. Kaplan, J. *Marijuana : The new prohibition.* World Publishing, New York, 1970. Pp. 92–146.
11. *Op. cit.* Pp. 80–82.
12. Meyers, F. H. In *The new social drug,* D. E. Smith, (Ed.), Englewood Cliffs, N.J.: Prentice-Hall 1970. Pp. 35–40.
13. Dahlberg, C. C. Sexual behavior in the drug culture. *Med. Aspects of Human Sexuality,* 1971, 5 (4): 64–71.

14. Margolis J. and Clorfene, R. *A child's garden of grass*. Pocket Books, New York, 1970. Pp. 53–64.
15. *Interim Report of the Commission of Inquiry into the Non-Medical Use of Drugs*. Crown Copyrights, Ottawa, Canada, 1970. P. 19.
16. Shepherd, M., Leder, M., and Rodright, R. *Clinical psychopharmacology*. Lea and Febiger, Phila., 1968. Pp. 67–75.
17. Ban, T. *Psychopharmacology*. Williams and Wilkins, Baltimore, 1969. Pp. 173–188.
18. *Interim Report of the Commission of Inquiry into the Non-Medical Use of Drugs*. Crown Copyrights, Ottawa, Canada, 1970. P. 55.
19. Ban, T. *Psychopharmacology*. Williams and Wilkins, Baltimore, 1969. Pp. 200–202.
20. Bleuler, M. In *Clinical Psychiatry*. G. Mayer, *et al.* (Eds.), Cassell, London, 1960.
21. Ban, T. *Psychopharmacology*. Williams and Wilkins, Baltimore, 1969. P. 200.
22. Howard, J. and Borges, P. Needle sharing in the Haight: Some social and psychological functions. *J. Psychedelic Drugs*, 1971, **4** (1).
23. Hopkins, J. Cocaine: A flash in the pan, a pain in the nose, in *Rolling Stone*. Issue #81, April 29, 1971.
24. Burroughs, W. *Naked lunch*. Grove Press, New York, 1959. P. 64.
25. *Op cit.* P. 249.
26. *Interim Report of the Commission of Inquiry into the Non-Medical Use of Drugs*. Crown Copyrights, Ottawa, Canada, 1970. P. 65.
27. Leary, T. *The politics of ecstasy*. College Notes and Texts, New York, 1968.
28. Yablonski, L. *The hippie trip*. Pegasus Press, New York, 1968. Pp. 224–237.
29. Students Association for the Study of Hallucinogens. *Capsules*. April 1970. Vol. 2, No. 1.
30. Burroughs, W. *Junkie*. Ace Books, New York, 1953. P. 106.
31. Burroughs, W. *Naked lunch*. Grove Press, New York, 1959. P. 35.
32. *Interim Report of the Commission of Inquiry into the Non-Medical Use of Drugs*. Crown Copyrights, Ottawa, Canada, 1970. P. 55.
33. Gay, G. R., *et al.* Short term heroin detoxification on an outpatient basis. *Intern. J. of Addict.*, 1971, **6** (2): 241–264.
34. Kaplan, J. *Marijuana : The new prohibition*. World Publishing, New York, 1970. P. 82.

Vocational and Social Adjustment of the Treated Juvenile Addict

ELLA J. HUGHLEY

INTRODUCTION

Treatment of the abstinent juvenile drug abuser presents greater difficulties than that of the hard-core addict because the adolescent is generally involved in addiction for a relatively short time, and the negative consequences of addiction such as imprisonment, total rejection by one's relatives, and physical ailments inherent in the use of drugs have not had their full impact. The young adolescent drug abuser is therefore still in what could be called the "honeymoon" stage of addiction. Society, his family, the schools, and police may define the youngster as having a "problem," but he has not yet come to accept this definition. This is particularly true of the alienated, economically deprived young drug user in urban areas. Socially acceptable alternatives within the milieu in which drug abuse occurs are singularly unattractive. Schools, especially in the ghettoes are seen as irrelevant and the youngster drops out, preferring the heroin-induced euphoria to classroom instruction which he finds dull and uninteresting.

Legitimate job possibilities for school dropouts are limited, thus tending to further alienate the youngster from the conforming world. The following picture of the youthful addict emerges: a high school dropout, lacking in work experience and/or skills, often possessing a criminal record, rejected by the family and non-drug using friends.

The youthful addict may handle large sums of money, becoming a street entrepreneur, i.e., selling stolen merchandise, drugs, pimping, stealing, etc. This, therefore, enhances his self-esteem. An alternative of a dishwasher's or porter's job would be unattractive to him. The lack of viable vocational opportunities is one of the greatest deterrents to successful rehabilitation. In addition, if the narcotic craving has a physiological component, as has been reported in the literature, the young addict's difficulty in remaining abstinent from drugs in the community may be further compounded (Dole and Nyswander, 1967).

Concern with and treatment of the teen-age drug abuser is a relatively recent development occurring in response to the drug abuse epidemic among the young. The number of teen-age drug abusers reported to the New York City Narcotic register through 1969 was 19,899. These figures are admittedly conservative. During 1970, there were 254 teen-age deaths from narcotism according to the office of the New York City Medical Examiner. At present, narcotic-related deaths constitute the principal reason for the mortality of young people between the ages of 15 and 35.

Legal considerations as well as a general reluctance to treat the teen-age addict because he is "unmotivated" have inhibited the development of treatment of addicts under the age of 18 years.

Presently two major modalities have evolved in the treatment of the teen-age drug abuser, namely, the drug-free model and the chemotherapeutic. Both modalities were developed in New York City where the problem of drug addiction has been most serious. Unfortunately, except for programs other than methadone maintenance, extensive evaluations have not been reported in the literature.

Therapeutic communities modeled after Synanon have been adopted with modifications as a prototype for drug treatment. Although initially established for the adult addict, therapeutic communities have recently been turning their attention to the teen-age drug abuser. These programs, in addition to group therapy, involve the removal of the patient from his environment and the substitution of a new anti-drug reference group. Most therapeutic community programs have built re-entry into the larger community as a final stated goal of treatment. However, if the same levels of successful completion of treatment obtain for the teen-age addict as have been reported for adult addicts, then the number and percentage of teen-age addicts maintaining abstention in the community will remain small (Lowinson and Zwerling, 1971).

Pilot studies using methadone with teen-agers are currently in progress. Preliminary findings indicate a measure of success in assisting the young patient in returning to school, seeking employment, abstaining from drugs and criminal behavior (Nightingale *et al.*, 1971). One basis for therapeutic intervention is reality-oriented counseling and assistance with problems of everyday living. Schoof and Stanczak (1971) report some success in using methadone and group psychotherapy with predominantly middle-class patients and their parents.

Millman and Nyswander (1971) are using long-term methadone detoxification with a teen-age addict population in conjunction with one New York City high school. The results have been promising in regard to school performance, abstention from heroin and criminality.

PROBLEMS FACED BY THE TEEN-AGE ADDICT UPON HIS RETURN TO THE COMMUNITY

Relinquishing drug-induced euphoria as well as related anti-social behavior is simply the first step in the total rehabilitation of the addict. Initially a patient may feel very proud about having given up narcotics, but once he comes face to face with the everyday world he is often in need of further assistance. Illustrative of the problem of re-entry is the case of an 18-year-old black male on the methadone maintenance treatment program who came to the author's attention while she was working with the Department of Social Services as a rehabilitation and employment counselor. W. J. was on the methadone maintenance treatment program for 6 months. Previously he had been in a drug-free therapeutic community and left because he felt that he was unfairly treated in regard to a job promotion. He succeeded in remaining drug-free for a period of 7 months, working as a clerk in a book store. Despite his employment, he was unable to cope with his narcotic hunger and he entered into the methadone maintenance program. When W. J. was first seen by the author he was extremely depressed because he had lost his job in the book store when his employer learned that he was a former heroin addict and accused him of taking merchandise from the store. Further records revealed that W. J. had been arrested, convicted of burglary and placed on probation.

W. J. was born in New York City (Harlem), where he grew up with his mother and two brothers. His father left the household when he was 4 years old. He was supported by his mother's minimal income from employment which was supplemented by Public Assistance. W. J. attended school up to the ninth grade and dropped out because he could not concentrate due to lack of adequate food, clothing, and a sense of inferiority due to his "shabby appearance." His two brothers also dropped out of high school, but did not take to drugs. W. J. tried to find work at age 16, but was not successful. He became despondent and disillusioned and started smoking marijuana. A few months later he started to experiment with heroin. He became addicted within 3 months.

Unfortunately, this client was not amenable to counseling. W. J.'s anti-social behavior gives evidence of an internal conflict stemming from his early childhood privations which were characterized by hard times, poor housing, and lack of adequate food. The absence of a father figure in the home with whom he could identify as a role model contributed in part to his lack of ambition and inability to choose a vocation. His need to seek solace in drugs to allay tension can be understood in terms of his poor social adjustment coupled with imperfections in the social system which restricted his possibilities of upward mobility.

A similar situation is the case of M. C. an 18-year-old white Italian male who was estranged from his family. He was referred to the author for counseling because he had dropped out of training through the Division of Vocational Rehabilitation. Initially, he was referred for rehabilitation from a mental hospital where he spent 3 years. He also had a history of drug addiction and was drug-free after his 3-year period of hospitalization. Unlike W. J. who was reared with his natural parents, but lost the love and attention of his father at age 4, who also wanted to work but could not find employment, M. C. was reared by adoptive parents and, upon learning about his status, he ran away from home for the first time when he was 14 years old. Unlike W. J., economic circumstances did not play a great part in shaping his involvement with drugs, but as we look into M.C.'s history we find that his behavior shows greater evidence of underlying psychopathology. M. C. used narcotics to cope with anxiety.

Initially, M. C. was very talkative, manipulative, and suspicious of people. Because of his immature personality makeup, he required firm guidance. He had virtually no work history and little motivation, so that the initial focus was to place him on a work training program in order to evaluate his potential as well as for him to gain experience. His attendance in the program was not good and he frequently reported to work late. He was given intensive counseling regarding his poor motivation and attendance. He was abstinent from heroin, but admitted that he did take amphetamines occasionally whenever he felt depressed so as to help him function better during the day.

As M. C. continued in counseling, his attendance and work habits improved. He was also able to work through some of his insecure feelings about himself. He was ultimately re-referred to the Division of Vocational Rehabilitation to pursue training as a commercial artist.

In both clinical surveys, we can see how two people from different ethnic backgrounds became involved with addiction and the problems they faced in their endeavor to give up drugs and cope with the demands of the work-a-day world.

ROLE OF THE SOCIAL WORKER

The social worker's role in treating the addicted client should first be supportive and, whenever necessary, the client must be offered a positive transferential relationship, and, most of all, the conveyance of empathy at all times in order to establish rapport. He must be allowed to ventilate his feelings about his past negative and/or positive experiences. It must be kept in mind, however, because of the life-style of this type of client, one's focus should be reality based, keeping in mind the psychodynamics involved, i.e., poor reality testing, immediate need for gratification, fear of loss of friends who have similar life-styles and survival mechanisms and/or techniques. Special emphasis should be placed on how the client feels about himself in terms of remaining drug-free. He must be an active force in shaping his own future and treatment goals.

Vocational counseling with this type of client constitutes a vital aspect of the treatment process. The patient will need help in coping with interpersonal relationships. His ability to accept employment and/or training will depend to a large degree on how he presently views himself as well as his past life experience, which is characterized by shooting heroin and eliciting funds from street crimes. The counselor must work on the positive aspects of his personality in order to help him take on different values, to want change, to envision himself in a different role. This will require overcoming the patient's preoccupation about past failures.

Because of his poor identification and lack of adequate nurturing in the past which are due in part to his poor adjustment to life and ultimately lead to his seeking solace in drugs, he will need intensive contact with an empathetic, caring worker whom he can identify with as a role model. The sex of the counselor may be important in establishing a relationship with certain patients. The worker must convey to the client that he is capable and deserving of living a healthy, well-adjusted life, as free from frustration as possible.

As we saw in the two case illustrations, one client was able to gain greater self-confidence and was able to think more realistically about vocational rehabilitation, and ultimately pursued a vocational goal.

The addict who is functioning well in the community may find it very difficult to adjust to the inadequate income offered in a low non-skilled job. The social worker must serve as an activist in finding resources available for the addict who shows promise and wants to train for higher paying skilled jobs. The clients must not be misled about the reality of the job market. The social worker must convey and verbalize his/her awareness of the lack of jobs, training, and other services to his/her clients so that the clients will get a sense of his honesty and can think realistically, knowing that he has support in his endeavor to move ahead despite the obstacles he may face. This honesty on the part of the social worker can help to build up the client's trust and feelings of strength to cope with information which is conveyed by someone he feels cares.

By reinforcing the client's trust, he can begin to think more realistically about his present choice and view it in terms of his previous life-style.

CONCLUSION

Successful vocational rehabilitation of the teen-age addict is two-fold: First, the counselor must play a major role in helping the young addict adjust socially and economically to the "square" world. This should include the remediation of vocational and educational deficits. Second, society must allow the addict to be accepted as a first-class citizen.

One of the deterrents to adequately rehabilitating the former addict upon re-entry into society is the lack of adequately paying jobs as well as the closing off of certain positions to persons with criminal records or history of addiction.

REFERENCES

Dole, V. P. and Nyswander, M. E. Heroin addiction — A metabolic disease. *Arch. intern. Med.*, July 1967, **120**: 19–24.

Lowinson, J. and Zwerling, I. Group therapy with narcotic addicts. In *Comprehensive group psychotherapy.* H. I. Kaplan and B. J. Sadock (Eds.). Baltimore, 1971, Williams and Wilkins, P. 611.

Millman, R. B. and Nyswander, M. E. Slow detoxification of adolescent heroin addicts in New York City. *Proceedings Third National Conference on Methadone Treatment.* U.S. Government Printing Office, Washington, D.C., 1971. Pp. 88–90.

Nightingale, S. L., Wurmser, L., Platt, P. C., and Michaux, W. W. Adolescents on methadone: Preliminary observations. *Proceedings Third National Conference on Methadone Treatment.* U.S. Government Printing Office, Washington, D.C., 1971. Pp. 91–98.

Schoof, K. G. and Stanczak, S. A methadone withdrawal program for young heroin addicts. *Proceedings of the Committee on Drug Dependence.* National Research Council, Washington, D.C., 1971. Pp. 1904–1915.

Some Approaches to the Treatment of Adolescent Drug Addicts and Abusers

D. VINCENT BIASE

INTRODUCTION

This chapter is presented in two sections. Section I is a brief commentary on current forms of treatment for the adolescent addict/abuser. In addition, a relevant bibliography has been generated which includes references to recent source material concerned with adolescent drug treatment. These are references to qualitative, descriptive material regarding treatment of adolescent addicts/abusers and to several quantitative studies as well. In addition to references from the author's own current bibliographic file, the following additional sources were used.

- PASAR (Psychological Abstracts Search and Retrieval Service)
- National Institute for Mental Health—Clearinghouse for Drug Information
- Reader's Guide to Periodicals

This bibliography should therefore serve as an adequate and current base for specific and related source materials.

Section II includes a germane research study conducted by the author. The data report on several aspects of adolescent addicts in a drug-free therapeutic community.

The research findings:

- demonstrate the feasibility of predicting adolescent absconders (splittees) from a drug free therapeutic community;

170

- highlight the role and significance of depression with adolescent addicts in treatment, and implicate the need for more effective clinical intervention;
- demonstrate the feasibility of obtaining reliable affect reports of adolescent residents in a drug free therapeutic community;
- compare the affect level of adolescent addicts in a therapeutic environment to adult and other adolescent clinical groups.

SECTION I   A BRIEF COMMENTARY

The results from both surveys of drug use and the drug histories, obtained from adult addicts who are presently in treatment, substantiate that early drug experiences are becoming more common phenomena in younger adolescents. Drug histories of adult addicts repeatedly indicate that between the years of 15 and 17 there is a high probability that they either will have experimented with or consistently used marijuana, barbiturates, alcohol, heroin, and hallucinogens. Thus, many treatment programs seek to interrupt this pattern of drug taking and seek to modify the attitude of the adolescent addict and abuser so as to prevent him from becoming a chronic adult addict who will tend to engage in an active cycle of related criminal activities.

The "adolescent addict" is a general reference term which includes those adolescents who are physiologically addicted as well as those adolescents who are compulsive chronic drug abusers. The significant issue is to differentiate between the adolescent whose functioning is impaired as a consequence of drug taking or addiction, in contrast with his counterpart who has occasional drug experiences which do not appear to significantly disrupt his appropriate personal and social functioning and development.

Frequently, any adolescent drug use stirs parents or guardians to refer and place an adolescent with "drug problems" in treatment programs. Consequently, treatment programs which do not have specific admission criteria accept the referred adolescent and frequently seek to treat him with their single approach philosophy. Underlying this phenomena is the position that most adolescent drug taking is inherently destructive and will lead to a total debilitation of the adolescent. This condition suggests the need to develop a more effective framework for differentiating adolescent behaviors and assessing the particular meaning drugs have for the current adolescent style of adapting, coping, reacting, or adjusting.

The range of treatment modalities also reflects the current attempts to structure an appropriate level of analysis for the drug problem and its parameters. We have yet to answer the question—Do we have a drug epidemic? A related issue is the type of information necessary for prevention and treatment program development. Should the emphasis be on the intra-psychic level, behavioral-performance level, biochemical level, or is relevancy only achieved by addressing sociocultural and socioeconomic vectors?

At present no single specific recognized treatment approach exists for adolescent addicts and chronic abusers. Because of the recent rise in adolescent addiction, new treatment programs have developed more times out of social necessity. In addition, the majority of adolescent treatment programs have been adopted from recently developed single modality adult addict rehabilitation programs. Since many of these latter programs are still in their own developmental process, they infrequently can provide information regarding their specific efficacy. Certainly many of the treatment programs both for adults and adolescent addicts indicate creative and unique responses to the problems of drug and social rehabilitation, but they still require evaluation of their treatment processes and outcomes. We do not have answers to the question—How do you best and most efficiently treat a particular adolescent with a particular type of drug history? After the critical phase of chemical detoxification for either opiates, hallucinogenics, barbiturates, and amphetamines the problem still remains—which treatment approach? Certainly every existing modality has its underlining rationale, but we must be careful not to generalize any specific treatment approach categorically to all drug abusing adolescents.

Because the behavior of the adolescent is somewhat less crystallized than that of the adult, he is more susceptible to the influence of social as well as psychological factors. The emerging adolescent is also forced to deal with such new impulses as his emerging self-identity, sexuality, aggressive impulses, and mood swings. Even though the adult addict may have an active emotional life, his responses to them will be somewhat more habitual and regular. The adolescent with his emerging social self is more likely to be influenced by peer pressure than is the adult. Recent data suggest that the adolescent addict is more likely to have demonstrated previous behaviors which were different from the adolescent non-addict. I refer here to delinquent behaviors, unrealistic life goals and aspirations, chronic feelings of alienation from family, depressive moods, and sometimes the selection of adult psychopaths as role models for his own developing notions of self. It is assumed that, particularly within a residential treatment program, these underlying "symptoms," which are frequently conceptualized as "motivation for drug taking," can be modified by presenting a more constructive set of goals, aspirations, peer group and role models.

Treatment programs which seek to modify attitudes and reconstruct personalities approach the adolescent by enforcing abstinence, controlling his environment, teaching him new interpersonal and social skills, helping him learn to better interpret his feelings and experiences, and ultimately hoping that this training will foster change sufficient to stem and prevent the need for drugs in the future. Although many of the nuances of drug-free or abstinent treatment programs are more subtle, they do anticipate a positive learning experience to occur. In addition to the above characteristics, they provide the adolescent with a new social network of adolescents and adults who are also seeking to modify their own drug-taking behavior.

Preliminary research findings with this self-help therapeutic community treatment approach indicate a high degree of selectivity in the type of adolescent who eventually embarks on such a treatment course. Recent investigation by the author has demonstrated a significant degree of psychopathology in such a group of adolescents. Related work has also demonstrated that the degree of expressed depression is very often a significant indication that the adolescent client will abscond from treatment if there is little opportunity for relief from these feelings.

The adolescent addict and chronic drug abuser, particularly one from a low socioeconomic and minority ethnic background, frequently presents a poor record in the areas of academic achievement and social skills. Thus, in an environment as highly structured as a therapeutic community with its strong social norms, there are provisions made for the adolescent to attempt reinforcing situations in these areas with the help of this new peer group support. Here he has the environment which, by means of social control, encourages accomplishments in the learning of academic, interpersonal, and vocational skills. For many, this regularity and personal accountability as well as personal responsibility is a new experience. Some adolescents for whom this type of regulated or structured environment is similar to their own early experiences see the opportunity for them to better learn and cope with their reactions to this unique rehabilitative family.

The use of a chemical substitute to treat the adolescent addict is frequently considered an ethical issue. The proponents do not seem to defend this approach as much as they suggest its expediency in treating widespread adolescent addiction. The use of methadone with adolescents younger than 18 years of age is not infrequently criticized as immoral, because it appears to reinforce the adolescent addict identity. A more important issue is not whether methadone is dispensed to adolescents, but under what conditions it is dispensed. It would appear that dispensing methadone to adolescents in an ambulatory outpatient treatment program may not provide the necessary social limits for the adolescent to learn new behavior patterns to deal with his negative emotional and social life.

Although there is a physiological imbalance in any individual who is addicted to an opiate, there is no demonstrated evidence of a physiological predisposition prior to opiate use. However, research has been able to demonstrate more frequently the presence of predisposing social, emotional, and personality factors. These findings have been more consistent than any physiological evidence. It would appear that a responsible approach to treating adolescents with a maintenance drug would require a full-time therapeutic residential setting during the periods of detoxification, slow detoxification, and short-term maintenance toward abstinence, if possible. The adolescent who is most susceptible to social and family pressures as well as his own underlying emotional life would more likely benefit from this specialized residential setting. In such an environment, with its social norms of learning responsible behavior, an accessible achievement hierarchy, and peer support, the adolescent can be encouraged to face the critical issues in his emotional life that appear related to his addiction pattern. Moreover, within such a setting he will have the opportunity for learning educational, vocational, and social skills which appear as a token aspiration when he is an ambulatory client. He will also have the opportunity to experience former drug addicts who now elect a drug-free life-style. The probabilities are great that he will seek to imitate this behavior and will try periods of abstinence. Even if this young person relapses and requires continued methadone maintenance he will continue to experience positive reinforcements from his own ego accomplishments in such a setting. To expect similar achievements to occur in the original neighborhood and social setting where the addiction pattern developed is expecting far in excess of what many of these young addicts can adjust to adequately. It also denies the evidence developed by researchers that demonstrates that such a neighborhood or social environmental setting can be a critical conditioning component and even a reinforcer to the maintenance of the addiction pattern. On the other hand, a therapeutic setting would permit some of the addiction patterns to be extinguished,

and permit important new learning to occur—a learning which is facili-
tated by living examples and direct participation—new modes of dealing
with the stresses that he previously assuaged by compulsive drug taking.
Hopefully, with more careful monitoring and evaluation of treatment
programs and continued study of the variety of adolescent addicts, we
will be better equipped to offer significant treatment recommendations.

REFERENCES

Bakewell, W. E., Jr. Nonnarcotic incidence in a university hospital psychiatric ward. *JAMA.*, 1966, **196**: 710–713.

Biase, D. V. Adolescent heroin abusers in a therapeutic community. *National Research Council Committee on Problems of Drug Dependence,* Thirty-third Annual Scientific Meeting, Toronto, Canada, Feb. 1971.

Bonfante, J. A town in trouble. *Life.* March 21, 1969, **66**: 48–54.

Brill, L. and Lieberman, L. *Authority and addiction,* Boston: Little, Brown, 1969.

Brotman, R., Silverman, L., and Suffet, F. Drug use among affluent high school youth. E. Goode, (Ed.). *Marijuana,* New York, 1969, 128–30.

Brotman, R. and Suffet, F. *Youthful drug use,* U.S. Department of Health, Education and Welfare, Social and Rehabilitation Services, Youth Development and Delinquency Prevention Administration, 1970.

Chambers, C. *Treatments for narcotic addicts,* Selected Literature Abstracts, New York State Narcotic Addiction Control Commission. Unpublished manuscript, 1971.

Chambers, C. and Brill, L. Some considerations for the treatment of non-narcotic drug abus- ers. *Indus. Med.,* 1971, **40**: 13–22.

Chatham, Lois R. The role of the National Institute of Mental Health in the field of drug abuse treatment and rehabilitation. *National Research Council Committee on Prob- lems of Drug Dependence, Thirty-third Annual Scientific Meeting,* Toronto, Canada, Feb. 1971.

Chien, I., Gerard, D., Lee, R., and Rosenfeld, E. *The Road to H.* New York: Basic Books, 1964.

Cohen, Y. The journey beyond trips: Alternatives to drugs. *J. Psychiat. Drugs,* 1971, **3** (2), 16–21.

Dawtry, F. (Ed.). *Social problems of drug abuse,* London, Appleton-Century-Crofts, 1968.

Drug abuse treatment and prevention—Religious activities and programs. *National Clear- inghouse for Drug Abuse Information,* June 1971, Series 6, No. 1.

Eliashop, E. Concepts and techniques of role playing and role training utilizing psycho- dramatic methods in group therapy with adolescent drug addicts. *Group Psychother.,* 1955, **8**: 308–315.

Fischmann, V. S. Drug addicts in a therapeutic community. *Psychother. and Psychosom.,* 1968, **16**: 109–18.

Gamso, R. R. and Mason, P. A hospital for adolescent drug addicts. *Psychiat. Quart. Suppl.,* 1958, **32**: 99–109.

Information on Five Drug Treatment Programs: Haight-Ashbury Free Clinic, California, Drug Abuse Self-Help Council, California, Christian Community Service Agency, Florida, Michigan State Department of Social Services, Michigan, and Arlington

County Department of Human Resources, Virginia. U.S. National Institute of Mental Health, 1970.

Jaffe, J. Whatever turns you off. *Psych. Today*, May 1970, **3** (12), 43–44, 60–62.

Jansson, B. Narcotic addiction in young people in Sweden. *Acta Psychiat. Scand.*, 1970, **217**: 17–18.

Jurgensen, W. P. Problems of inpatient treatment of addiction. *Int. J. of Addict.*, 1966, **1**: 62–73.

Lennard, H. L. and Allen, S. Issues in the evaluation of drug addiction treatment programs, New York, N.Y. 1971. Unpublished manuscript.

Levitt, L. Rehabilitation of narcotic addicts among lower class teenagers. *Amer. J. of Orthopsychiat.*, 1968, **38**: 56–62.

Lindesmith, A. R. *The addict and the law*. Bloomington, Indiana: Indiana University Press, 1965.

Maurer, D. and Vogel, V. *Narcotics and narcotic addiction*. Springfield, Illinois, Thomas 1954.

McCollum, S. Education and training of youthful offenders. *The Transition from School to Work Manpower Symposium*. Princeton University, May 9–10, 1968, pp. 108–118.

McKean, W. Encounter: How kids turn off drugs. *Look*, April 15, 1969, **33**: 40–43.

McNaspy, C. J. Fighting drugs in Puerto Rico. *America*, 1969, 121–61.

Meyers, D. I. (Ed.). A new adolescent? *Psychosocial Process* Issues in Child Mental Health 1971, Vol. 2, No. 1.

Newmann, C. P. and Tamerin, J. S. The treatment of adult alcoholics and teen-age drug addicts in one hospital. *Quart. J. of Studies on Alcohol.* 1971, **32**: 82–93.

Nobel, P. and Barnes, G. Drug taking in adolescent girls: Factors associated with the progression to narcotics use. *Brit. Med. J.*, 1971, **2**: 620–623.

Paterson, G. C. and Wilson, M. R., Jr. A perspective on drug abuse. *Mayo Clin. Proceedings*, July 1971, **46**: 468–476.

Preamble of the White House Conference Drug Task Force. *White House Conference on Youth*, Boulder, Colorado, 1971.

Proceedings, Third National Conference on Methadone Treatment, U.S. National Institute of Mental Health, November 14–16, 1970, Chapter IV.

Proceedings, Fourth National Conference on Methadone Treatment, NAPAN, Jan. 8–10, 1972, 41–58.

Ramirez, E. A new program to combat drug addiction in New York City. *Brit. J. of Addict.*, 1968, **63**: 89–103.

Rasor, R. W. The institutional treatment of the narcotic addict. *J. of Miss. Med. Assoc.*, 1965, **6**: 11–14.

Rosenthal, M. S. and Biase, D. V. Phoenix House: Therapeutic communities for drug addicts. *Hosp. and Comm. Psychiat.*, Jan. 1969, **20**: 27–30.

Sanders, Marion. Addicts and zealot. *Harper's*, June 1970, **240**: 71–73, 76–80.

Supplemental Statement to the Task Force on Drugs. *White House Conference on Youth*, Boulder, Colorado, 1971.

Telson, S. Counseling the adolescent addict. *Rehabilitation*, 1964, **30**: 10–12.

The teacher's role in Alpha School, *Addiction Services Agency*, New York, Unpublished manuscript, Jan. 1971.

Vandervort, J. Treatment of drug abuse in adolescents. *Third National Conference on Methadone Treatment, National Institute of Mental Health*, Public Health Service Publication Nov. 1970, No. 2172, 87–88.

Varilo, E. On the etiology of drug addiction in youth. *Acta Psychiat. Scand.*, 1970, **217**: 19.

Voluntary action and drug abuse: Some current highlights. *National Clearinghouse for Drug Abuse Information.* Feb. 1971, Series 5, No. 1.

Wainwright, L. A town deals sternly with its own. *Life*, Nov. 6, 1970, **69**: 40–42, 44, 46–47.

Wolfe, R. and Boriello, R. Drug addiction: An effective therapeutic approach. *Med. Times,* 1970, **98**: 185–193.

Wong, R. C. Ambulatory treatment of drug addicts. *Brit. J. Addict.,* 1965, **61**: 101–114.

Yurick, S. The political economy of junk. *Motive*, March 1971, **31**: 46–51.

SECTION II ADOLESCENT HEROIN ABUSERS IN A THERAPEUTIC COMMUNITY*†

USE OF THE MAACL TO ASSESS EMOTIONAL TRAITS AND SPLITTING FROM TREATMENT

The widespread "epidemic" of heroin abuse among young persons has become a cause for national concern, and has also pointed to the scanty empirical data related to the psychology of adolescent addicts. The New York State Narcotic Addiction Control Commission reports that in 1960, 15 adolescents died of heroin related deaths and by 1969 that number grew to 224. In New York City, for the age group 15–35, narcotic-related deaths are now the leading cause of deaths as reported by the Chief Medical Examiner's Office. These alarming facts would seem to encourage further study of this recently acknowledged problem, a problem which has direct societal and psychological implications. An overview of the adolescent drug abuser is presented in a monograph edited by Harms (1965) in which Laskowitz presents data of adolescent addicts in a hospital treatment program. The present study was conducted in a peer self-help therapeutic community rehabilitation program for adolescent heroin drug abusers. The Phoenix House programs part of New York City's Addiction Services Agency is designed to modify the addictive behavior pattern chiefly through emotional development within a

*These findings were presented to: National Research Council Committee on Problems of Drug Dependence Thirty-third Annual Scientific Meeting, Toronto, Ontario, Canada, February 17, 1971.

†The author wishes to acknowledge the helpful assistance given to this study by Sherry Holland, Mary Wynn, and Fred Levine. He wishes to also acknowledge the cooperation of the staffs and residents of Phoenix House, Boerum Street, Brooklyn, New York, 85th Street Phoenix Center, the Adolescent Educational Unit of Creedmor State Hospital and Cathedral Prep Seminary, Brooklyn, New York, and all the adolescent subjects whose participation was necessary for this study to be realized.

therapeutic community environment. In September 1970, the Phoenix House adolescent unit was authorized by the New York State Board of Social Welfare of the Department of Social Services to care for addicts under the age of 16. This study investigated the feasibility of obtaining reliable self-reports of emotional traits from drug-free adolescent addicts who were participants in this residential setting. Another goal of the study was to explore the possible relationship between self-reported emotional traits and early termination from the rehabilitation program (splitting). Previous research has demonstrated the usefulness of the MAACL (Today form) as a measure of affect with adult male heroin addicts in a group encounter situation (Biase and DeLeon, 1969). The MAACL (General and Today form) was also used successfully in an assessment of emotional traits of adult addicts on welfare and those seeking treatment within the Phoenix House program (Biase, 1970).

METHOD

Subjects

The Ss were adolescent male and female heroin addicts who were drug-free while being full-time live-in residents in an ASA Phoenix House therapeutic community for adolescents. They were essentially from the lower economic stratum and included Blacks, Puerto Ricans, and Whites. This therapeutic community, because of operational demands, provided for the active participation of 10 adult ex-addict residents along with the adolescent residents. The operations of the house are conducted by rehabilitated ex-addicts, working under the direction of professional personnel. The Phoenix House program uses the process of confrontational encounter coordinated with a work and education program to assist the addict in modifying his negative behavior patterns. A more complete description of the Phoenix House Therapeutic Community can be found in a paper by Rosenthal and Biase (1969). The Ss in the present study were tested twice in a test-retest paradigm of a 7-day interval. The first sample of 30 consisted of 19 males and 11 females. The males had a mean age of 16.53 with a mean completed school grade of 9.37. The mean age for female Ss was 15.91 years and the highest mean grade completed was 8.91. The 1-week retest sample included a total of 33 Ss – 20 males and 13 females. These included 3 female Ss and 2 male Ss not tested in the first sample: 2 male Ss from the first sample were not available for the retest session. The mean ages were 16.75 years for the males and 16.23

years for the females. The mean highest grade completed was 8.91 for males and 8.62 for females. The mean time period of full-time residence in the therapeutic community was 5.49 months.

Instrumentation

Several considerations suggested the use of the Multiple Affect Adjective Check List (MAACL) developed by Zuckerman and Lubin (1965). Although the test is still in a research phase, the general or trait form permits assessment of three affects: Anxiety, Depression, and Hostility. The possibility of using the MAACL with an adolescent addict population to measure emotional traits was considered feasible since it is a self-administered instrument which has been made as simple as possible for the respondent to complete; all words are at or below an eighth grade reading level. The MAACL contains 132 adjectives. The full scale scoring includes 21 adjectives for the Anxiety scale, 40 for the Depression scale, and 28 adjectives for the Hostility scale. The remaining adjectives are non-scale related, except for two adjectives which are part of the brief Hostility scale.

*S*s were also administered a 9-item Lie Scale from the Eysenck Personality Inventory Form B (EPI L) (1963 edition) in an attempt to assess a reliable test-taking attitude and to insure against gross falsification of the MAACL.

Procedure

The General form of the MAACL and EPI L scale were administered in a group setting. *S*s were informed that their scores would have no consequent effect on any aspects of their involvement in the program. *S*s were instructed to indicate on the face sheet the number of siblings in his family of origin and his birth order within that family. The MAACL Check Lists were scored for Anxiety, Depression, Hostility, and total number of items checked. The MAACL was administered first, the EPI L scale was administered after all *S*s had completed the MAACL. After a period of 6 months, a comparative analysis of Anxiety, Depression, and Hostility scores was performed between voluntary dropouts from the program (splittees) and adolescent residents who continued in full-time treatment.

Results and Discussion

Table 1 shows the mean MAACL scores for both testing sessions and the test, retest reliability correlation coefficient (7-day interval) along with

Table 1   MAACL general form full scale scores.

	N	Anxiety		Depression		Hostility		Total Items	
		$\bar{x}$	σ	$\bar{x}$	σ	$\bar{x}$	σ	$\bar{x}$	σ
Test 1	30	11.60	3.56	17.93	4.90	11.50	4.23	50.90	20.77
Retest	33	11.14	2.84	16.90	6.49	11.19	4.19	53.96	26.50

Test Retest Reliability Coefficients

	N	Anxiety	Depression	Hostility	Total Items
7-day Interval	27	0.62*	0.71*	0.67*	0.77*

Note: All probability values are two-tailed.
*$p < 0.01$, $df = 25$.

the two-tailed probability values. The reliability coefficients were all significant: $r = 0.67$ ($p < 0.01$, $N = 27$) for Anxiety, $r = 0.71$ ($p < 0.01$, $N = 27$) for Depression, and $r = 0.67$ ($p < 0.01$, $N = 27$) for Hostility. The present mean MAACL scores were compared to compatible addict and psychiatric samples (Biase, 1971). No significant MAACL differences were found between the present sample and (1) adolescent addicts seeking treatment in Phoenix House Therapeutic Community Program; (2) adult drug-free addicts who were active residents within a Phoenix House Therapeutic Community; (3) adolescent psychiatric patients at a state hospital. Although the MAACL scores of the present study are within the range of normative scores from other psychiatric groups, we cannot at this time evaluate the clinical or psychopathological significance of the present scores.

Eysenck (1968) reports that the L scale measures a faking good response set. He considers scores of 4 or 5 the cut-off point for an invalid response set. The comparatively low L scores ($\bar{x} = 0.57$, $\sigma = 1.21$) of the present sample suggest a contrary test taking set. It might be considered a self-disclosure set, one in which socially undesirable items of the Anxiety, Depression, and Hostility scales would be checked. Such a response distortion might inflate the MAACL scores. This proposed set is congruent with the milieu of the Phoenix House Therapeutic Community Program. Residents are encouraged, particularly in the group encounters, to express their negative feelings in order to increase self-understanding and interpersonal objectivity. Such a schedule of social reinforcement for affect-laden words and self-disclosure might well influence the responses to an adjective check list.

Six months after testing, a statistical comparison was made of the Anxiety, Depression, and Hostility scores among a group of 22 of the sample who had chosen to prematurely terminate their rehabilitation period (split). Their data were compared to 15 residents who continued in the program at least 6 months beyond the last date of testing. A series of t tests indicated that the splits had significantly higher Depression scores than the residents who remained in treatment ($t = 2.18$, $df = 35$, $p < 0.05$). No significant differences were found between these two groups on Anxiety or Hostility scores. An analysis of Anxiety scores for all Ss yielded no significant differences between first born (including only children) and later borns. A subsequent analysis yielded no significant difference in the number of children in the families of origin of the split and resident groups. The mean number of children was 3.5.

Conclusion

The present study has demonstrated the feasibility of obtaining reliable MAACL self-reports of emotional traits from adolescent drug-free addicts in a peer self-help therapeutic community setting. The data suggest that a self-disclosing response set unique to this type of rehabilitation program may be operating with self-report measures. The findings indicate that the MAACL has the potential to predict those residents who split from such a treatment setting within the first year of program.

Moreover, although additional research is required to assess the full implications of these Depression findings, they do suggest the importance of this affect in treating adolescent addicts in self-help therapeutic communities.

REFERENCES

Biase, D. V. Adolescent drug abusers normative data and word comprehension for the multiple affect adjective check list. Unpublished manuscript, 1971.

Biase, D. V. A comparison of trait and state affect levels between two groups of adult drug abusers, welfare recipients and candidates seeking treatment. Unpublished manuscript, 1970.

Biase, D. V. and De Leon, G. The Encounter Group — Measurement of some affect changes. In, *Proceedings of the 77th Annual Convention of the American Psychological Association, 1969*. Washington, D.C.: American Psychological Association, 1969.

Eysenck, H. J. and Eysenck, Sybil. *Eysenck Personality Inventory*. San Diego: Educational and Industrial Testing Service, 1968.

Harms, E., (Ed.). *Drug addiction in youth*, International Series of Monographs on Child Psychiatry, Vol. 3. London: Pergamon Press, 1965.

Laskowitz, D. Psychological characteristics of the adolescent addict. In *Drug addiction in youth*, International Series of Monographs on Child Psychiatry, Vol. 3. London: Pergamon Press, 1965.

Rosenthal, M. S. and Biase, D. V. Phoenix Houses: Therapeutic communities for drug addicts. *Hospital and Community Psychiatry,* 1969, **20**: 26030.

Zuckerman, M. and Lubin, B. *Multiple affect adjective check list manual.* San Diego: Educational and Industrial Testing Service, 1965.

Withdrawals and Methadone Treatment

HAROLD L. TRIGG

The technique of withdrawal from drugs most commonly abused by youthful drug-dependent individuals does not differ significantly from the withdrawal approaches to the adult drug-dependent individual. However, in the opinion of the author, the younger drug-dependent person is much less motivated for voluntary withdrawal than the adult and, to go back a step, is most often not convinced that his drug dependence (abuse, addiction) is virtually out of his control. For example, when confronted with the probability of addiction to heroin, the response is very often, "I'm not really hooked; I can go a whole weekend without using any stuff." This ability on the part of the adolescent to deny the seriousness of drug involvement is greatly enhanced by elaborate processes of denial by his guilt-ridden and frightened parents. To further complicate matters, the adolescent is often rebellious and probably operates under what seems to be the contemporary misconception that people are entitled to do whatever they want with their own bodies.

THE OPIATES

The most commonly abused opiate is heroin. In the younger age group it is quite unusual to find abuse of dilaudid, demerol, or morphine. However, abuse of cough mixtures containing codeine is common. The abuse of heroin generally begins around the age of 12 or 13, though abuse beginning in earlier age groups is not rare. The two most common reasons for

beginning heroin abuse are: "curiosity" and "My friends were using it."
The use of heroin may or may not be preceded by smoking marijuana. At
the present time, there is absolutely no scientific evidence that marijuana
smoking, in and of itself, leads to the use of heroin.

Patterns of heroin abuse vary widely. At one extreme there is the adolescent whose first use of heroin is by intravenous injection ("mainlining").
Such an individual may fall into an immediate pattern of intravenous
injections of heroin several times daily and in a matter of weeks or months
be thoroughly addicted ("hooked," "strung out"). At the other extreme is
the adolescent who begins heroin use via the nasal route ("snorting,"
"sniffing") only on weekends and, perhaps, not even consecutive weekends. However, as time passes, the intervals between usage become
smaller and smaller. Generally, after a period of months, either in order to
achieve a greater degree of euphoria and/or as a result of peer pressure, he
begins to inject subcutaneously ("skin-popping"). Here again, this particular route of administration can be limited to weekends for many months.
However, almost inevitably, regardless of the length of time the subcutaneous route is maintained, the next jump is to intravenous injection of
heroin. Injection of heroin via the intravenous route produces a tremendous degree of euphoria and seems to be the preferred route of administration by the majority of heroin addicts. The heroin abuse patterns between
the aforementioned extremes are endless.

It may be instructive to cite one such other variation. The adolescent
may inject heroin several times daily, with clock-like regularity. In as
short a period as a few weeks, he may awaken one morning with symptoms of the opiate abstinence syndrome, but not recognize the significance of such symptoms. He telephones a peer, describes his symptoms,
and is advised to take an injection of heroin. The opiate abstinence symptoms are relieved in a matter of a minute or two. More often than not, it is
at this point that the heroin user, on the one hand, realizes that he has
become addicted and, on the other hand, is simultaneously able to deny
the seriousness of his illness. However, at this juncture, he may cease
abruptly the use of heroin and attempt to "mask" the withdrawal symptoms by switching to another drug, particularly one of the barbiturates.
(Currently the consumption of very inexpensive wine is in vogue.) Assuming, however, that barbiturates have been substituted, the inherent
tragedy may very well be that the adolescent then finds the abuse of
barbiturates quite pleasurable. In a matter of months, and depending on
the amount consumed, the adolescent finds that he has substituted barbiturate dependence for heroin dependence, albeit perhaps unwittingly.

Having been warned of the danger of convulsions which may occur following abrupt cessation of barbiturates, the adolescent at this point may decide to "level" with his parents about his drug involvement and ask for whatever medical assistance is needed. Very frequently, however, he returns to his peers in the street and relies on their advice in tapering down his barbiturate dependence. In the latter instance, one can assume that he is still interested in concealing his drug involvement from any kind of authority. If he is successful in achieving drug-free status at this point, he may with great sincerity and conviction decide never again to use drugs. This resolution is, more often than not, short-lived.

The actual treatment of the opiate abstinence syndrome is quite simple. Methadone hydrochloride, in liquid form, administered by mouth, is the drug of choice. The amount of methadone prescribed depends on the amount of heroin consumed, and the methadone detoxification schedule is geared to match the stated heroin intake. The stated heroin intake is, of course, not always reliable. However, should the patient appear over-medicated (excessively drowsy) on the prescribed schedule, the likelihood is that the amount of heroin consumed ("the size of the habit") has been overstated. In such a case, the methadone schedule should be downward-ly adjusted usually by decrements of 5 mg. On the other hand, if objective withdrawal symptoms are present, an upward adjustment of the metha-done schedule is indicated. Failure to make the opiate abstinence syn-drome as tolerable as possible often causes the patient to panic and sign out of the hospital prematurely. Admittedly, the heroin addict undergoing medically supervised withdrawal is highly manipulative and the physician must learn to strike a balance between providing competent and com-passionate care and avoiding being "conned." In the author's experience, it is rarely necessary to exceed a total of 40 mg of methadone per day. This should be equally divided into an a.m. and a p.m. dose for 2 full days, then reduced by 5 mg per day. Using such a schedule, the actual number of days the patient is on methadone is about 10. If the methadone with-drawal schedule starts at a level of 10 mg in the morning and 10 mg in the evening (a total of 20 mg per day) then, obviously the number of days the individual is on methadone is considerably fewer. Some patients elect to go through the opiate abstinence syndrome without the use of methadone. If the patient is young and physically healthy there is no objection to such a patient making this choice. In such cases, when this method is elected, the withdrawal symptoms are generally quite mild and seldom amount to anything more than lacrimation, rhinorrhea, diarrhea, loss of appetite, and stomach and leg cramps. The clinical picture improves rapidly and symptoms of the opiate abstinence syndrome have virtually completely subsided after 72 hours. This method of withdrawing from heroin is often referred to as "kicking the habit cold turkey." The adolescent who elects to "kick cold turkey" should be reassured that if he develops discomfort several hours or even a day or so later, he will be given methadone in sufficient quantities to control his symptoms. In such instances, a single dose of 10 mg of methadone by mouth will bring the symptoms under control in a matter of 10–15 minutes. If the administration of methadone by mouth is precluded because severe vomiting has developed, then the methadone should be administered intramuscularly. Also, if the symptoms which do occur are not severe enough to require the administration of methadone, one should consider the use of Thorazine, 30 mg q.i.d., for 3–6 days. The Thorazine should be in liquid form made up from the hospital concentrate.

The withdrawal procedure is probably best accomplished in a drug-free hospital environment. Following the last dose of methadone, it is preferable to continue the patient in the hospital for an additional 14 days. In actual practice, however, once the patient has received his last dose of methadone, he is more apt to sign out of the hospital against medical advice rather than complete a fuller course of hospitalization. The aforementioned figure of 14 days can be considered an arbitrary one, but hopefully can be used by some patients to reflect upon their lives and work with hospital staff in appropriate post-discharge plans. It is clear that detoxification is a simple but important humanitarian gesture and that following detoxification every effort should be made to assist the patient in getting involved in a long-term rehabilitation program.

BARBITURIC ACID DERIVATIVES

The barbiturates (and opiates) are central nervous system depressants. There are many barbiturate preparations, though the most commonly abused are Nembutal, Seconal, Tuinal, and Sodium Amytal. Abusers may take barbiturates by mouth, intramuscularly, and intravenously. Adolescent abusers seem to prefer Nembutal probably because of its rapid onset of action.

As with heroin, patterns of barbiturate abuse vary widely. There can occur sporadic use resulting in acute intoxication with symptoms resembling those of acute alcohol intoxication. There can occur daily use in quantities sufficient to produce addiction. The symptoms of chronic barbiturate intoxication resemble those of chronic alcoholism, with sensorial clouding, slurred speech, staggering gait, etc. Whatever the pattern of abuse, it is important to emphasize that the barbiturates in question have a high addictive potential. Even with regular abuse, it probably takes longer to become addicted to barbiturates than to heroin. However, absolutely no implication is intended that barbiturate addiction has a better prognosis than heroin addiction.

Detoxification from barbiturate addiction is best done in a hospital setting because of the danger of convulsions. It is important to emphasize that when addiction to barbiturates is clearly established or strongly suspected their use should never be discontinued abruptly. It is equally important to emphasize that only barbiturates should be used in barbiturate withdrawal. Anti-convulsants, including Dilantin sodium, are not effective in preventing or controlling the convulsions which may occur as part of the barbiturate abstinence syndrome.

The author prefers either Elixir of Nembutal or Elixir of Seconal in the treatment of the barbiturate abstinence syndrome. Setting up a barbiturate withdrawal schedule is more complex than determining a methadone schedule for the heroin addict. Also, it can take as long as 3 weeks to complete a barbiturate withdrawal schedule. Appropriate references at the end of this chapter provide valuable material on setting up a barbiturate withdrawal schedule. When available it is probably desirable to call in a consultant if the physician attending the case is inexperienced in this area.

GLUTETHIMIDE (DORIDEN)

Another commonly abused drug among adolescents is Doriden (very often known only to the patient as "Cibas"). Though not a barbituric acid derivative, its clinical effects and symptoms are not distinguishable from those of barbiturate intoxication. The glutethimide abstinence syndrome also resembles the barbiturate abstinence syndrome including the occurrence of *grand mal* type convulsions. As with the barbiturates, when addiction to Doriden is established or strongly suspected their use should not be discontinued abruptly. The author's preference is for the use of Doriden itself (in gradually decreasing dosages) in the treatment of the glutethimide abstinence syndrome.

In setting up a withdrawal schedule a pretty good rule of thumb is to cut the daily intake by 50 percent and proceed from there with gradual reduction. For example, if the daily intake is 4 g, then begin the withdrawal with 500 mg of Doriden q.i.d. for 2 days, then reduce by 250 mg every second or third day. If convulsions occur, additional Doriden should be administered as soon as possible, and consideration should be given to pace the withdrawal more slowly, simply by adding an additional day before the next decrement is scheduled.

METHADONE MAINTENANCE

It should be made clear that methadone hydrochloride can be used as a substitute drug in the treatment of the opiate abstinence syndrome. It is also used on a very protracted basis in high doses, administered by mouth, on a daily basis in order to effect a blockade against heroin in certain cases of heroin addiction. Since 1965, methadone maintenance treatment programs have sprung up throughout the United States and abroad. Their protocols vary greatly; however, the author's preference is for the protocol developed by Dole and Nyswander (1965, 1966). Originally, heroin addicts under the age of 21 were not accepted for the Dole–Nyswander high dosage methadone maintenance program. However, as experience accumulated, the lower age limit was dropped to 18 years as long as the minimum length of addiction to heroin was 2 years and the applicant showed no evidence of dependency on drugs outside the opiate series.

Though the lower age limit was dropped to 18 years in 1969, the first admission of an 18-year-old did not occur to any of the Beth Israel Medical Center (New York City) Methadone Maintenance Treatment Units until September 1970. Admissions in the younger age group have continued in a steady stream, the bulk of them via the ambulatory induction route. In the author's clinical experience, the rehabilitation of the younger patient on the methadone maintenance program has been most impressive. Obviously, more time and experience are needed for a more complete assessment. Also, it would seem to be of the utmost importance to investigate the use of methadone maintenance in the age group below the age of 18. There is enough clinical evidence amassed over the years to indicate, for example, that the child who begins the use of heroin at the age of 11 or 12, and sustains that use for a year or two, will also be a heroin addict at the age of 30. Why one must wait until the youthful addict has been incarcerated several times or has demonstrated numerous non-chemotherapeutic treatment failures before being considered for methadone maintenance is not explicable on medical grounds. As matters now stand, professionals from various disciplines need to spend more time on rehabilitative approaches to heroin addicts, regardless of their ages, and much less time on professionals from various disciplines who are addicted to immobilizing argumentativeness.

REFERENCES

Dole, V. P. and Nyswander, M. E. A medical treatment for diacetylmorphine (heroin) addiction. *JAMA* Aug. 1965, **193**: 646–650.
Dole, V. P., Nyswander, M. E., and Kreek, M. J. Narcotic blockade. *Arch. Intern. Med.*, Oct. 1966, **118**: 304–309.

Suggested Reading
Goodman, L. S. and Gilman, A. (Eds.). *The pharmacological of therapeutics.* New York, Macmillan, 1970.
Wikler, A. Diagnosis and treatment of drug dependence of the barbiturate type. *Amer. J. Psychiat.*, Dec. 1968, **125**: 758–765.

Attitudes Toward Methadone Maintenance

BERNARD LANDER

In this paper we shall examine the attitudes of hard core heroin addicts toward the treatment program of methadone maintenance. The data under consideration comes from 10 in-depth interviews taken in 1969 on the social block of 100th Street between First and Second Avenues in New York City. We cannot extrapolate our findings to a universe of hard core heroin addicts, and we doubt the validity of attempting to construct such a universe. But, we do believe that the following descriptive study represents common attitudes of the urban ghetto addict toward methadone.

According to the sponsors of the maintenance program, methadone given in adequate doses blocks the euphoric effects of heroin and, once the patient has become stabilized on his standard maintenance dose, does not itself produce euphoria, sedation, or distortion of behavior. It is stated that the patients remain alert and functionally normal. This may be true in the case of those addicts who undergo complete "social" rehabilitation through the methadone maintenance program.

The question under consideration is to what extent complete social rehabilitation occurs for the average addict exposed to methadone maintenance. That is, does methadone always succeed in drawing the heroin addict out of the life cycle of de-addiction, away from the addict community, criminal activity, and the use of alcohol and other drugs as substitutes for heroin? Or is methadone simply a half-way house within which non-heroin drug use is reduced, but not terminated, criminal activity is eschewed only as long as the patient is able to hold his job, and alcoholism as a problem runs rampant?

Our following evaluation does not emanate from disinterested scholars or from committed social workers, but rather from hard core street addicts who are scrutinizing the behavior of the "methadone boys" in trying to decide if they themselves should apply for the methadone program. One of our respondents, an ex-addict turned social worker gave us the following testimony.

> I know some methadone boys and I know them well so they tell me honestly. They take methadone and they also use other things. They use bambito. They use liquor, bambito and liquor especially. And they use dope, too. Some shoot dope, too. Bambito is a liquid amphetamine. It's like dexedrine and benzedrine only it's in liquid form. It's a desoxiser. It makes you feel peppy. They call them bams. The methadone boys, some of them, use the bams. They shoot it with a needle to give them a rush. You see methadone keeps you straight, but some fellas are not satisfied with that. Some are. They like the rush and they like the needle. They miss that. You take methadone orally. And some go along with it, usually the old timers, because the kick of the needle and the hustle and all is over for them. They just want to be well. So they get along okay. This is my interpretation. But guys who are still looking for something extra; they want to do something. They shoot the bambito for the rush. They drink and they nod. In other words, they sort of reach the dope high.

The following exchange seems to indicate the same problems.

Q. Now the fella that you were talking about that looked so bad, was he just using methadone or was he doing some other things?

A. He was drinking some wine sometimes and smoking pot, too. Methadone you drink, too. Now, on Friday they give you two small bottles to take home with you. To carry you over the weekend. He used to shoot that up.

Q. From what you hear about shooting it, do you get the rush?

A. You feel better than when you drink it, but not much.

Q. When they have that on the weekend and they shoot it, how much of that do you think is just the idea of the needle, the whole thing that goes with it, the waking up and all that . . .?

A. That's right.

Q. Getting your work out and cleaning your works and getting the cooker and all that — is that part of it, do you think?

A. It's part of it. It's in your mind, too. Sometimes you're not that sick, but you start thinking about it and you think so much about it that you want to get high, and you get worse and you're not really that sick. It's all in your mind.

Q. It's almost like a little ritual. You've got to go through all these steps.

A. Right, to be satisfied.

Q. How many other guys do you know on the methadone program?

A. A few.

Q. How long did they stay on it?

A. I don't know how long they stay on it, but I know they also take drugs. They stay on methadone so they don't get sick; maybe they don't have no money and it comes in pretty handy. But when they got money they don't really care for the methadone. They just want to feel good, to get high.

Q. And they go for dope too?

A. Right, They don't really want to kick the habit, to get a better life or anything. I just want to cut off everything, get a nice little job, and get married, that's all.

Q. Now, a guy could be on methadone and, if he's already straight, he only needs maybe 1 bag a day to get high.

A. Yeh, you're right. He doesn't get sick. He wants to feel that rush. Methadone helps a little bit because when you're sick you get desperate. You do anything so that methadone holds you and you could plan better. You are less likely to hold some one up.

A third respondent also testified to the methadone patient's desire for a rush.

Q. If an addict is on methadone he's probably happy to get a rush once a day.

A. Yeah, that's probably right.

Q. Would it be a surprise to you if a guy who is on the methadone program shot 4 or 5 bags a day?

A. No, I wouldn't be surprised. If they've been taking methadone and they got $30 in their pocket, they're still going to spend it on dope.

Q. Are they going to go looking for that $30 as hard as if they were not on methadone?

A. They're going to shoot it.

Q. Are they going to go looking for that $30 as hard as if they were not on methadone?

A. No. If they are on methadone they won't look for it that hard.

Q. If it falls in their lap they squat on it.

A. Right. They won't take the chance of being busted because they really don't need it.

Though the de-addiction process may not be complete for several methadone patients, the street addict is well aware of the advantages of the program, as the next interview indicates.

Q. How long does the program last in the hospital?

A. A couple of months.

Q. A couple of weeks, I think?

A. No, you got to stay there a couple of months. If you sign out before that you won't get it, because they know that you're not interested.

Q. Do you know any guys on the methadone program, and let's assume that they shoot dope or bams, but who are working and getting by?

A. Yeah. This Robles; he never worked before when he was using drugs, but since he's on this methadone program he started working right away.

Q. How hard is it to kick a methadone habit?

A. Right. I know a guy who was on the methadone program for 8 months and he got busted. It took him 2 or 3 months to get it out of his system. To feel good, right . . . it affects the bowel, too.

Another respondent who declined to go on the methadone program stated:

> They asked me over here if I wanted to get on the program. I said no; I didn't want it. I didn't want to kick one habit to get back to a worse habit.

This attitude until very recently has been quite prevalent among the general population, but most heroin addicts are well aware of the differences between heroin addiction and methadone maintenance.

In the follow-up study (1969–1970), of 29 former heroin addicts from the same block (100th Street), most demonstrated some support for the methadone program although only 2 of them had themselves been methadone patients. Only 6 replied "no" to the question: "Do you consider someone doing well on the methadone maintenance program to be an ex-addict?" All 6 gave the same reason, that one was still hooked on a drug if he took methadone. Eighteen of the 29 former heroin addicts rated the methadone maintenance program as being somewhat effective to very effective. Of all the 6 treatment programs mentioned in our ex-addict questionnaire, methadone maintenance was given the best evaluation. Phoenix House and Synanon were rated as "somewhat effective" by 10 of these respondents.

Attitudes of heroin addicts and ex-heroin addicts toward methadone maintenance are usually determined by a philosophy of life that is fostered by the treatment program within which they have found the most success. The following excerpts indicate that each addict is drawn into the program that most fulfills his emotional and physiological needs. However, it is also evident that a long period of exposure to a definite de-addiction philosophy and some success under a corresponding treatment program are largely responsible for the following attitudes expressed toward the methadone maintenance program.

Manhattan State Hospital

#1. **Q.** What have you heard about other programs?
A. Methadone: I like what I've heard and seen. I'm kind of enthused with it. Synanon and Daytop are a lot of shit, Ramirez included. First you get put down and then you become dependent on them.
Q. What do you think is the best way of handling drug addiction?

A. First detoxification. Then group and individual therapy where the patient is ready, but I feel that the patient must have gotten his lumps to get the message.

#2. **Q.** What have you heard about other programs?

A. The methadone maintenance program isn't any good. It's a habit. I would never send anyone to it. It's like a high; it gives you a false sense of security. All those programs are alike; they're all treating the narcotics problem as a business.

Damascus

#1. **Q.** If addicts can't become Christians, at least they can accomplish something with Synanon and Daytop's programs.

A. Philosophically, I don't agree with Synanon. I don't agree with other anti-society philosophy. An addict should be able to come back into society and be able to function. As for the methadone maintenance, I saw patients at Lexington who were stoned all the time. It's like heroin. If there was ever a panic, I'd tell addicts to go to the methadone program.

#2. **Q.** What have you heard about other programs?

A. The methadone program isn't any good; you're just back on the streets with the same problem. Synanon could be good, since they have a philosophy that you can use as a foundation. If a program has a philosophy, then it's good. With a philosophy, you can build a foundation so you can confront society. Then you could go on the street.

#3. **Q.** What have you heard about other programs?

A. Most of the other programs may get at the symptoms, but they do not try to change a person deep down. Living up heroin and drinking is no solution. Groups like Phoenix House do not accept the religious approach; in fact they are somewhat anti-religious. Psychology cannot get at the moral or spiritual problems. Many persons, addicts, go in and out of hospitals and its unending cycle. Addiction is a symptom of sin, a symptom of spiritual disease. The real problem is to change the addict's nature totally.

Cyclazocine

#1. What have you heard about other drugs?

A. I was offered the methadone maintenance program, but to me that's another drug. I really don't think that there is one way to clean up drugs. It's important to find the best program to suit each individual. Drug addiction is a personality problem and good therapy is important.

#2. **Q.** What have you heard about other programs?

A. I've heard about different programs. Synanon is very good, if you want to be swallowed up in that way of life; however, you lose your identity and that's why this program would not be good for me. Methadone isn't for me either, because I want to be drug-free. At the end of this month I expect to be able to be free of cyclazocine, too. Methadone is great for the street junkie; it's the only answer. Methadone patients should be encouraged to go on cyclazocine, but those that can't and those that lack the motivation should be continued on methadone. As far as the religious programs are concerned, I have no interest whatsoever in them.

Methadone Maintenance

#1. **Q.** How do you feel about your last program, and others which you have experienced?

A. Methadone maintenance program at Rockefeller Institute. It's the greatest thing going. It's concrete; it works if a person sticks by the rules; he's got a real good chance.

Q. What have you heard about other programs?

A. I've heard about a number of programs. They are all good if they can benefit someone. Synanon: they break your spirit, like they shave people's heads. If they don't want a husband or wife to associate with each other, they send them to different places. Who the hell do they think they are?

#2. **Q.** How do you feel about your last program and others which you have experienced?

A. Methadone maintenance: I think it's great. I'm no longer in jail, stealing, or having to hustle. All the other programs I was in were at best so, so.

#3. **Q.** How do you feel about your last program?

A. The methadone maintenance program is only good for one type of individual. That is for people who can work and function if they're off drugs. Places like Synanon are good for those who can't function even if they are off drugs.

Q. What do you think is the best way of handling drug addiction?

A. I think there should be different programs for different people, depending on their needs and problems. Synanon is good for those who can't take care of their hang-ups and they've been taken off heroin. Sometimes I resent the way the methadone program treats a patient like a child. If you're going away for a weekend you have to prove it, and they make you bring in the same bottle so as to prevent people from selling the methadone. I'd say that's pretty stupid 'cause you don't have to sell the methadone in the same bottle that they gave you.

The purpose of quoting these interviews at length was not simply to reveal the misconceptions and antagonisms that patients of these various treatment programs have toward Methadone Maintenance, Synanon, and Damascus House.

A close examination demonstrates that there is a common thread throughout all these partisan statements, especially those that seem to contradict each other. This common thread lies in the area of emotional and physiological dependence, a central problem in the life situation of both the heroin addict and ex-heroin addict. The hard core heroin addict who desires to kick is well aware of his dependence on heroin and, at least on some level, is aware of his needs to transfer this dependence from the totally destructive use of heroin to some other healthier preoccupation of the mind and body. For the most part, the heroin addict is ambivalent toward this need for successful substitution.

At certain points in his career of heroin use the hard core addict is willing to try anything to achieve temporary periods of abstention, but gnawing at him is the deep conviction that there is a weakness within him that has reduced him to this complete state of dependence. Therefore, it is important for the heroin patient's self-image that he feel he is exerting a latent power of self-reliance as he continues through the process of de-addiction.

But the American fundamentalist world view holds that independence or self-reliance can only emerge after a long period of pain, struggle, and suffering. This explains the Synanon and Damascus patient's attitude that the methadone maintenance program is only for lazy addicts, or desperate street addicts, and even if one kicks heroin on methadone, he is addicted; that is, he is still in a state of dependence. Synanon patients would cringe at the charge by any methadone patients that Synanon is a complete cop-out on life and is for people who could not even function normally in society when they are not under addiction to heroin. Neither allegation is more valid than the other. The need for this mechanism of transference or substitution is intrinsic to the process of de-addiction.

From this study we can learn that it is vital to the image of the heroin patient to see his own power of self-reliance as the most crucial element in making a final abstention from heroin. The fact that in almost every situation and treatment program he will at least initially be dependent on therapy, religion, or medicine, does not diminish the importance of the addict's strong sense of self-reliance. In the case of Methadone Maintenance we feel it is necessary that heroin addicts be given a more accurate description. It is true, as the first excerpts quoted in this paper pointed out, that it is possible to "cheat" on methadone although the better administered programs diminish this practice. The important point is that Methadone Maintenance does have a philosophy – simply, it is that if the physical demand for heroin is blocked, the patient then has the potential to be socially rehabilitated. At that point it is a combination of the heroin addict's personal strength in conjunction with the program's offering of job training and therapy that will determine the success or failure of the de-addiction process. Though relying on a synthetic drug, the methadone maintenance program can no longer be considered to be an "easy" or "dehumanized" treatment to achieve successful completion of the de-addiction process.

Group Therapy in the Treatment of the
Juvenile Narcotic Addict:
A Review of the Findings

JOHN LANGROD

Relatively little work has been done until recently with the juvenile narcotic addict, who, for the purposes of this paper, will be defined as a person under 20 years of age who has abused and/or has become addicted to heroin and/or other narcotic drugs. The first treatment response to this problem was group therapy led by trained professionals at Riverside Hospital in New York City. However, the results of treatment as measured by abstinence in the community subsequent to discharge showed an extremely high rate of relapse. In response to the current heroin epidemic, other forms of treatment are being tried; these include therapeutic communities on the Synanon model which utilize the rehabilitated former addict as both group leader and role model. In addition, research involving chemotherapy, generally long-term detoxification with methadone in low doses of 20–40 mg per day has been widely carried out.

In the absence of a systematic evaluation and follow-up in the literature, the author proposes to review some of the available findings with the purpose of assessing the effectiveness and applicability of group therapy in the treatment of the juvenile narcotic addict. Group therapy will be defined as therapy occurring in a group context designed to accomplish attitudinal and behavioral change. In terms of orientation, it may range from psychoanalytically oriented groups led by professionals to encounter therapy led by ex-addicts or other lay persons.

We shall now examine some treatment programs which utilize group therapy or encounter techniques in treating the adolescent addict.

197

SURVEY OF PROGRAMS

The first facility to deal exclusively with the treatment of the adolescent addict was Riverside Hospital in New York City. This was a residential program for adolescent addicts, referred through the courts, where the
tools of treatment were individual and group therapy coupled with
vocational and educational remediation. The program was adequately
funded and staffed. Patients were treated by a team of psychiatrists,
psychologists, and social workers. Research was done into the feasibility
of mixing addicts and non-addicts in groups. These results showed some
promise according to Einstein and Jones (1965). However, follow-ups
done by Trussel *et al.* (1959), Gerard *et al.* (1956), and Amsel *et al.* (1971)
show that despite the intensive psychiatric treatment and vocational
training, the rate of relapse to heroin was high. For details see Table 2.

Odyssey House — Adolescent Treatment Unit

Odyssey House, as a treatment agency, has been in existence since
1966 and was designed originally to treat the adult narcotic user. The
establishment of the adolescent treatment unit grew out of the concern of
Odyssey's founder Dr. Judyanne Densen-Gerber about the lack of treatment facilities for addicts under the age of 16.

At the present time, Odyssey House has two adolescent treatment
units, one for boys and the other for girls. Dr. Densen-Gerber believes
that addiction is an epidemic disease which spreads from one person to
another, and that it is a peer group phenomenon reflective of drug oriented
values found in society, rather than simply a symptom of individual
psychopathology (Densen-Gerber and Murphy, 1971).

Odyssey House combines the use of ex-addicts and professionals in a
therapeutic community setting. The average age of the patients in the
adolescent treatment group is 16.4 years. Treatment results have not as
yet been described in the literature.

Encounter therapy including peer group pressure is used in a drug-free
setting as a principal tool for treatment. The type of drug abused is not
considered as important as the fact that drug abuse is indicative of destructive social behavior which interferes with maturation.

Bayview Rehabilitation Center

The New York State Narcotic Addiction Control Commission
(NACC) in response to the heroin epidemic has also developed a special-
ized treatment program for court committed adolescent addicts at the
Bayview Rehabilitation Center. Calof (1971) reports that 54 percent of

adolescents are being treated on a specialized ward. Paraprofessionals and narcotic corrections officers who work on this ward are selected because of their maturity. Groups are conducted by counselors who are college graduates as well as by some specially trained narcotic corrections officers and successfully treated graduates of the NACC program. Groups are reality oriented and leaders are trained and supervised by the staff psychologist. Bayview residents are committed by the courts. Adolescents are confined for a longer period of time than older addicts. For further details see Table 2.

Encounter, Inc. grew out of a community meeting held in 1966 to discuss drug abuse problems in Greenwich Village. Initially, a day treatment center was established with the assistance of a small grant from a private foundation with the Greenwich Village Peace Center providing rent free offices. Initially, Encounter served as an induction center for hard core addicts into Daytop Village, in addition to being a counseling day center for youthful pre-addicts.

Encounter has shifted its focus from referral and treatment of the hard core addict to the problem of the youthful non-narcotic drug abuser and his adjustment in the community. There has been a shift away from the severe encounter techniques which were developed by the therapeutic communities such as Synanon, Daytop, and Phoenix House. It was felt that these techniques adversely affected many of the young patients who sought help and caused others to drop out.

The retention of persons under the age of 18 has been lower than for older patients. Attempts are being made to find new ways of reaching those under 18 years of age. At present, the groups are reality oriented without the sharp confrontations and head shavings found in the traditional therapeutic communities.

Cage Teen Center for Drug Prevention

Cage Teen Center, Inc. was organized in 1962 by a group of residents of White Plains, New York who were concerned by the lack of recreational facilities for young people. The Cage Drug Prevention project was organized in 1968 as a result of increasing drug abuse among young people. At present, the Cage treatment program consists of an all-day therapeutic community. Parents and relatives are also participants.

It is expected that the patient will break with his drug oriented life. Reality therapy is used and traditional therapeutic community techniques such as shouting, verbal abuse, and head shaving are avoided. The Cage program is oriented to returning patients to full community life. Ex-addicts serve as rehabilitation aids with primary responsibility for treatment residing with professional staff members. Clientele served is predominantly white (77 percent), and middle class, reflective of the population of Westchester.

Only half of the treatment population (51 percent) was using heroin as the principal drug of abuse. Plans are being developed for a residential treatment center as well as a follow-up study to learn more about patients who have left the program. (Yomtov, 1971.)

Lafayette Clinic, Detroit, Michigan

The last program to be examined will be the Lafayette Clinic which treats a predominantly white middle-class patient population. This program, in addition to providing compulsory group psychotherapy for both the patient and his parents, assists the teen-age addict in coping with his addiction problem by maintaining the patient on low doses of methadone (5–70 mg per day). Although one of the final goals of treatment is withdrawal from methadone, a great deal of stress is placed on resolving problems which the patient encounters in school, social life, and interpersonal relations. Economic deprivation appears to play a less prominent role with this group, since the cost of treatment was $30–$40 per week. Groups are directed by the psychiatrists and psychiatric social workers.

An examination of treatment programs must address itself to at least three areas—screening criteria, retention in treatment, and social adjustment in the community.

In the case of voluntary treatment programs, screening criteria play a role in determining the extent to which applicants follow through and enter treatment. Only two programs have published this data.

Table 1

Program	Time period	Number of applicants	Number and % admitted to treatment	Source of information
Encounter, Inc.	12 months (1970)	321	64 (20%)	Encounter, Inc. 1971
Cage Center for Drug Prevention	12 months (1970)	248	124 (50%)	Yomtov 1971

The above statistics indicate that a substantial proportion of applicants, at least in the case of two programs, did not enter treatment because they were unable to meet the screening criteria of the programs. Encounter, Inc. required at least two visits prior to admission, and Cage required applicants to remain drug-free and attend groups for 3 days to 1 week.

Encounter is presently reassessing its screening criteria so as to involve a higher percentage of applicants in treatment.

PATIENT RETENTION IN TREATMENT

On the basis of the limited data available, Lowinson and Zwerling (1971) have found treatment retention and successful completion of treatment rates to be rather low for adult narcotic addicts in abstention oriented programs which use group or encounter therapy. Table 2 shows results of an examination of available data for programs treating the youthful addict with group or encounter therapy.

The limited data available on treatment completion by adolescents in drug-free programs utilizing group therapy appear no more promising than for adults. This has led some of the programs treating the adolescent to seek out the social and psychological correlates of retention in treatment. Biase (1971) reports that adolescent heroin addicts who left Phoenix House prior to completion of treatment received significantly higher Depression scores on the Multiple Affect Adjective Check List than those who remained in treatment. No significant differences were noted between the two groups on Anxiety and Hostility scores. Heller and Mordkoff (1972) have found that patients with a history of heroin abuse are more likely to leave treatment earlier than non-narcotic drug abusers.

These findings would suggest a need to develop specialized therapeutic techniques to enhance retention in treatment. Biase's (1971) findings regarding the depressed patient's greater likelihood of leaving an ex-addict-run therapeutic community (Phoenix House) reinforces Harms' warning elsewhere in this book about some of the pitfalls inherent in ex-addict-run encounter groups. The appropriateness of encounter therapy for depressed addict-patients should be carefully evaluated.

The third area, social adjustment in the community, including abstention from addictive drugs is the final measure of treatment effectiveness. This is also the area in which least data are available because longitudinal follow-ups present great methodological problems.

The final problem areas that a treatment program should address itself to are the relevance of the treatment to therapeutic goals. In addiction treatment this would mean acceptable social functioning in the community, including at the very least not becoming re-addicted to drugs. An

Table 2 Summary of treatment follow-up of adolescent patients.

Name and Location of program	Type of program	Age at admission to program	Number of patients	% With History of narcotic abuse	% Fully completing treatment	% Leaving prior to completion of treatment	% Remaining abstinent on follow-up in community	Length of observation	Source
Riverside Hospital New York City	Residential treatment program for court referred adolescent narcotic addicts	"Adolescents"	30	100%	Not stated	Not stated	7% No relapse, no police trouble, 13% unknown	12 months	Gerard et al. 1956
Riverside Hospital New York City	Professionally run group therapy used	Mean age 18.1 years	247	100%	Not stated	Not stated	4% lost to contact	$2\frac{1}{2}$ to 3 years	Trussel et al. 1959
Riverside Hospital New York City	Professionally run group therapy used	Mean Age 18.1 years	247	100%	Not stated	Not stated	30% had no reports as addicts to the Narcotics Register for at least 7 years	13 years	Amsel et al. 1971
Encounter, Inc. New York City	Day center using modified encounter techniques	Under 18 years 25% 18–21 years 60%	71	Not stated	8%	68%	Not stated	12 months	Encounter, Inc. 1971

Encounter, Inc. New York City	Day center using modified encounter techniques	Mean age 19 years	67	33%	Not stated	16%	Not stated	2 months	Heller & Mordkoff 1972
Cage White Plains, New York	Day center using modified encounter techniques	Mean age 19 years Median 18 years	124	56%	4%	52%	Not stated	12 months	Yomtov 1971
Lafayette Clinic Grosse Point, Michigan	Compulsory group therapy and long term methadone detoxification	Group 1 19.4 years Group 2 18.9 years	20 patients 10 in each group	100% for both groups	—	Group 1 10% Group 2 30%	*Group 1 84–90% in treatment *Group 2 76–80% in treatment	5 months Group 1 3 months Group 2	Schoof & Stenzek 1971

*During the last month of follow-up percent of urines taken on a twice weekly basis free of heroin or quinine.

204   John Langrod

evaluation of treatment outcome requires a follow-up of the patient in the
community. O'Donnell (1965) discusses some of the methodological
problems involved in this endeavor.

Of the studies summarized in Table 2, only three — Gerard *et al.* (1956),
Trussell *et al.* (1959), and Amsel *et al.* (1971) have followed up the patients for an appreciable period of time after initiation of treatment. In all
three studies the rate of relapse to drugs has been high, ranging from at
least 70 percent to 92 percent of the patients. It should be noted that the
Amsel *et al.* (1971) study is the longest post-treatment follow-up of
adolescent narcotic addicts. Thirteen years after receiving group therapy
at Riverside Hospital, only 30 percent of the original 247 patients *might*
be considered abstinent from drugs. Presumptive abstinence is based on
the fact that the patient's name was not reported to the New York City
Narcotics Register as an addict for at least 7 years. Whether this pre-
sumed abstinence is a result of the patient's having received group therapy
is not as important as the fact that 70 percent of the original sample of
adolescent patients was either still addicted, or dead 13 years later.

DISCUSSION AND IMPLICATIONS FOR TREATMENT

On the basis of the limited data available, group or encounter therapy
alone does not appear to be effective in keeping the adolescent narcotic
user from becoming re-addicted. Other forms of treatment should be
utilized in addition to groups. Methadone maintenance treatment appears
to show some promise for the hard core adolescent addicts. See Millman
and Nyswander (1971) and Nightingal *et al.* (1971).

Brill (1968) has pointed out that "It is necessary to develop a variety of
treatment modalities geared to help the various types of addicts." As long
as professionals continue to remain inflexible in the face of new approaches
and techniques it will be more difficult to cope with the drug epidemic
which afflicts society.

REFERENCES

Amsel, Z., Fishman, J. J., Rivkind, L., Kavaler, F., Krug, D., Cline, M., Brophy, F., and
Conwell, D. The use of the narcotic register for follow-up of a cohort of adolescent
addicts. *Int. J. Addict.*, June 1971, **6** (2): 225–239.
Biase, D. V. Adolescent heroin abusers in a therapeutic community. *Report of the 33rd
Annual Scientific Meeting Committee on Problems of Drug Dependence*, Washington,
D.C. 1971. P. 1008.
Brill, L. Three approaches to the casework treatment of narcotic addicts. *Social Work*,
April 1968, **13**: 2, 25–35.

Calof, J. *Observations on five residential facilities of the State of New York Narcotic Addiction Control Commission.* New York, July 1971. Community Service Society (mimeographed report). Pp. 29–43.

Densen-Gerber, J. A. and Murphy, J. P. *The changing face of addiction: An adolescent confrontation.* Presented at the Annual Meeting of the American Psychiatric Association, Washington, D.C., May 3–7, 1971.

Einstein, S. and Jones, F. Group therapy with adolescent addicts. *Drug addiction in youth.* E. Harms (Ed.), Pergamon Press, New York, 1965.

Encounter, Inc. *Personality drug abuse and treatment: Recent research findings.* New York, March 1971 (mimeographed report).

Encounter, Inc. *Statistical summary of growth (January 1, 1971–June 30, 1971).* New York, 1971.

Gerard, D. L., Lee, R. S., Rosenfeld, E., and Chein. I. *Post-hospitalization adjustment: A follow-up study of adolescent opiate addicts.* Research Center for Human Relations, New York University, Oct. 1956. P. 26.

Heller, M. E. and Mordkoff, A. E. Personality attributes of the young non-addicted drug abuser. *Int. J. Addict.,* Jan.–Feb. 1972, 7: 1.

Lowinson, J. H. and Zwerling, I. Group therapy with narcotic addicts. *Comprehensive group psychotherapy.* H. I. Kaplan and B. J. Sadock (Eds.), Williams and Wilkins Baltimore, Md., 1971. Pp. 602–622.

Millman, R. B. and Nyswander, M. E. Slow detoxification of adolescent heroin addicts in New York City. *Proceedings of the Third National Conference on Methadone Treatment.* U.S. Government Printing Office, Washington, D.C. 1971. Pp. 88–90.

Nightingale, S. L., Wurmser, L., Platt, P. C., and Michaux, W. W. Adolescents on methadone: Preliminary observations. *Proceedings of the Third National Conference on Methadone Treatment.* U.S. Government Printing Office, Washington, D.C. 1971. Pp. 91–98.

O'Donnell, J. The relapse rate in narcotic addiction: A critique of follow-up studies. *Narcotics.* Wilner and Kassenbaum (Eds.). McGraw-Hill, New York, 1965. Pp. 226–246.

Schoof, K. G. and Stanczak, S. A methadone withdrawal program for young heroin addicts. *Proceedings of the Committee on Drug Dependence.* National Research Council, Washington, D.C. 1971. Pp. 1904–19.

Trussel, R. E., Alksne, H., Elinson, J., and Patrick, S. A follow-up study of treated adolescent narcotic users. Columbia University School of Public Health and Administrative Medicine, New York, May 1959 (mimeographed report), p. 42.

Yomtov, J. *The Cage Center for Drug Prevention.* White Plains, New York, 1971 (mimeographed report).

Psychotherapy With the Juvenile Drug Addict*

ERNEST HARMS

Proposals for open discussion of psychological involvement in addiction and expressions of belief in applying psychotherapy have often met with claims that psychology has little to offer in the treatment of addicts. The reasons given are many, but the decisive statement seems to be that for the most part dogmatism has prevailed and addiction continues to spread. There seems to be little willingness to study the psychology of the drug abuser who needs and wants the kind of assistance psychology has to offer. To charge that Freudian psychoanalysis is meaningless is like saying that a cancer can be suppressed without the aid of medical therapy administered by a physician.

I believe that the strongest forces behind addiction are psychological in character and that the practitioner who wishes to help his patient, especially the youthful addict, extirpate his craving for drugs must feel the challenge posed by what is still, for the most part, a riddle. Armed with nothing more than some of the patent medicines of psychological treatment now in use, of course he is doomed to fail to lift the burden from his patient's back. Addiction psychotherapy, like criminal psychotherapy, involves a great deal of highly individual attention. As one psychiatrist has said, "Each of these young people has in him more problems and confusion than you will find in my entire hospital ward." A therapist must listen intently, and be willing to probe with a mind open to all the means

*Because of the special structure given to this volume, the Psychological and Psychotherapeutic sections have been separated and appear in different places in the book.

within his experience. He must also be sensitive enough to see and have the quick wit to grasp opportunities for applying necessary psychotherapy.

Three areas of pathology which must be given deep concern are: (1) the psychopathology which might have existed prior and parallel to the addiction psychopathology. This might be constitutional, or environmentally induced; (2) the actual addiction pathology—its history, its withdrawal problems, and possible after-effects; and (3) the social pathology—the upheavals with jobs, social relations, religion, school, and profession.

These targets are two-faceted, involving the present picture of disintegration and the frustrations of past futile attempts to reconstruct relationships or to develop some where none existed before. I hear a psychiatrist sitting with a patient thinking, "How can one deal with all these problems simultaneously?" The answer is that one cannot; it takes time to sift through them, to chart a plan of action, and to battle against them. However, one does not need to "fill out" a 45- or 60-minute session by routine inventory questioning. Five or 10 minutes on a street corner, on the stoop of a brownstone, or at a coffee house table can do as much or more than a dozen full sessions of the "swivel chair" type. Some therapists have used the academic term "subculture" to describe addicted youth. This is a basically wrong use of the term. Addiction is not inherent in the concept of culture. Despair, poverty, distrust, disorientation, and a narcotic-supported unreality bind thousands of American youths into a similar behavior group to make their existence more bearable.

The idea that therapy lifts people "out of the mud" must be abandoned. This attitude is disparaging and patronizing. If one wants to be psychotherapist to teen-age addicts, one must also abandon the jargon of psychiatry textbooks and the technology of the social worker. A new, undogmatic approach must be developed in which the therapist functions on a direct human level, using his creative imagination to project himself into the addict's life design to understand the elements that prevent some from being able to open themselves to the wider world in which most of us cope. This is an important step in helping youth get back on their feet. Many psychotherapists are put off from treating addicts by this test of their personal stamina and art.

It has been said that many addicts are hostile to the psychotherapeutic approach. If this is so, it may be due in large part to the psychotherapist. Clearly, the process of transference in addiction is difficult, unstable, and one which cannot proceed with predictable continuity. The shifting evolvement of adolescence coupled with the weaknesses of the addictive personality demand what I call "floating transference." This requires agility in adjusting to the quickly changing conditions. Transference may start in the way to which we have become accustomed, but then be interrupted, lightning-like, by episodes of violent doubt and distrust; absurd questions seemingly remote to the point at issue may be asked. The therapist's pursuit of a cue will be arrested as he himself may suddenly feel caught up in the fleeting mood changes, but he will have to recover his equilibrium to go back, undiscouraged and with calm demeanor, through a perilous period of starting all over again with his patient.

Most addicts we meet want help, want to escape from dependence. This is a promising beginning. It is our task to build from this impulse, insecure though it may be, a personality edifice made up of inner self-confidence and an outgoingness to others. Catharsis is only one ingredient of the formula for fitness; for catharsis alone presents the danger of depressive withdrawal.

Most addicts are afflicted by a variety of phobic elements: fear of being caught, of being punished, of losing last holds, of not getting the "dope" desperately needed, of being without funds, and so on. These phobias seriously resist or interfere with psychotherapeutic attempts at healthy inner consolidation.

Of course, the overcoming of these phobic states, especially in the young, are greatly dependent on trust and transference to the psychotherapeutic agent. A relationship with a professional cannot be replaced by one with a group, relatives, or friends. Phobias need professional handling to be dissolved; otherwise, they may transfer to others. I have encountered several cases where a phobia created by the addiction transferred inappropriately; in one case it transferred into claustrophobia.

Guilt feelings, which tend to remain half conscious or unconscious, because they are more intimate and ego-involved, should not be dealt with until a certain trust has been established.

Viewed psychotherapeutically, drug addiction is a specific syndrome in the approach to which certain basic procedures are to be followed. Later on, we shall enumerate the differences among the varieties of addiction and the specific therapeutic approaches to them. Here we must establish first some basic similarities among the forms of addiction.

Psychopathologically, drug addiction is an externally and chemically induced pathology. We mentioned above the need to differentiate between drug psychopathology and any previously existing pathology of constitutional or environmental origin. Drug addiction is always a kind of toxic neurosis or psychosis. We have to view it in its active state. Of far-reaching importance are the after-effects drugs produce. We frequently find in adolescents, especially females, a pre-addiction neurotic phobic state resulting from a fear of change of consciousness which is initiated by a feeling of insecurity. Someone has compared this experience with stage fright, or the fear of entering an airplane. In this we encounter the engagement of the unconscious in drug addiction, which is still totally virgin land.

We have had countless reports from addicted individuals about their experiences when "they are high" or "on a trip." There is no doubt that even in the frequently unpleasant initial stage of drug taking the desire to "become doped" is strong.

Questions which I believe should be probed seriously by the psychotherapist are: What are the elements involved in the desire? In what way can one influence, overcome, or eliminate them? There is a variety of drives leading to the initial experience, depending on the drugs used; but underlying them is the basic one of motivation. One can apply counter-motivations, reason with an addict, take the emotional approach, offer him warmth, or threaten him with exposure and imprisonment. All of these have the same basic motivation. They all are pretty much within conscious experience.

Today, many people working to eliminate drug addiction claim that conscious motivations are unable to overcome the dependency impulse. They believe that only a chemical counter-agent can eliminate craving. They also claim that methadone medication can eliminate heroin addiction. Unfortunately, turning the addict away from heroin and on to methadone does not solve the major prior problem which is to turn the addict away from all drugs. General addiction to methadone is developing. Bottles with methadone taps are floating in the underground market. A new drug wave is underway.

There is only one certain way to extinguish drug dependency, and that is through abstinence prompted by a self-motivated desire to be "clean." We already know much of the complexity of the motivational sphere surrounding drug abuse. Clearly, it is not a simple matter to design a workable rehabilitation program.

A great deal has been written to the effect that drug habituation has its causes in the impact of modern technology on our way of life – our government, our social circumstances, our education, ourselves. Blame can be placed on many factors outside ourselves. We may have a president with whom we disagree strongly, and we have inflation and poverty, but you cannot blame them for everything. The problems we attribute to unhappy conditions are the reflections of our own discontent. In this respect, an important goal of therapists should be the coordination of individual psychotherapy with adjustment to the social environment, or improvement of that environment. General motivation studies and statements regarding the desperate conditions causing drug abuse will achieve nothing so long as they are not immediately applicable. They must be applicable not only to the conditions but also to the individual personalities. The major reason for our lack of success in spite of enormous effort is the creation of generalized and abstract plans instead of a willingness to work on a one-to-one basis with each to whom we wish to extend help.

There are three considerations which have to be emphasized in a preliminary approach. First is that a tangential approach ought not to have the form of sterile, dogmatic questioning. Even an inventory of a person must be undertaken with the specific individual who concerns us at that moment. A student may be a student, but he is a student of a special kind. We are overwhelmed today by a mass of tests which do not leave room for contemplation of individualized psychological impulses. They may be determined by latent or unconscious impulses, but they are the primary ones.

The second aspect concerns the specification of drug therapy. Most of the case presentations we read, whether they have the personality profile in view or psychopathology, are not clearly designed for any therapeutic task. Much of the material we find in such case histories is devoid of any prescription for eliminating drug dependency. Effective drug psychotherapy demands a disciplined program with the individual therapeutic aim clearly in mind. This is the only way we can hope to treat successfully.

A third view admits the clear differences among the various kinds of addiction. In most treatment facilities, all dependencies are dealt with alike. Whether the dependency is on a solvent, marijuana, heroin, amphetamines, barbiturates, or LSD, no psychological differences are acknowledged. In general medicine, when treating virus patients afflicted with different bacterias, do we simply treat the fever, or do we administer serums for the specific virus causing the fever? The concern should be the same in drug treatment. We must learn to see the variety of conditions caused by different drugs. Even this is not totally satisfactory if we wish to succeed. I have made it my job to separate the various types of cravings. I have pointed up three specific types of marijuana addiction and four types of heroin addiction. Similar differentiations can be made among other drugs. If we wish to achieve a full cure we must treat different addictions differently. There is a further differentiation to be made among beginners, "drug-heads" (those severely addicted), and individuals in an after-care state, following detoxification treatment, or in a withdrawal state.

In outlining the basic phases of psychotherapy with drug addiction, we should mention here the role psychotherapy is assuming in handling the young addict. We must differentiate between main and supporting treatment. Supporting treatment is questionable if the youth is otherwise under medical care or is institutionalized for educational or penal purposes, or if he has been admitted to institutionalized detoxification treatment. Supporting treatment must adjust itself to the given circumstances and also may be considerably limited in time. Certain institutions make various forms of group treatment the major psychotherapeutic impact. At the end of this presentation we shall have a discussion of our view regarding group therapy in general and a comparison with individual therapy. Most of the institutions emphasizing group or encounter therapy limit individual psychotherapy to a minimum, or push it totally into the background.

On the following pages we will outline some fundamentals of such differences in treatment. We feel we should remind the reader again that this is merely an outline for familiarization with the basic concepts. It cannot be extended to include advice for application in any individual treatment attempt.

The earliest type of drug abuse we see is the sniffing of solvents, beginning with the sniffing of glue by junior airplane builders. Playfulness and adventure seeking are part of the scene, just as secret cigarette smoking was in earlier generations. In my youth we were forced to smoke a big heavy cigar (which resulted in a vomiting spell) to cure us of our desire to smoke. Youngsters today seem to have little difficulty withdrawing from solvents even when punitive corrective means are applied. "Insight," if it is not merely intellectual, but also emotion- and achievement-oriented, will, for most, eliminate such habituation. There is one limitation to this, however, namely, if the youngster is in the second "no saying" period. In this case, one may have quite a struggle. Suggestions made by Benjamin* and Spitz,† designed for normal youngsters, may do the trick here: the double negative. "I myself don't like to go to bed or clean my plate, but this or that disagreeable or unfortunate thing may happen to me as a consequence of this." Turning away. After a while the desired result will be achieved.

Pre-adolescents who have started with ether or paint remover or other

*Benjamin, E., Hanselmann, H., and Iserlin, M. *Lehrbuch der Psychopathologie des Kindesalters*. Rotapfel Verlag, 1938.
†Spitz, Rene. *A genetic field theory of ego formation*. Intern. Univ. Press, 1959.

such inhalants, and who may show physical damage, have done so chiefly because they have failed in some ways to achieve what they are striving for, or feel unable to make headway in their studies. They suffer from constant headache. Therapeutically, one may be successful by substituting some kind of compensatory impulse. Students have been induced to replace ether with eau de Cologne.

The problem of euphoric addiction may be explained in a limited discussion of the marijuana problem. There are contradictory opinions about marijuana, but one thing seems to be valid—that most of the psychological impact of marijuana is of an euphoric character. I have previously tried to show that some of the contradictory claims result from the fact that there are different types of marijuana influence. We were clearly able to establish three types. Of course, these three types must also—and this is the purpose of our presentation—receive different therapeutic approaches.

However, before we can present this therapeutic differentiation, we must outline the psychological characteristics which distinguish one drug of euphoric effect from another. Euphoria is fundamentally a psychic activation which rests on a positive "uplifting" impulse. If this effect becomes—as it does in marijuana smoking—negatively directed, our therapeutic task is clearly to turn the negative impulse into a positive one. In other words, we have to transfer the desire for marijuana into another euphoric impulse with no negative side effects of the type described in our presentation of pathology. It means that we leave the addict his euphoria, but try to create it in some other way.

This kind of psychotherapy is not simple to accomplish and it is not likely to be successful if executed by dogmatic psychotherapeutic concepts as, for instance, psychoanalysis. We must fulfill a fourfold approach—physiological, individual and social psychological, and educational. There is the theoretical technical view to which must be added what is strongly active in the somatic picture of addiction, namely, specific typological difference. We have differentiated (1) the intoxicative marijuana smoker, (2) the collective smoker for whom marijuana is an expression and outlet of togetherness, and (3) the actual marijuana addict who cannot function without it.

Briefly, (1) the intoxicant is a lone smoker who doubtless needs an immediate and personal approach. His euphoric marijuana desire is always tied to certain personal tendencies and impulses. Therefore, we have to go into his specific character traits and desires to find material for redirecting his impulses. He is also apt to acknowledge negative impact. He may have experienced unpleasant effects from marijuana and he might be receptive to avoiding these impacts by exchanging the marijuana intake for something more pleasant that we might be able to suggest to him. Social and professional contacts may also be important in playing a certain role in his decision to give up his habit.

(2) Adolescents who smoke in groups have a strong need for togetherness, which, to a certain degree, is prompted by the age tendency to balance individualism in development. Loneliness is disagreeable and these meetings to smoke offer relief. Marijuana's euphoric impact, the emotional "easing up," the impulse of grouping, and especially the influence of the need to forget, provide the support for marijuana use. For the most part, especially at younger age levels where such smoke meetings last only a short time, the psychopathological drive is rather limited and the danger of dependency lies in habitual use and the taking of progressively larger amounts, or switching to other, harder drugs. Such groups are also breeding grounds for morally objectionable, delinquent tendencies.

The therapeutic approach can be dual in nature. We can try to pry the individual youth from the group relationship and replace it with another type, or we can try to influence the entire group. The first way, of course, is the easier. One or more therapists would be needed to carry an entire group to other activities. If the meetings are of the club type with long night sessions, as they frequently are with post-adolescents, the individual and group approach together may be necessary.

(3) The "pot head" marijuana smoker who needs at least half a dozen "joints" daily to keep him out of misery actually falls within the area of psychopathology and needs treatment accordingly. He cannot be handled in the same manner as the individual or group smoker. Some therapists have achieved partial success with pharmaceutical treatment alone. However, in order to accomplish true rehabilitation, psychotherapy must be added.

A large number of pharmaceuticals which the addict refers to as "ups" are euphoria producing. These are known as anti-depressants, the pitch ups, the psychological reinforcers. Among these are dexadrine, amphetamines, benzedrine, desbutal, and dexamyl. Dexedrine seems to be the most widely used; amphetamines are most abused and appear to cause most side effects. Neither are usually used for euphoric pleasure. Dexedrine is usually used to extend work or functioning ability. Any psychopathology rarely occurs. Amphetamines are used by severely or chronically depressed individuals and cause frequent overdose psychopathology. Also, amphetamine has little real euphoric quality. The main task here for psychotherapy is to overcome the depression and to induce the drug user to take a less dangerous medication. As is widely known, placebo treatment has proved rather successful with many patients suffering from depression. In some cases, persuasion and taboo therapy — something developed by this author — have proved successful if applied intensively. Most of these "up" patients call for similar psychotherapeutic treatment.

The largest group of addictive substances by far is that which aims at calming or pacifying, seeking a state of tranquillity or oblivion. At the center of this group stands heroin, presently the most used addictive.

However, to repeat what we have mentioned above because we feel we must, ether abuse has become rather common with pre-adolescents. Ether sniffing and, even more, ether drinking can have a devastating effect in dependency. Thinking and memory disturbances occur as well as emotional trauma. The craving, for instance, among medical students and nurses, may become so strong that they prefer it to any of the finest perfumes. They are often not frightened away even by parapathological insight. It takes a long time with social psychological therapy to overcome the addiction once they have determined for themselves that they wish to be free of this dependency. An English writer claimed that ether addiction is as difficult to overcome as morphine addiction, perhaps more so. A slow detoxification with intense psychotherapy may, after many weeks, prove successful.

There are an almost unlimited number of pharmaceuticals which ought to be listed as tranquilizers. They begin with sleeping aids and nerve medicines sold over the counter. Next come the barbiturates, codeine, other pain killers and, finally, the opiates.

One substance, phenobarbital, presents a characteristic portrait of addiction. However, we must point out that the basic conditions of phenobarbital dependency are not valid for all of this group. More detailed descriptions will reveal considerable differences among these substances. All individuals who take these drugs do not do so solely for their euphoric effect. They all take them to combat or overcome a more or less disagreeable, more or less pathological condition. They are nervous, more or less neurotic, psychopathic personalities or actual psychotics. Those who crave sleeping pills, barbs, codeine, or heroin have some kind of disagreeable pathological predisposition to a particular drug. In our psychotherapeutic approach we must focus on the pathology existing prior to the intake of drugs. Therefore, we must deal not only with drug addiction as such, but also the psychopathic condition which we must view as the basis for the actual drug abuse. We face a complicated task. Either we have to treat this underlying psychopathology separately from the drug psychopathology, or we have to view it as part of the drug addiction. It is actually this problem which helps us to understand why most of our crude detoxification methods do not work. However, there are other lacks in our therapeutic approaches which we shall discuss.

I feel strongly that many addictive drugs actually have, even in small doses, a certain toxic character, although this does not immediately make itself known. Because of this, the demand for barbiturates has recently diminished. Barbiturates are not properly eliminated from the body and build up to a point where they become seriously toxic. In general pathological processes, this often causes new depressive conditions in addition to the physiopathology.

This double-headed demon demands considerable adjustment of the entire psychotherapeutic approach. As I have stated above, we need to deal with the addiction relationship and, at the same time, consider the prior existing psychopathology. In other words, we cannot deal with the addict as though he had been normal before he developed a dependency on the drug.

In a discussion of heroin psychotherapy, we confront what I consider to be one of the greatest challenges to overcoming the present run of failures in drug therapy efforts. This is the lack of interest in distinguishing the differences among drug dependencies. The four types of heroin addicts require four different therapeutic and psychotherapeutic approaches. We simply do not reach the specific character of any heroin habituation if we try to meet all heroin addiction in the same way. Indeed, it is always heroin abuse we are dealing with, but each type is different and must be treated according to this difference.

I have designated the first of these heroin types as the *Intellectual* or *Rational*. It is made up of students, young white-collar workers, and others who lean toward a rational and speculative inner life. Their drive to heroin abuse results from conflicts in thinking, empty speculation, and professional problems. They like to "knock out" or "knock off" their heads. They want to "put themselves out" or into a state of forgetfulness; and heroin seems to do it the way they need and like it. When their minds are not clouded, they tend to irony, skepticism, and a depressive desire for the banal. They want to throw all "the nonsense of knowing" out the window. Therapy is "quite an intellectual job." It means building up an intellectual confidence and trust in ideals, society, and the purpose of man. They may rationalize themselves through to the acknowledgment and acceptance of detoxification treatment; however it must come from themselves; it cannot be imposed on them. They must work it out alone. They are not too receptive to group treatment. In the sphere of heroin addiction, this group has the highest suicide rate. If they are unable to stop their addiction drive through reasoned motivation, or to get the necessary help, they most easily reach the point of "cutting the rope." However, from my experience, it seems they represent the group with the best therapeutic hope for cure because when their speculative reconstruction succeeds they really "get out of the mud."

The second type of heroin addict is primarily *emotionally motivated.* This group is composed mostly of women, artists, "poetical souls," and strongly introverted individuals. They are emotionally adrift. They are always seeking friends, but cannot adjust to them easily. Therefore, they are miserably alone. They are very much afraid of the drugs they badly need; and while they are easily guided, they are still more easily misguided. Therapeutically, they make good patients if one understands how to direct their emotionalism into the right kind of transference. They need a lot of attention. In the beginning, they need a great deal of emotional feedback. "If the thing works," they may be free of their dependence in a few weeks, but for a while they need the continued emotional guidance of the therapist. Frequently, one is able to transplant the transference to someone else. However, if they "split" with the other, the start of a new therapeutic relationship is considerably more difficult. Sometimes it is better to turn them over to another therapist whose emotional difference may give rise to a new, more fruitful approach. It is most important to find for them an attractive occupation or profession into which this type of addict can release his emotional needs. Emotionally motivated addicts make the best material for any kind of group therapy. We shall discuss this later. It is also important that they break away from relationships with friends who are still drug dependent, as these relationships, almost without fail, push them back into heroin use.

The third heroin addiction type is the one I have classified as *Volitional.* This includes lower-class youths with no intellectual or professional intentions or interests. They do not wish to finish high school, or early become dropouts. They make up the crowd of "loafers," those who "hang around;" if forced by need they become occasional and manual laborers. They live on a primitive, volitional level. They are politically belligerent. In this group also is the sports gang, youths with low-grade mechanical interests, or youths who have fallen away from religious and social relationships. They make up the largest contingent of heroin addicts in rural districts, and are the juniors from workingmen's circles. They are bitter, rude, and rough. When they do not drown themselves in liquor, they get to the "needle." Therapy can hardly reach them when they come "to the end of the rope," realizing that they need help, or are transferred from courts and social agencies. The best settings for their treatment are communes and houses which take over the reshaping of their life-style. They need a stable environment to build a volitional pattern of existence. They must be given tolerable alternatives to their former habits, whether through strong professional guidance or otherwise. After a few weeks of structured direction, group therapy will have considerable value, primarily in developing human relationships. One should not underestimate the addict's hunger for comradeship. Teaching them to ignore or forget the past is a good method of therapy, and one which I earlier described as "taboo therapy."* It can be most beneficial with this group. It is also important, through vocational testing, to discover and encourage their abilities so that they may become self-sufficient. This type of addict requires far more attention than either of the other two types discussed.

The fourth type of heroin addict is the "*heroin head.*" In this group are individuals totally submerged in addiction, more often older persons than teen-agers. Elsewhere, I have designated this type as the *ego heroin addict.* These individuals cannot function on a primitive level in any respect unless "under the influence" or, better still, during the after-effect stages of heroin. Most of them vegetate and are able to exist outside of institutions only if they have independent means. Sooner or later, most of them end up in institutions or detoxification centers. Their stay may be for a limited time; they go back into society, and revert to their habit again, living through endless cycles of misery until they die. Most of them do not grow old. There are many suicides among them. I have seen very few cured. Even if they are cured of their addiction, they are like dark shadows in a room lit by small sputtering candles, and they appear mentally retarded, defective. They require constant vigilance because there is always the danger they will turn to crime or back to addiction.

A third kind of addiction, and one which we discuss with reluctance, is that of *hallucinogenics.* Anyone planning to do psychotherapeutic battle in this area must realize that he is stepping into a circle of completely unreliable forms of experience which grow from a deeply rooted mental design that is partly religious, partly psychotic in character. When C. G.

*Harms, E. Taboo as therapeutic tool. *International Mental Health Research Newsletter.* XII, **3**, 1970.

Jung started his scientific career at the beginning of this century, he wrote a small book calling attention to the similarities between psychotic and metaphysical episodes. Today, one faces the same problem of separating the elements in dealing with those at the mercy of hallucinogens. I have spent time with dozens of people who were "hooked" by LSD. There is no experience in the entire field of psychopathology to be compared to this. Even when they are "mortally afraid," they have a deep desire to "take a trip again," a trait which recalls the self-inflicting torments of medieval martyrs. I have met young post-adolescents who have assured me they would commit any crime in order to have "a set." Therapeutically, one is limited to those cases who seem, if only temporarily, determined to get help, to "get away from it." Those who have a severe illness and are near death are more likely to accept psychotherapeutic help. I am only familiar with a few where there occurred a definite release from dependency. Some switched to heroin and went on to a longer period of abuse. A few young artists, who had previously achieved considerable professional success, came to feel that the drug interfered with their abilities; therefore they stopped using it.

The moat between the fortress-like hold of hallucinogenics and any therapeutic approach lies in the large amount of writing attesting the metaphysical reality of their use. To a certain degree, these drugs leave the intellect intact, and the profuse literature gives addicts much questionable information which gives support to their addiction. An LSD addict almost always must experience the horrors of beginning dementia before he will be convinced of how much he hurts himself. By then he may not be able to restore his full rational abilities, and is left with his thinking and memory impaired. I have seen persons whose thinking became so impaired that they had to be retrained from the most elementary level such as one of a mentally defective child. Severe fear techniques, while unpleasant, have proved successful in young persons. Almost all hallucinogenic addicts live with a basic phobic feeling. In spite of this the dependency rules them. I have met only a very few who, after taking LSD more than once, have not confessed that they felt "burnt." We do not know how it takes place, but LSD does do injury to the nervous system which takes more remedial skill than we have available now to overcome. The best we can do is to make intensive preventive and educational efforts to limit the spread of this horrible addiction.

A therapeutic technique which has received great acceptance is group therapy. The reason for its acceptance and frequent use cannot be satisfactorily explained.

Group therapy with addicts, in the form in which it is mostly applied, consists of sessions with fewer than twelve members and an experienced therapist as the "leader." Some groups have one or two so-called cured addicts conducting them. For the most part, the participants are not carefully screened and selected. Sometimes these are open groups in which anyone may participate.

The basis for these group assemblies is, first, to enhance the feeling of belonging, and sameness. It is claimed that fears that block much desired communication are removed. Also encouraged are relatedness, the release of suppressed feelings, and confessions of guilt. Accusations, expressions of self-pity which occur because of the knowledge that there are others who have had the same experiences are given free outlets. Finally, feelings are awakened for the possibility of therapeutic relief and even improvement and cure. Unfortunately, alteration of the real personality structure is not quite that simple to achieve by such meetings. Basic and individual differences among addict types, which must be seriously considered, are not taken into account. Individuals do not all respond alike because they are all addicts. One does not get a "confession atmosphere" from a mixture of intellectual students, emotionally overloaded women, and rough underdogs. On the contrary, I have witnessed great harm done by a vulgar response of ridicule to a display of deeply felt emotion. A group with a therapeutic purpose must be carefully assembled and should never have any but an experienced group leader in charge. Only a limited number of presently conducted groups have trained, experienced leaders. Others are presided over by former presumably cured addicts, a practice borrowed from "Alcoholics Anonymous." There is no insight into the basic difference between drug abuse and alcoholism. So-called cured addicts know only their own very specific patterns of cure from drug abuse which they try to apply to completely different people. During their cure they have gone through a very narrow experience which, quite naturally, they rely on, but they know this and nothing more. They are frequently dogmatic, fanatic, and lacking in empathy for others. As group leaders, thus, they can do more harm than good.

It is true that group therapy applied with care and in small doses can have considerable therapeutic value. This value is mainly in its ability to build and reconstruct lost or impaired human relations. Of course, the awareness of our sameness with others is essential to the security of the ego. Our personality is to a great degree the product of environment and it unfolds in our relations with others. In this respect, group therapy is an unique tool, if it is properly applied. Nevertheless, in addiction, a therapeutic system must be soundly coordinated by medical, social, and individual influences, without which most of our efforts to help or cure the drug addict will prove to be in vain.

I feel something must be added regarding professional didactics before closing this paper. I have placed emphasis on the failure of attempts to stem the tide of drug addiction. This leads us to question, "Why this failing?" Is it a lack of realistic insight, clear thinking, or proper education? On one level, all three are involved. The major factor, however, is more embarrassing. It is tied to the personal quality and social conditioning of addiction care. We have heard much about the social and cultural causes of drug dependency. It is difficult to believe the charge that addiction is beyond control under existing social conditions. It appears that those dealing with addiction are themselves much influenced by the atmosphere in which they are working. I will not claim that one could not encounter worse restrictive conditions in government and other bureaucracies. The basic tone of society is set by those in political and administrative authority and by those who follow them to forward their own careers. Punitive and authoritarian patterns, avoidance of personal involvement to achieve social gains block the progress of science and psychology. Any advance in the proper handling and treatment of the addict, especially the juvenile, demands a rigorous, sharp fight against professional attitudes which stand scrupulously rigid against humane, responsible efforts to stimulate work in this field. This could be changed if a large enough group could be united in this task. Details of the means needed for this fight are beyond the scope of this paper.

REFERENCES

Bell, R. G. *Escape from addiction*. McGraw-Hill, 1970.
Bejerot, N. J. *Addiction and society*. Thomas, 1970.
Biase, V. and De Leon, G. The Encounter Group. *A.P.A. Proceedings*, 1969.
Brenner, J. H. *Drugs and youth*. Liveright, 1970.
Caldwell, W. V. *LSD Psychotherapy*. Grove Press, 1968.
Cameron, D. An overview of the problems of drug abuse. *J. Hillside Hosp.*, 1967, **16**.
Caroff, P., *et al.* The drug problem. *Social Case Work*, 1970, **51**.
Cohen, S. *The Drug dilemma*. McGraw-Hill, 1969.
Dole, V. B. and Nyswander, M. E. Rehabilitation of the street addict. *Arch. envir. Hlth*, 1967, **14**.
Duncan, T. L. *Understanding and helping the narcotic addict*. Fortress Press, 1965.
Fouquet, P. Psychotherapie Individuelle. *Taxiconaniscs*, 1969, **2**.
Freedman, A. M. and Sharoff, R. L. Crucial factors in the treatment of the narcotic addict. *Amer. J. Psychotherapy*, 1965, **19**.

Glatt, M. M. Psychological basis of the treatment of the addict. *Praxis of Psychotherapy*, 1965, **10**.

Glatt, M. M. Group-Therapy with young drug addicts. *Nursing Times*, 1967, **63**.

Goldstein, K., *et al*. Interpersonal exchange at a residential drug addiction center. *Proceedings A.P.A. Convention*, 1969.

Hartman, D. Study of drug-taking adolescents. *Psychoanal. Study of the Child*, 1969, **24**.

Holmberg, M. B., *et al*. Experiences from an outpatient department for drug addicts in Gothenborg. *Acta Psychiat. Scandin.*, 1968, **44**.

Horman, R., *et al. Drug awareness*. Avon, 1970.

Kadushin, L. and A. The ex-addict in the therapeutic team. *Comm. Mental Health*, 1969, **5**.

Krinsky, L. W. and Jennings, R. M. Treatment of the acting-out adolescent. *Hospital Comm.*, 1968, **19**.

Kurland, A. A. The narcotic addict. *Md. Medical J.*, 1966, **15**.

Lesser, B. Behavior therapy with narcotic users. *Behavior. Research Therapy*, 1967, **5**.

Levy, N. J. The use of drugs by teenagers. *Amer. J. Psychoanalysis*, 1968, **28**.

Louria, D. B. *Overcoming drugs*. McGraw-Hill, 1971.

McNeill, E. B. *Neuroses and personality disorders*. Prentice-Hall, 1970.

Maddoux, J. F. *Treatment of drug addicts*. U.S. Government Printing Office. 1967.

Masserman, J. H. *Transcultural psychiatric approach*. Grune & Stratton, 1969.

Meyerson, D. J. *Treatment of drug addicts*. Mass. Medic. Soc., 1968.

Nat. Library of Medicine. *Psychotherapy with drug addicts*. U.S. Government, 1969.

Nyswander, M. *The drug addict as a patient*. Grune & Stratton, 1956.

Pierre, C. *Motivating the drug addict in treatment*. Mass. Med. Conference, 1969.

Rado, S. The Psychoanalytic point-of-view of drug addiction. *Arch. Neurol. & Psychiatry*, 1933, **30**.

Ramirez, E. The existential approach to narcotic addiction. *Review of Existent. Psychol*, 1968, **8**.

Raskin, H. A. Rehabilitation of the narcotic addict. *JAMA*, 1964, **189**.

Riebling, C. Intoxication psychosis. *Med. Clinic of North Amer.*, 1939, **35**.

Solomon, P. Medical management of drug dependence. *JAMA*, 1968, **206**.

Uhr, L. and Miller, J. G. *Drugs and behavior*. Wiley, 1960.

Westman, W. Ch. *The drug epidemic*. Dial, 1970.

Wilmer, H. A. *Social psychiatry in action*. Thomas, 1958.

The Religious Problematic of the Juvenile Addict

EDWARD M. BROWN

"... living dreams of vision, mystic crystal revelation ... Aquarius"

Musical, *Hair*, 1968

Drug addicts generally have a problem with authority; we would expect that they would have a problem with a Final Authority. The religious problematic will be discussed in three sections: religion and opiate addiction; religious mysticism and hallucinogens; and the crisis in the church and family.

RELIGION AND OPIATE ADDICTION

Narcotic addicts elevate people in authority, render them attributes which they do not have, give them roles to which they are not entitled, and give them power by which they are not legitimately endowed. At the same time, addicts denigrate authorities by ascribing to them heinous motives, portraying them as abusive and seeing them as punishing, scheming, and guilt-invoking even when they are not. It is an old game of setting them up to knock them down, exaggerating their omnipotence and destructiveness in order to justify hating them. Addicts do the same thing with concepts of the deity. They shun the God of mainstream religions. Instead, their god is very real to them, but is inhumane, unforgiving, and a figment of their imagination based upon their own personal experiences with human authorities.

Experience at the Lower Eastside Service Center, Inc. bears out that narcotic addicts have relatively little affiliation with church institutions, but a high degree of hidden religious ideation. The Center in New York

City sees a broad cross-section of drug abusers through its walk-in social service and outpatient psychiatric clinic. In the past, many of the clients were referred by churches, or parents of the clients were affiliated with local churches. Most of the patients themselves, however, had no direct church ties from which they could receive social support. Nonetheless, in art, writing, poetry, and bull sessions abundant religious material has been elicited from which emerge the distortions inherent in their internal authority problem.

The Lower Eastside Service Center has also noted that some clients have found the most help in recovering from their addictions through church organizations considered outside of the mainstream Judaic-Christian religions. Especially Pentacostal, Church of God, and Black Muslim churches have appealed to their patients. Instantaneous conversions were marked by a severe self-punishing trend, and exaggerated exclusiveness, and elevated importance of the group. The god-head is conceived as a harsh judge who accepts them because of their self-abnegation and a magical connotation of a special group conferred through the institution. These patients identified with God so that the lines between their identity and the divinity were blurred. The Service Center often found them obnoxious patients because of their militant proselytizing, their preoccupation with religious thoughts, and their refusal to accept responsibility for planning (educational or vocational) on the grounds that "God would provide."

However, it has been the more orthodox churches, especially Protestant ones, that pioneered and provided services for drug abusers since the adolescent drug problem began after World War II. It was St. Marks Episcopal Church in Chicago and the East Harlem Protestant Parish in New York City that began work with addicts early in the 1950s, that campaigned for government action, and stimulated many other churches to initiate programs. It is interesting that although the more orthodox churches presented a benign image and receptive attitude toward drug abusers, and succeeded in attracting them into services, they have had very little success with the particularly religious aspects of their programs in effecting rehabilitation. Only the more religiously conservative fundamentalist institutions like Teen Challenge effectively utilized religion for rehabilitation.

On the one side, narcotic addicts have heretical or unorthodox religious ideas; on the other side, we now examine how the addicts are making a religion out of their drugs.

Drug addicts, especially of the heroin type, are using opium as a religion. The opiates are their god-head. This god commands their complete devotion, their absolute loyalty, their unswerving respect, their full attention, and their unchallenged satisfaction. Only the traditional religions demand equal or greater fealty. Heroin addicts will die for their god, an attribute most clergy would like to use to measure their parishioners.

This religion of the heroin god brings with it a whole way of life which is another characteristic of the great religions. The cycle in which the addict lives has a short time span and a larger orbit. The 8-hour period is determined by the length of time heroin takes to diminish its chemical effect and for which another injection is needed to prevent withdrawal symptoms. This time dimension includes taking the "shot," going on the "nod" in a euphoric sleep, emerging to a waking state in which the preoccupation begins with obtaining the next "fix," and then preparing for the next injection.

The larger cycle involves an orbit outside the mainstream of society, the way of life of the criminal, the rules of the game in the underworld culture, the search for illicit forms of finance, occupation in illegitimate practices, and planning income beyond the 8-hour intervals. There is a concentration on immorality equal to the fervor of morality often accompanying the religion of the very orthodox.

The reader will note the argot used in quotation marks two paragraphs above. This use of symbolism is vivid and parallels the traditional religions. Those phrases, as well as others such as, the tools of the trade (needle, eye dropper, bottle top, spoon, etc.) and the signs of the addiction (the pusher, the connection, the unseen dealer, the "fence" who accepts stolen merchandise, etc.), all take on exalted and mysterious qualities not unlike the awe of the traditionally religious images. Certainly heroin takes on the same holy characteristics that evidence other divinities, perhaps more so; it has no rivals for producing a dream-less bliss. It is important to remember that mainstream religions have a dream-like bliss, not dream-less; the contentment is usually filled with story content, e.g., fantasies, memories, sensations in contrast to the opiate religion.

Morphine religion also has its ritual aspects. A repetitive system of physical motions is practiced every 8 hours, more happily if regularly, and laden with intangible meaning and satisfaction. The whole enterprise of taking an injection is preceded by preparation and accompanied by actions that possess a routinized and mechanical labor engaged for its own sake as well as the pleasure to which it leads: preparing the ingredients, igniting the cooker, applying the tourniquet, inserting the needle, squeezing the dropper, suctioning blood into the eye dropper and needle to wash out all the contents, pressing the pacifier on the end of the dropper to ebb and flow blood from the vein into the glass tube. The latter especially may be done by addicts when they have no drugs available, or while they are trying to be abstinent.

As I see it, the flaw in the religious analogy, more in mainstream religion than in chemical stimulated religious experience, is that heroin addicts are more driven to their religion than they are fulfilled by it. They are like so many moths flying into the candlelight and burning to death because they are driven and not satiated by the satisfaction of the light. They cannot curb or limit their gratification. Greed is all-consuming. They have not given of themselves, but only plunge on to take what they can get. What is absent is love, faith and hope; what is absent is personal concern and social justice, human closeness. To me, their religion is an addiction. To them, religion is nothingness. To me, their religion is nihilistic, destructive, denial of selfhood, and empty of fulfillment. To them, my religion does not pack instantaneous pleasure of the flesh and bones. To me, their religion is suicide of the self. To them, my religion is death itself. We are very close, the addict and I, except that he cannot appreciate me.

RELIGIOUS MYSTICISM AND HALLUCINOGENS

In contrast to the religious addiction of opiate users, very likely a much larger proportion of the drug-taking youth population is seeking religious mysticism from psychedelic drugs. The opiate religion is concentrated in the urban slums and among the underprivileged, despairing, and minority groups and, to a growing extent, among the emotionally impoverished in the suburban and middle-class communities. However, as one gets away from the northeast United States urban complex and from the industrial population and into suburban and Middle America, there is a greater interest in mood-altering drugs. Both the drug consumption and treatment approaches are markedly different between New York and California, albeit there is an appreciable overlap. Instead of a "high" to counter the urban despair, middle-class youth are seeking the "self" to counter their emptiness.

The appeal of psychedelic drugs to youth is essentially a religious quest. It is a much maligned and misunderstood activity in the eyes of adult society. The dangers of psychedelic drugs have been greatly publicized. The accidental suicides and the instances of psychosis have confirmed the public myth that such partakers are "crazy" and that the intention of such persons is unconstructive.

When such mind-expanding drugs are taken unilaterally and without supervision and when they are made an end in themselves, they become destructive. It is not that it is "wrong" which makes drug-taking destructive; it is the method of playing doctor and of taking on an illegitimate role of omnipotence. It is not that conscious-expanding drugs are themselves, *per se*, harmful, or that the person is necessarily suicidal.

Hallucinogens which can give a psychedelic experience include marijuana, sniffing glue, and inhaling other solvents, peyote, LSD, and certain other similar chemicals. I am excluding the intravenous use of amphetamines and methamphetamines, (nicknamed "meth") because of their undesirable side-effects of irritability and agitation, because of the extreme reactions due to injection directly into the blood stream, because of the dangerous behavior incited by the increased feeling of having "nerve," because excessive and prolonged usage can sometimes lead to death, and because the social conditions under which they are taken usually do not include peer group control over the hallucinations and delusions of persecution which may occur. Similar dangers can be cited for the other hallucinogens, but usage within a group often provides some controls and supervision. Crash pads, talking-down bad trips, supervision of individual LSD trips by sympathetic previous users are frequent forms of social control within peer groups seeking psychedelic experiences.

To yearn to know oneself is an honorable philosophical quest running from Socrates through Shakespeare. The hippie subculture which blossomed in the decade of the 1960s gave forth that renewed credo as stimulated and reinterpreted by drug taking. The psychic effect, however, carries dimensions that proved broader than merely mind-expanding and the unmasking of the unconscious under the influence of drugs. Both the effects of the drug and the needs of the takers promoted more far-ranging goals. Consciousness expanding provoked an awareness of the self, of others, and of the environment that can only be described as mystical. The seekers felt that they had arrived at their truth and this truth is their faith, their being, their commitment to live. Such formulation fulfills some definitions of religion.

Not all psychedelic users may have that same experience. However, a body of experience and literature is gaining scientific credibility and delineates structures which can be duplicated to study chemically induced mysticism. Although research at this time cannot show that most psychedelic users have been having the same experience, evidence is mounting that identifiable and reportable experience can be described by a number of people which would meet the criteria of mysticism.

The therapeutic use of LSD has been studied with terminal cancer patients, alcoholic patients, and heroin addict patients. In a therapeutically supported atmosphere, under medically supervised conditions, the psychedelic experience can best be described as a mystical consciousness which reveals the inner truth about the self and the outer truth about the meaning of life, and a harmony between the self and the infinite.

The psychedelic experience under the influence of therapeutically controlled administration of LSD produces a mystical consciousness that can best be described as a dimension of religious experience that when expressed on paper by experimental subjects, and subsequently content-analyzed, corresponds to 9 inter-related categories:* These mystical qualities described are:

1. Unity

The hallmark of mystical consciousness is the experience of undifferentiated unity, either internal or external, depending upon whether the dichotomy transcended is between the usual self and the "inner world" or between the inner self and the external world of sense impressions outside the experiencer. Sense impressions and ego identity fade and consciousness expands and merges with the inner world or external entities.

2. Objectivity and Reality

Insightful, illuminating, intuitive, non-rational knowledge gained by direct experience is combined with the authoritativeness and certainty that such experience is ultimately real in contrast to a subjective delusion. The sense of ultimate truth is achieved.

3. Transcendence of Space and Time

This category refers to the loss of a person's usual space-time orientation to the environment and the gaining of a radical change in perspective in which he feels outside of time, in eternity or infinity and beyond past and future.

4. Sense of Sacredness

A response of holiness felt to be of special value, capable of being profaned and producing an awareness of finitude, humility, and reverence in the presence of inspiring realities as though one had stood before the Infinite.

*Pahnke and Richards p. 176ff.

5. Deeply-Felt Positive Mood

Oceanic feelings of joy, love, and peace.

6. Paradoxicality

Significant aspects of the experience are felt to be true despite their violation of the laws of logic, e.g., simultaneously feeling dead and alive or being in one's body and out of one's body.

7. Alleged Ineffability

Feeling that language symbols are inadequate to describe the experience because of its uniqueness.

8. Transiency

The temporary duration of mystical consciousness contrasts with the relative permanence of the level of usual experience, and also contrasts with psychosis when the unusual state of consciousness is sustained.

9. Positive Changes in Attitude and/or Behavior

Persons who experience the preceding 8 categories also report concomitant changes in attitudes toward themselves, others, toward life and toward mystical consciousness itself. They report feelings of personality integration, enhanced self-worth, and relaxation of defense mechanisms.

These common qualities of the psychedelic experience indicate a deep mystic yearning and a religious character. Sometimes the experiencers are not beyond describing their drug subculture as a new religion. Although the experience is not institutionalized, there are marked parallels to traditional churches with regard to the properties of unity, insight, transcendence, holiness, joy, ineffability, transiency, and attitude changes.

CRISIS IN THE CHURCH AND FAMILY

The generation gap has taken a new dimension, namely, adolescent emancipation. The community must seek new answers and religion re-examine the foundation of family life.

The adolescent emancipation is signified not only by the experimentation with drugs and the developing hippie subculture, but also by the easy access of teen-agers to mobility away from unhappy homes, by transient residences in communes and group living, by identifiable alienated groups usually in inner cities, and by the visibility given to opportunities for adolescents to meet like-minded associates by the mass media. There are informal underground social-service middlemen who, while helping to reconcile youth with their parents, also provide avenues for running away. Such phone numbers have been seen in New York City communes. Legitimate social welfare agencies have begun to protect youth with residential sustenance, legal advice on independent habitation, and with a buffer on legal action taken against runaways. More and more youth are escaping family conflicts earlier and earlier.

The generation gap has always been with us. It will continue long after the fad of drugs has disappeared. However, it can be a source of enrichment, a fountain of new ideas, and a model of innovation and change. Children bring forth new horizons unimagined by their fathers. But the resolution of many family interactions breeds disharmony instead of harmony, deviance instead of unity, and despair instead of individual fulfillment. The culture which has served as the bulwark and preserver of family life now needs to articulate the basis of its heritage for this age.

A new interpretation of family life must take into account the contemporary crisis. Youth no longer will perpetuate the form of family life without its vitality. Youth will no longer succumb to parental ideals unless the relationship warrants affection and imitation. Youth will simply leave their homes in greater numbers. The exception of the decade of the 60s is on the way to becoming the pattern of the decade of the 70s in the twentieth century. In the fast changing tempo of our times, the church has an opportunity to respond because of its historic connection with family life.

The nature of the crisis within the family today deserves exploration. Examination of existing tensions can take into account the implication of the signs found in drug misuse by adolescents. From the broadest perspective, drug activity is a form of rebellion. No matter what other meanings, motivations or satisfactions, self-prescribed drug use is illegal and risks apprehension of the user. Against what experiences are youth rebelling?

A second question raised by drug use is that of the unashamed hedonistic pleasure. The pleasure takes many directions — ups and downs, sedation and intoxication, depressants and stimulants, hallucinogens, and pain killers. Chemicals are giving these youth what many of us take to be inalienable rights of happiness. What has happened to the family so that the natural joy which children should experience is gone?

There are also the deeper pathologies represented by the flirtation with insanity by the use of some drugs, and the total isolation and insulation created by opium drug derivatives. These expressions of severe emotional problems indicate that a profound reinterpretation of family life must also resolve the problems of mental illness. The widespread self-destruction from nicotine, alcohol, drugs, criminality, and poverty has its derivates from family impoverishment. What can be done about replenishing the deep roots which are missing?

The preoccupation with psychedelic drugs by youth is a religious concern. These young are not so much people of great faith as they are people of great religious fervor—seeking the ultimate in life, to pursue steadfastly the way of the final quest, and with the great hope that drugs will meet their ultimate fulfillment. Their concern and yearning are all-consuming, a religious zeal, sometimes manifested in ritual and religious fabric, but rarely if ever connected with the mainstream religious traditions, not to mention the institutional church. (A notable exception is the Glide Methodist Church, San Francisco.) The weaving of religious thought with theological framework and moral practices is invariably a departure from the conventional church if not, in fact, from the church's viewpoint, a perversion and heresy.

Because our society does not define drug experimentation, drug use, and drug addiction in religious terms, we fall short of understanding the problem and finding viable alternatives. Only if one can understand the religious implications can we then begin to see the complexities and find medical answers.

Karl Marx was getting at something with his often quoted aphorism that religion was the opiate of the people. The reverse is equally true: some drugs are the religion of the people. This is not just peyote use by American Indians. Narcotic drugs are perhaps the truest rivals of orthodox religion. Atomic bombs can instill great fear, but they cannot provide the allure of opiates.

In a puritanical society such as this, the fabric of institutional religion cannot absorb the challenge of pleasure-seeking and bliss. The traditional religions in Western society are still shackled by Victorian self-denial of the body. Hence, they cannot address themselves to the basic problems and yearnings of drug enthusiasts. For example, it is very difficult to get people who should stay on medically prescribed tranquilizers to do so because of the frequent fear that they will become addicted. It is nearly impossible to get American society to approach a drug problem initially other than punitively, punishing the victims and prohibiting the drug. It is virtually impossible to address a parent audience about drug infiltration and to get them to give up their rage in order to consider expanded opportunities for adolescents.

Adults prefer to do nothing and to enjoy the fascination with drug culture because it meets their secret pleasure-seeking wish inhibited by Western religions. They are stimulated by ex-addicts; they get excited learning about narcotic usage; they like to focus on the addict so as to exclude the implication of the drug lure to themselves. Therefore, public policy changes slowly and community interest is invariably two-faced.

The neurotic illusion that exists for these people is that there really is a happiness pill. The magical idea is that one pill (shot in the arm) will bring all happiness. True enough, the addict has reduced life to one solution. It is a fallacy that for most of us, puritan churchmen included, life can have one solution: generally we have many needs and many ways to meet them. However, the desire to have a happiness pill, like finding the fountain of youth, is a vision which lingers. The fear that it is missed because adherents make claims for their narcotized state of being leads to fascination instead of study.

Religious and public education are being asked to carry the illegitimate role of interrupting drug abuse. Neither the churches nor the education system nor the educational function of youth-serving institutions are capable of doing much education by way of preventing experimentation with drugs. Education is in the twofold business of imparting information on the one hand and "educating" or leading out of the mind interpretive and integrated responses. Education can provide facts about drugs, their danger and dependencies, and can provoke a questioning mind, but it cannot persuade a mind which is seeking emotional and physical satisfactions distinguished from intelligence. Education presumes the existence of an objective, rational, open mind which is not the state of persons prone to drug misuse.

Education can, therefore, be helpful to parents and to leaders who truly wish to do well by their children and who, armed with facts and guided by reason through education, can interact with their children in as helpful a fashion as possible.

Now, then, authorities so armed with education will be successful and persuasive, like education itself, significantly with persons who emulate them. Those persons will change through education who identify with the authorities and model themselves after the values of the teacher, or the style of the leader. Such readily responsive persons will be youngsters, either pre-schoolers or in early elementary grades, or those in upper grades whose relationship with their parents is unusually harmonious, docile, and mutual. Education about the dangers of drugs will have a beneficial effect upon early schoolers as has the effect of cancer-tobacco campaigns on developing inhibitions of smoking among the emerging generation.

In contrast, education about the facts of drugs, the damage of addiction, and the harmful effects of drug misuse is met in later schoolers by a new set of mind appropriate to an age which is more conducive to rebellion than compliance, experimentation than coercion, and to independence rather than conformity. Education may not only be a waste but initiate suggestions for new explorations in the discovery of the world.

Education cannot substitute for persuasion, attitude-changing, mental health growth, or what church institutions refer to as religious faith. Personal growth can be encouraged by the present programs of churches and youth serving agencies, which have been accomplishing this for years, or by accelerating and institutionalizing the inter-personal experiences geared to changing value attitudes. The current vogue in encounter groups, sensitivity training or rap sessions, can be used to initiate, to build on, or to expand human relations experiences to provide alternative human satisfactions and displace the chemical solutions so readily available.

These are personal growth opportunities of religious dimensions and are not to be confused with education nor with treatment. Education is for the person who wishes to be persuaded. Treatment is for the drug-dependent person who cannot be persuaded but wishes that he could be. And personal growth experiences are for persons who wish not to be persuaded, but wish to persuade themselves in the sanctity of their own consciences. We cannot deal then with the drug-dependent persons who cannot be persuaded to give up drugs and who also do not wish to be persuaded. Personal growth programs are directed to the individual who sees himself (herself) as independent and who values autonomy.

Currently, there is a large void in society for the required type of personal growth programs attempting to be described here. The effect of mass media upon youth, the effects of rapid transportation and mobility of teen-agers, and the effect of exposure to the ambiguities and complexities of life, ethics, and authority have given rise to an adolescent emancipation which not the church, the home, the school, nor youth-serving institutions have been prepared to meet. Too often, such institutions, or leaders, have been frightened away from this function by the problems of runaways and drug abusers. However, it is for this function and for these groups that the church and similar institutions are best geared.

Adolescence is a struggle. The period of adolescence grows longer as experience occurs earlier and life commitments educationally, vocationally, and maritally are delayed. With a pluralistic society, the struggle of adolescence becomes more varied and of longer duration. It is to this struggle that the church and family can address themselves.

The drug question points the way to broadening the scope of church life. Church schools have been excellent enough to develop personal growth among unemancipated youth, but they are insufficient for many young people struggling with adolescence and asserting themselves in society. The issues of racism, women's rights, family life, marriage, child rearing, parent rearing, child bearing, sex, contraception, abortion, drugs, careers, human relations, selfhood, and other choices deserve the time, place, and setting in programs to facilitate personal growth. When these struggles exist, as they do more frequently, new programs and departures are needed. The novel use of encounter groups may succeed today, but tomorrow their novelty may wear off and new techniques sought. Openness of the leadership will be the hallmark leading to the openness of the participants; the church and family addressing themselves to the adolescent religious quest will determine whether these institutions will continue to be models or become obsolete. The religious problematic of the juvenile addict is the spiritual problem of the church.

REFERENCES

Brown, E. The juvenile narcotic addict, A profile. *The Pastoral Counselor*, Vol. I, No. 2.

Brown, E. Treating heroin addicts with medically supervised narcotics. *Classmate Mag.*, Methodist Church, April 1967.

Brown, E. Guidelines for programs for drug abusers. *The YWCA Magazine*, National Board of the Young Women's Christian Association, Oct. 1971.

Glide Urban Center. Glide in/out, Vol. 1., No. 1–5, 330 Ellis St., San Francisco, Calif. 94102, Glide Memorial United Methodist Church, *Newsletter*, 330 Ellis St., San Francisco. Calif. 94102.

Kolansky, H., M.D. and Moore, W., M.D. Effects of marijuana on adolescents and young adults, *J. of the Am. Med. Ass.*, April 19, 1971, Vol. 216, No. 3.

Kron, Y. J., M.D. and Brown, E. M. *Mainline to nowhere, The making of a heroin addict,* Pantheon, 1965.

Kron, Y. J., M.D. and Brown, E. M. Profile of a narcotic addict, *Christianity and Crisis,* Nov. 15, 1965, Vol. XXV, No. 19.

Land, H. *What you can do about drugs and your child,* Holt, New York, 1969.

National Clearing House for Drug Abuse Information. Drug abuse treatment and prevention—Religious activities and programs. *Report Series,* June 1971, Series 6 No. 1.

National Sex and Drug Forum. *News Releases,* Glide Foundation, 330 Ellis St., San Francisco, Calif. 94102. (*Psychedelics and Religious Experience,* Allan Watts, 50¢ copy.)

Pahnke, W., M.D., Ph.D. The psychedelic mystical experience in human encounter with death. *Harvard Theological Review*, Jan., 1969, Vol. 62, No. 1.

Pahnke, W., M.D., Ph.D. and Richards, W. A. Implications of LSD and experimental mysticism. *J. of Religion and Health*, July 1966, Vol. 5, No. 3.

Pahnke, W., M.D., Ph.D., Kurland, A. A., M.D., Unger, S., Ph.D., Savage, C., M.D., and Grof, S., M.D. The experimental use of psychedelic (LSD) psychotherapy, Paper presented at the Symposium on Psychedelic Drugs, American Medical Association Annual Meeting, New York City, July 17, 1969.

Simon, W. and Gagnon, J. H. Children of the drug age. *Saturday Review*, Sept. 31, 1968.

Smart, R. G., Whitehead, P., and LaForest, L. The prevention of drug abuse by young people: An argument based on the distribution of drug use, *Bulletin on Narcotics*, United Nations, April–June 1971, Vol. XXIII, No. 2, p. 11.

Student Assoc. for the Study of Hallucinogens, Inc. *Capsules*, Dec. 1970, through Vol. 2, No. 5, 638 Pleasant St., Beloit, Wisconsin 53511.

Zaks, M. S., Ph.D., Hughes, P., M.D., Jaffe, J., M.D., and Dolkart, M. B., M.A. Young people in the park. Paper presented at the American Orthopsychotic Association, 46th Annual Meeting, March 30, 1969, New York City.

Aftercare Problems With the Juvenile Drug Addict*

ARTHUR GRUBER

Drug addiction rehabilitation, as it is presently practiced, can hardly claim that it is able to totally extinguish dependency and drug cravings in the addict. As we see drug addiction today, to a great degree it is a socially conditioned pathological state of mind which demands a longer process of social adjustment or readjustment following the actual withdrawal from addiction as a period of aftercare.

However, if we wish to survey the total aspect of aftercare, we must widen our vision considerably. We must include the various forms of relapse to drug addiction and the switching from one drug to another, or to a drug-like dependency. Although we may sometimes think we have found definite means of terminating the use of a specific drug, this may not be permanent. Unconscious dependency and dependency through memory may remain alive for quite some time. Often, we are not aware of the shock which was a major element during withdrawal periods. If this shock loses its impact, desires for addictive experiences may return. The impact of the shock or other terminating effects may last for a few weeks, months, or even years, and then the desire for drugs may return. Outside factors, such as contact with active addicts, may become motivations for new addictive desires and a return to the wants of abuse. Of course, all of this does not need to occur if the addict is given an aftercare relationship

*This closing chapter comes from a 24-year old former teen-age drug addict who, after having achieved a B.A. in social work, is now an instructor in a professional school of social work. (Editor.)

powerful enough to prevent such reoccurrences. Careful consideration
should be given to the selection of this effective human support on whom
the addict must be willing and able to rely. A proper bond of confidence
and trust must be developed as the basis of such a therapeutic aftercare
relationship. This person need not be an addiction specialist or a psychiatrist. It can be anyone with the didactic ability to handle the situation.

Beyond the termination of a specific addiction, there may—and
frequently does—occur a switch to an addiction to another more or less
potent substance. It means that the aura of the original addiction is
removed, but the craving for the addiction experience is still alive and
wants to be satisfied. This factor is frequently not observed nor treated
by the therapist who has not looked beyond the one drug relationship
into the psychology of his client. Our presently sanctified methadone
treatment is based upon such a switch or replacement. We cannot be quite
sure whether we really terminate psychological dependency in this way.
This writer, from his own experience and observations, is very dubious of
the methadone treatment as it is applied today. Even if one replaces a
dangerously addictive substance with a less addictive or non-addictive
one, we still nurture the basic tendency. Even a placebo leaves a certain
tendency alive which can act like a sleeping dragon and awaken and gain
strength. We certainly have not brought an end to the addiction problem
if we have not solved the aftercare problem.

This narrower aftercare problem turns directly into the wider one of
actual adjustment or readjustment of the addict to normal and safe
living.

As with any human being, we must see two fields of the addict's life:
the inner and the outer. Addiction does not come from nowhere. There
are psychologically disturbing experiences which may sometimes even be
physiologically conditioned that call for an addictive release. Very little
notice has been taken of these psychological factors which I believe
essential to deal with in overcoming the dependency. The psychological
factors are not terminated when the actual drug intake ceases. Their
elimination by psychological therapy is a necessary task for addiction
aftercare. If we do not eliminate such psychopathology—however mild it
may be—we cannot eradicate the tendency to addiction. This must be
taken very seriously in light of any reawakening or repetition of addiction.
Psychologically weak or neurotically disposed individuals need help.
It is not farfetched to suppose that a psychological upset can reawaken an
addiction tendency. We need a definite awareness of the dangers which
must be considered for an effective application of aftercare. One is only

confirmed against addiction if one is firm and secure in one's psychological expressions. Without this, no addiction didactic is meaningful.

Our second major aspect concerns the outer world adjustment of the convalescent drug addict. Here again maladjustment appears as a conditioning factor. An educational journal raises the question whether more dropouts become conditioned to take dope or whether the taking of dope is the reason for dropping out of school. The exact figures do not matter, but there is a considerable amount of adolescent maladjustment which acts as a cause of drug dependency.

The aftercare life adjustment is of considerably greater importance. During addiction treatment, efforts should be made to find occupation for the treated and to offer practical guidance for a way of life. In most addiction centers, when asked what they wish to do with their lives, the majority of teen-agers reply that first they want to return to school and get a diploma. There is no doubt that the most important factors in any treatment of the young addict are giving their lives meaning, a job for the present, and an acceptable goal for the future. One of the wisest and most successful addiction workers I ever met told me that the first thing he asked the young addict was what he wanted to become in life. Most of the current crop of addiction workers do nothing more than try to find the young person "a job." The addict has no or little meaningful existence. Giving him something he can believe in is the real medicine for addiction. The addict is not really cured until he has found a meaningful life and well-fitting occupation. Efforts to build a sound and adjusted personality ought to start during withdrawal treatment, and must continue as a major task of aftercare. On the one hand, we have youths who led a defective social existence and, because of this, were vulnerable to addiction, and, on the other hand, we have youths who had no proper professional education and need professional guidance "from the bottom." Some addiction programs are lax in this respect. They claim that some art, music, or novel reading may do the trick as occupational therapy. Adolescents often take life more seriously than adults. They need reality experiences, especially if they have been dislodged by drug dependency. In most cases, withdrawing and detoxification treatments do not last as long as they should to set the youth up properly in life. This is a major consideration for aftercare of the addict. Such aftercare is the real means of overcoming addiction in youth. We have to give them a view of a healthful existence in which there is no need for drugs, "kicks," and "doping away." It is only if we approach drug addiction from this wide view that we will have any sound means of overcoming it.

BEYOND DRUGS

By Stanley Einstein, Ph.D.

Dr. Einstein looks upon the contemporary drug situation not as an isolated phenomenon but as a facet of a world wide change in social values and institutions. Based upon this premise the author: (1) offers useful insights to those concerned about the increasing drug problem which have either not been presented before or are in need of clarification; (2) challenges a wide variety of drug abuse myths and untested assumptions which continue to act as a "smoke-screen" surrounding the thoughts of many; (3) Serve as a catalyst which may cut through much of the hopelessness and despair experienced by young and old concerning drug abuse; and finally (4) points out some alternatives to take the place of the usual "cut and dry" reactions to a whole spectrum of private and public behavior. Each of the twelve chapters is followed by a series of questions which will aid and challenge the reader to: determine or clarify his own thoughts and roles, weigh non-drug alternatives that can influence his life, and act as a guide to a useful understanding of the "backbone" of this current social crisis.

PERGAMON JOURNALS OF RELATED INTERESTED . . .

ART PSYCHOTHERAPY
BIOCHEMICAL PHARMACOLOGY
NEUROPHARMACOLOGY
NEUROCHEMISTRY
PSYCHIATRIC RESEARCH